'THE LITTLE COMMONWEALTH OF MAN':
THE TRINITARIAN ORIGINS OF THE ETHICAL
AND POLITICAL PHILOSOPHY OF RALPH CUDWORTH

STUDIES IN PHILOSOPHICAL THEOLOGY
42

Philosophical theology is the study of philosophical problems which arise
in reflection upon religion, religious beliefs and theological doctrines.

'THE LITTLE COMMONWEALTH OF MAN': THE TRINITARIAN ORIGINS OF THE ETHICAL AND POLITICAL PHILOSOPHY OF RALPH CUDWORTH

by

BENJAMIN CARTER

PEETERS
LEUVEN – PARIS – WALPOLE, MA
2011

A catalogue record for this book is available from the Library of Congress.

© 2011 – Peeters, Bondgenotenlaan 153, 3000 Leuven, Belgium.

ISBN 978-90-429-2214-3
D/2011/0602/44

CONTENTS

For my parents and first teachers,
Richard and Awena Carter.

ACKNOWLEDGEMENTS

This study is based on my Ph.D. thesis 'Politics, Theology, and Cambridge Platonism: The Trinity and Ethical Community in the thought of Ralph Cudworth' which I completed under the supervision of Prof. Sarah Hutton as a member of the, now defunct, History Section of the School of Arts at Middlesex University. My first and greatest thanks go to the former members of the History Section, in particular John Hope Mason and Keith McClelland, who awarded me a full scholarship which allowed me to undertake this programme of research. In addition I would like to acknowledge the help and support of Francis Mulhearn and Anna Pavlakos at Middlesex. This work is, however, the culmination of a decade of work in early-modern intellectual history which I began as an undergraduate at The University of Exeter. I particular I would like to thank Iain Hampsher-Monk who first fired my interest in the relationship between theological principles and ethical and political ideas. My academic curiosity was further encouraged by Douglas Hedley at the University of Cambridge who first introduced me to the work of Ralph Cudworth and who encouraged me in the completion of this volume. I was able to complete the research which allowed me to convert my thesis into this study thanks to the award of a British Academy Small Research Grant. Also I would like to acknowledge the financial support I received from the Dowager Countess Eleanor Peel Trust and the Trustees of the Priory Hall, Lancaster.

I am very grateful to the following institutions and libraries for permission to consult and quote from manuscript sources. To the Master, Fellows, and Scholars of Christ's College, Cambridge for use of: MS B.1.10, 11, and C.6.13.1 held in college archives, and Christ's College MS Box 77, 188 and John Mitchell, 'Personalities of Christ's' held in the college library. To the Master and Fellows of Emmanuel College, Cambridge for use of MS 48. To the Syndics of Cambridge University Library for permission to cite from: MS Mm.1.38 and MS Mm.5.24, 45, 48. To the Bodleian Library, University of Oxford, for use of: MS D'Orvile 471, MS Rawlinson A28, A.38, A.43, A.58, A.63, B.375, C.982, D.1104, MS Selden Supra, 108, 109, MS Tanner, 39, 44, 46, 49, 58, 92, 290, and MS Western, 52546.

I was first encouraged to convert my thesis into a full length study by my doctoral examiners, G.A.J. Rogers and Leslie Armour, and I am very grateful for the help an encouragement they have subsequently given me. I was enormously fortunate that my work on this volume fell during four very happy years I spent in the generous intellectual culture of the University of Bristol. At Bristol I benefitted from conversations with Robert Bickers, Alexander Bird, Fernando Cervantes, William Doyle, Brendan Smith, Andrew Pyle, and the late Trevor Johnson (of the University of the West of England). Kenneth Austin, James E. Force, Charles Taliaferro, and Finn Spicer have given me helpful and constructive comments on earlier versions and drafts of this study. Oliver Crisp gave me characteristically generous, honest, and good humoured comments on the whole text and Awena Carter helped with the correction of my prose, however those errors that remain are entirely my own. My final, and greatest, intellectual thanks goes to Sarah Hutton who has acted first as my supervisor and, more recently, as my intellectual guide and friend. I hope that this study adds, in a small way, to the enormous body of work that she has produced which has helped raise the profile and importance of the Cambridge Platonists in the intellectual history of the seventeenth century. Her kind, generous and learned support has made all of my time coming to grips with the theology and philosophy of Ralph Cudworth not only a less daunting prospect that I had originally envisaged, but a more enjoyable occupation that I could have hoped for. Finally I would like to thank those who have helped and supported me through the final completion of this study. Firstly to Stephanie Carter whose love, encouragement, and cajoling has always allowed me to retain my focus on the completion of this work. Secondly to my parents, Richard and Awena Carter who have always taught me to approach the world with an open, honest, and inquisitive mind; it is to them that I dedicate this study, with love.

BHC
Durham, September 2009.

ABBREVIATIONS OF WORKS CITED IN
THE TEXT AND NOTES

FM	British Library Additional Manuscripts, 4978-4983, *Ralph Cudworth Freewill Manuscripts.*
EIM	Ralph Cudworth, *A Treatise Concerning Eternal and Immutable Reality*, edited by Sarah Hutton. Cambridge: CUP, 1996.
Enneads	Plotinus, *The Enneads*, translated by A.H. Armstrong. Cambridge MA: Harvard University Press, 1967-1988.
First Sermon	Ralph Cudworth, *A Sermon Preached before the House of Commons, March 31st 1647*, in *The Cambridge Platonists*, edited by C.A. Patrides. London: Edward Arnold, 1969.
Institutes	Jean Calvin, *Institutes of the Christian Religion*, 2 vols, translated by Henry Beveridge. London: James Clark & Co., 1962.
Intellectual System	Cudworth's incomplete project of which *TISU* was the only published volume.
Letters	Benjamin Whichcote and Anthony Tuckney, 'Eight Letters of Dr Anthony Tuckney and Benjamin Whichcote,' in *Moral and Religious Aphorisms*, edited by Samuel Salter. London: 1753.
Leviathan	Thomas Hobbes, *Leviathan*, edited by C.B. MacPherson. Harmondsworth: Penguin, 1968.
Second Sermon	Ralph Cudworth, *A Sermon Preached to the Honourable Society of Lincolnes-Inne*. London: 1664.
TISU	Ralph Cudworth, *The True Intellectual System of the Universe: The First Part; Wherein, All the Reason and Philosophy of Atheism is Confuted; and Its Impossibility Demonstrated*. London: 1678.
TFW	Ralph Cudworth, *A Treatise on Freewill*, in *A Treatise Concerning Eternal and Immutable Reality*, edited by Sarah Hutton. Cambridge: CUP, 1996.

INTRODUCTION

This study provides a reading of the ethical and political ideas of Ralph Cudworth in their historical and theological, particularly Trinitarian context. In particular I will argue that Cudworth's practical philosophy develops directly out of his Trinitarianism. One of the major problems in placing Cudworth's ideas in their context is we know very little about the details of Cudworth's life. Unlike his more famous contemporaries, such as Thomas Hobbes and John Locke, we do not have extensive collections of private papers and correspondence with which to plot, with any, accuracy the state and trajectory of his life.[1] Even compared to the other Cambridge Platonists we no much less about Cudworth's life than we do, say, about the life of Henry More whose extensive correspondence with Anne Conway remain and whose biography was written shortly after his death.[2] However, when we try to come to terms with early modern lives the richness of material we have for the lives of Hobbes, Locke, and More make them exceptions rather than the rule. The information we have for Cudworth's life is gleaned from college records, from surviving letters, and from later biographical texts particularly the one written by Thomas Birch 1742. However, even this source is limited as it plagiarised heavily from an earlier anonymous account of Cudworth's life, the anonymously written 'Memoirs of Ralph Cudworth D.D. *Author of The Intellectual System*' published in 1736.[3] Consequently, as with so many early modern lives, what evidence we have gives us a sense of the shape of Cudworth's life but little in the way of exact detail.

---

[1] Thomas Hobbes, *The Correspondence*, 2 vols, edited by Noel Malcolm. Oxford: The Clarendon Press: 1994-97; John Locke, *The Correspondence of John Locke*, edited by E.S. de Beer. Oxford: The Clarendon Press. 1976-89.

[2] Anne Conway, *The Conway Letter: The Correspondence of Viscountess Anne Conway, Henry More, and their Friends*, edited by M. H. Nicolson, revised by Sarah Hutton. Oxford: The Clarendon Press, 1992; Richard Ward, *The Life of the Pious and Learned Henry More*. London: 1710.

[3] Thomas Birch, 'An Account of the Life and Writings of R. Cudworth D.D.' in Ralph Cudworth, *The True Intellectual System of the Universe*. London: Richard Priestly: 1820. Also compare with British Library MS Additional. *4297*, 'Miscellaneous papers of Thomas Birch' and 'Memoirs of Ralph Cudworth D.D. *Author of The Intellectual System*' Article II, *The Present State of the Republick of Letters*, XVII (1736): 24-38. The best modern account of Cudworth's life is David Pailin's biography in the Oxford Dictionary of National Biography, see: David Pailin, 'Ralph Cudworth' in *The Oxford Dictionary of National Biography*. Oxford: Oxford University Press, 2004: 14.562-565.

What then do we know about Cudworth's life? In short Ralph Cudworth was, in all things, a product of the University of Cambridge. Not only did the University provide him with his education, it was also his home and place of work from 1632 till his death in 1688. More than this, the intellectual climate and religious culture of Cambridge in the early decades of the seventeenth century provided the defining context for the development of Cudworth's theological and philosophical works. In addition to this we can even trace the influence of the University of Cambridge on Cudworth from his birth in 1617. His father, also Ralph Cudworth, was of fine Puritan stock, a former student and later fellow of Emmanuel. At the time of Cudworth's birth he was Vicar of Aller having previously served at vicar of St Andrew's church in Cambridge and as a Chaplain to James I. Cudworth's father was a acquainted with the great Puritan theologian William Perkins and achieved limited recognition as the author of a supplement to Perkin's commentary of the Epistle to the Galatians.[4] The author of the 'Memoirs' written in 1736, comments that Cudworth's father 'wanted neither for Genius or Learning [but] he had not Ambition of appearing in Public as a Writer.' Cudworth's father died in 1624 and, therefore, had a limited influence on Cudworth's early development. Cudworth's mother, who had previously been a Nurse to James I's eldest son Prince Henry, remarried a Dr John Stoughton who, like the elder Cudworth, was a fellow of Emmanuel.[5] Stoughton oversaw Cudworth's early education and it was from him that he received, what he would later describe to Peter van Limborch as, a 'diet of Calvinism.'[6] In many ways Cudworth's initial intellectual development can be characterised as a rejection of this early diet of Calvinism. However, it would be wrong to see Cudworth, and the general position of Cambridge Platonism, as developing *ex nihilo* against a Calvinist hegemony. Rather Cudworth should be understood as existing first within a Puritan world view of which Calvinism was the dominant but not exclusive form of theological expression.

Despite the conscious rejection of the Calvinism of his up-bringing, Cudworth maintained good relations with his step-father as evidenced by

---

[4] Ralph Cudworth, the elder, *A Commentarie or Exposition, upon the first Chapters of the Epistle to the Galatians: penned by... Mr. W. Perkins. Now published for the benefit of the Church, and continued with a supplement upon the sixt chapter, by Rafe Cudworth.* Cambridge: 1604.

[5] 'Memoirs of Ralph Cudworth': 24.

[6] Powicke, *The Cambridge Platonists: A Study*. London: J.M. Dent and Sons, 1929: 111.

a series of enthusiastic letters which Cudworth sent to his step-Father in the late 1630s. Like his Father and step-Father, Cudworth went up to Emmanuel College, Cambridge, matriculating there in 1632. There he was tutored by Benjamin Whichcote who introduced him to Neoplatonic philosophy. Cudworth took is BA in 1632, and MA in 1639, 'with unusual Applause.'[7] He was later awarded a D.D. in 1651. In 1639 Cudworth followed the family tradition and was elected to a fellowship at Emmanuel. At Emmanuel Cudworth stood out as an unusually successful and popular tutor, having at one point 28 pupils, which was, so the author of the 'Memoir' comments, so rare as not to have been remembered in living memory at Emmanuel. During this period Cudworth quickly gained a reputation for expertise in questions of Jewish prophesy. This brought Cudworth to the attention of the English Jurist and scholar of Judaism, John Selden who corresponded with Cudworth on matters of Jewish prophesy in the early 1640s. Cudworth career changed with the outbreak of the English Civil War. In 1644 the Earl of Manchester was ordered by Parliament to purge Cambridge of those masters and fellows who refused to take the 'Solemn League and Covenant' which proposed the imposition of a Presbyterian model on the English Church. William Sancroft the younger described, in a letter to the then imprisoned Master of Emmanuel Richard Holdsworth, how Mancester's purge had 'beheaded whole colleges at a blow; nay, whole Universities and whole Churches too.'[8] Sancroft's assement of the purge is largely correct, ten heads of colleges and 212 fellows were ejected. Of the ten heads of colleges filled by the Earl of Manchester nine were already members of the Westminster Assembly and seven of these fellows of Emmanuel. A year later, in 1645, Cudworth, at the age of 28 was appointed as Master of Clare Hall and to the Regius Chair of Hebrew at the same time that Whichcote was created Provost of King's. Neither were the first choices for these posts, and both took them up reluctantly.[9] Cudworth later resigned the Mastership of Clare Hall when he was elected Master of Christ's in 1654.[10]

Up until his election as Master of Christ's Cudworth's financial situation was precarious, nearly causing him to quit University life at the end

---

[7] 'Memoirs of Ralph Cudworth': 24-5.

[8] Quoted in Twigg, *University of Cambridge*: 97.

[9] Twigg, *University of Camridge*: 88-93, 101-103.

[10] John Worthington, *The Diary and Correspondence of Dr John Worthington*, 3 vols, edited by James Crossley & Richard Copley Christie. Manchester: The Chetham Society, (1847-1886): I.52; CUL MS Mm.5.45, 'Notes on the Masters of God's House & Christ's College': 59.

of the 1640s.[11] His personal finances were, though, greatly enhanced by his appointment, in succession to Whichcote, to the living of North Cadbury in 1650, which carried with it the not inconsiderable income of £300 per annum.[12] What finally brought Cudworth financial security was his marriage in 1654 to Damaris Andrewes, the widow of one Thomas Andrewes. This marriage brought with it three step-children. Cudworth's wife then had three more children, John, Damaris and Charles.[13] Although Charles Cudworth died in 1683 in India, contrary to the claim made in both the 'Memoir' and Birch's 'Life,' Cudworth's eldest son John survived Cudworth, as did his daughter Damaris.[14] Cudworth's election at Christ's aided his career in two ways. Firstly, as Cudworth was elected to this position he immediately held more legitimacy in the University than he had as the Earl of Manchester's appointee at Clare Hall. Secondly, at Christ's he came under the influence and patronage of Heneage Finch, who later, as Lord Chancellor, was the Dedicatee of the *True Intellectual System of the Universe* (*TISU*). It appears that these preferments came with the blessing leading members of the interregnum regime. Cudworth's wife, as already been stated, had previously been married to Thomas Andrewes whose father was Sir Thomas Andrewes, one of the judges at the trial of Charles I and the first Lord Mayor of London following the Regicide. Cudworth also corresponded with John Thurloe, Cromwell's secretary on state appointments. Cudworth also advised Cromwell on the readmission of the Jews in 1655. It is unclear whether or not Cromwell knew or approved of Cudworth, but it is clear that Cudworth recognised the benefits of his relationship to the Lord Protector. On Cromwell's death in 1658 Cudworth wrote to Thurloe expressing his sorrow and professing his support for Cromwell's son and nominated successor Richard. Cudworth even suggested to Thurloe that he might dedicate a work to

---

[11] In a letter dated 12 April 1647, Robert Brownrigge comments, rather scathingly, to Edward Martin, the President of Queens', that: 'tis said that Mr Cudworth preached to yᵉ house of Commons last Fastday, & for his reward hath a grant of 150 out of ye revenues of oʳ Church of Ely to enable him to act yᵉ Mʳ of Clare Hall more comfortably. He hath got more at fast than others can gett at a feast.' Bod. MS. Rawlinson. D. 1104. 2b.

[12] 'Memoirs of Ralph Cudworth': 27, 29.

[13] Cudworth's wealth from his marriage is shown by the extensive properties, mostly in Suffolk, outlined in his will which he left to his wife and subsequently his eldest son John. Christ's College MS. Box 77: 'The Will of Ralph Cudworth D.D., Master of Christ's' and 'The Will of Damaris Cudworth.' In addition to his own children Cudworth cared for his three step-children, namely Thomas and Richard Andrewes and Damaris Abney (née Andrewes). For a rough Cudworth family tree see Christ's College MS.77.

[14] 'Memoirs of Ralph Cudworth': 29; Birch, 'Life': 9.

Richard Cromwell (probably one of his unpublished manuscripts on Jewish prophesy) 'to whose noble father I was much obliged.'[15]

Following the Restoration in 1660 Cudworth was quickly confirmed in his position at Christ's. Despite this Cudworth appears to have been continually under attack during this period from those who wished to remove him from Christ's and his close association with the regimes of the interregnum affected Cudworth's reputation till the end of his life. In the 1660s Cudworth moved away from his interest in Jewish prophesy to his earlier interest in ethical philosophy. This move famously brought Cudworth into dispute with Henry More who, at the same time was preparing the text of his *Enchiridon Ethicum* which was published in 1666. For the remainder of his life Cudworth juggled his academic interests with his responsibilities as Master and also Bursar of Christ's College. Possibly because of the onerous nature of these administrative jobs Cudworth, unlike the other heads of houses, never served as Vice-Chancellor, a role which was passed in yearly cycle between the heads of the college. In 1688 Cudworth was taken ill whilst travelling to London and returned to Christ's to die in his college on 26 June, 1688. He is buried in the college chapel.

The limitations presented by the lack of biographical information mean that it would be impossible to construct an intellectual biography of Cudworth, and it would be incorrect to view this study as such. Although there is inevitably a partial chronological ordering to the chapters, beginning with influences and ending with legacy, the central purpose of this text is to reconstruct Cudworth's ideas primarily in their theological context. For this reason the main sources for this book are Cudworth's published and unpublished writings. These sources provide their own problems which need to be accounted for. Cudworth's work can be broken down roughly into three sections. Firstly his early published works: beginning with his *A Discourse Concerning the True Notion of the Lord's Supper*, and *The Union of Christ and the Church in a shadow*, both published in 1642; then followed by two sermons: *A Sermon Preached before the House of Commons (First Sermon)*, from 1647, and his *A Sermon Preached to the Honourable Society of Lincolnes-Inne (Second Sermon)*, from 1664. Secondly we have Cudworth's *TISU*, which was written as the first volume of an incomplete three volume work. *TISU* was completed in 1671 and published in 1678. Thirdly there are works that remained unpublished in Cudworth's lifetime. These include both his

---

[15] Bod. MS Rawlinson 63: 43.

Treatise on Eternal and Immutable Morality (*EIM*) published in 1731, and his unpublished manuscripts on freewill, which are held in the additional manuscripts of the British Library; a section of these were published as *A Treatise of Freewill* (*TFW*) in 1838.

When one considers Cudworth's theology and philosophy there is a danger of focusing solely on the texts. Arguably many of the problems of appreciating Cudworth's place in early-modern thought has been born, in part, from an over emphasis on the texts without due attention being paid to the context in which they were written. This is shown in the manner in which many studies of Cudworth's life have ignored or passed over his early works, disregarding them as biographical necessities, and choosing instead to focus on the larger, later, works. Some recent commentators have argued that a focus on Cudworth's early texts shows a change in his philosophical opinion.[16] This claim, I would argue, is bogus. In fact there is a remarkable consistency in all of Cudworth's theological and philosophical output both in theory and temper. For this reason I have used these early texts in two ways in this study. Firstly I have used them, combined with what biographical information we know, as vital evidence for Cudworth's intellectual development. In particular the consistent and sophisticated rejection of the voluntarism of seventeenth-century Calvinism found in these early publications provides the central theme and impetus for all of Cudworth's work. This theme is developed in Chapters One and Two of this study. His advocacy for Neoplatonic intellectualism, which provides the philosophical core of all of Cudworth's writings, is present in, and develops through, these early writings into his mature work, particularly his *TISU*. Although these early works differ markedly at times in style and form from his later, more overtly philosophical writings, these early publications give a vital insight into not only the theological form, but also the ethical imperative that exists in all of Cudworth's work. Secondly, because of the intellectual consistency that exists throughout all of Cudworth's work I have felt it possible to introduce themes and principles from these earlier works in support of arguments which are only partially sketched in Cudworth's later writings. This is particularly the case with the political implications of many of Cudworth's ethical ideas. As will be shown in Chapter Five, Cudworth's conception of, what I term, the 'ethical community' can be

---

[16] See, Michael B. Gill's texts, 'Rationalism, sentimentalism, and Ralph Cudworth', *Hume Studies* 30 (2004): 149-182, and *The British Moralists on Human Nature and the Birth of Secular Ethics*. Cambridge: CUP: 2006.

found not only in his later explicit ethical and political utterances, but also throughout his earlier writings.

The main danger in dealing with Cudworth's output, however, is an over emphasis on the second section of Cudworth's writings, his voluminous *TISU*. From only a brief survey of Cudworth's work it is not difficult to see why this text has become the central focus to of Cudworth as a philosopher. The first published version of text runs to well over 900 pages and easily dwarfs all of Cudworth's other published works put together. In addition to this, *TISU* is a difficult and complex text to interpret. It is hard not to concur with Ernst Cassirer's assessment that it owes more to the humanism of the sixteenth-century than it does to the more progressive philosophical styles of the seventeenth. However, to view *TISU* merely as a literary artefact, and an antiquarian one at that, is to dismiss it too easily.[17] When dealing with *TISU* two caveats needed to be born in mind. Firstly it is, as Cudworth himself admitted, an unsatisfactory text. It is almost overburdened with the number of long and verbose quotations from ancient philosophy. Such is its length that it has often proved simplest to read the text at face value simply as a rejection of atheism in all its guises, and of Thomas Hobbes in particular. Such is the concentration on Hobbes in modern scholarship, it has become all too common to view Cudworth simply as the 'anti-Hobbes'.[18] However, this interpretation of *TISU* ignores both its place in Cudworth's intellectual development, and the philosophical importance of the text as a whole. Such is the importance of *TISU* to the understanding of Cudworth's thought that I have reserved two chapters in this study to discuss it. In Chapter Two I argue against the traditional characterisation of the text as simply an antiquarian and academic rejection of Hobbes. In the light of the discussion of Cudworth's intellectual development in Chapter One, I argue that all of Cudworth's work provides, in some form, a rejection of, what I term, arbitrary authority. In Cudworth's early writings this takes the form of a rejection of Calvinism, in *TISU* this rejection of Calvinism remains, but with an added attack on Hobbist materialism which

---

[17] Ernst Cassirer, *The Platonic Renaissance in England*, translated by James P. Pettegrove. London: Thomas Nelson and Sons, 1953. For a discussion of this problem in the historiography of the Cambridge Platonists see: Sarah Hutton, *Anne Conway: A Woman Philosopher*. Cambridge: CUP, 2004: 11.

[18] See for instance, Samuel I. Mintz, *The Hunting of Leviathan: Seventeenth-century Reactions to the Materialism Moral Philosophy of Thomas Hobbes*. Cambridge: CUP, 1962. Jon Parkin, *Taming the Leviathan: The Reception of the Political and Religious Ideas of Thomas Hobbes in England 1640-1700*. Cambridge: CUP, 2007.

had, in Cudworth's eyes, inherited and extended many of the vices of Calvinist voluntarism.

TISU is, however, not simply though a rejection of atheism and arbitrary authority, but a text of philosophical and theological importance in its own right. So once the form of Cudworth's negative dismissal of arbitrary authority has been discussed in Chapter Two, Chapter Three will discuss the positive arguments of *TISU*. This discussion is drawn in the light of the second difficulty with the text; that *TISU* is only the first part of an incomplete work. Although Cudworth argued that *TISU* could stand alone, it was intended to be the first of three volumes. Therefore to view the text merely as a rejection of atheism is to read the text simply at face value. Instead it should be viewed as the foundational volume of Cudworth's incomplete *Intellectual System*.[19] Cudworth's *TISU*, therefore, provides the most complete extant philosophical account of the thought of the Cambridge Platonists. Building on the themes of Cudworth's early works, *TISU* develops the principles of reason taught by Benjamin Whichcote, to present a comprehensive philosophical account of the created realm. Central to this system is the doctrine of the Trinity. Built on the foundations of Whichcote's defence of reason in religion I argue that the Trinity is, for Cudworth, the consummation of the Cambridge Platonic dictum, from Proverbs 20:27, 'the spirit of man is the candle of the Lord.' For Cudworth, the tri-unity of God provides the most eloquent, and reasonable, explanation God's relationship with his own creation. Central to this is Cudworth's argument that God, through his triune form, expresses his implicit wisdom and reasonableness to the world. Constant throughout this account of the Trinity in Cudworth's theology is a linking of each of the persons of the Trinity to different 'expressions' of the God's reason. So the first person is the creator, the second person, the *Logos*, is the perfect embodiment of that reason, and the Spirit is evidence of the constancy of that reason manifested through the unfolding of history and creation. Cudworth's Trinitarianism, therefore, makes a direct link between his theology and his philosophy. Just as God as Trinity presents to man the perfection of divine reason, so philosophy, correctly understood, could bring man into a participation with the reasonableness of God's creation. Cudworth's argument, particularly in his explicit linking

---

[19] The full title of the *TISU* is: *The True Intellectual System of the Universe: The First Part; Wherein, All the Reason and Philosophy of Atheism is Confuted; and Its Impossibility Demonstrated.* Consequently there is the possibility of confusion between this text and the incomplete project from which it derived. Therefore I will term this single volume the *TISU* to distinguish it from the project of the *Intellectual System*, throughout this text.

of reason to the second person of the Trinity, makes a link between reason and God's grace. Returning to 'the Candle of the Lord', Cudworth's
Trinitarianism gives a fuller theological working out of Whichcote's dictum: that reason is the God-given means by which man comes closer to
God. Cudworth's Trinitarianism, therefore, provides a development of
his rejection of Calvinism as he argues that God's grace is not given
exclusively to the elect, but constantly and unquestioningly to all.

Cudworth's Trinitarianism not only unlocks the philosophical importance of the *TISU* but also shows the ethical imperative that exists
throughout Cudworth's thought. The theological question that Cudworth
asks in *TISU* is not who will be given grace, but the practical question of
what will they do with when man recognises he has it? The explicitly
practical nature of Cudworth's theology is particularly important in the
interpretation of the third grouping of Cudworth's writings, those works
that remained unpublished in his own lifetime. It would be incorrect to
view these texts — primarily his *EIM* and freewill manuscripts — as
completing Cudworth's *Intellectual System*. However, as argued above,
there is a consistency in Cudworth's work which allows us to view these
texts as developments on, and completions of, many of the arguments in
his published works. For this reason this study, unlike other accounts of
Cudworth's writing, will interpret these texts in the light of the theological
insights of his early works and *TISU*. I will argue throughout Chapters
Four and Five that the Trinitarianism of Cudworth's *TISU*, particularly
his advocacy for the God-given nature of human reason, helps unlock and
develop the ethical and political principles that are present throughout all
of Cudworth's theology and philosophy.

The establishment of not simply a religious basis, but also theological
and particularly Trinitarian logic to Cudworth's ethical thought is a central part of the argument of this book. That Cudworth's thought contained
an important ethical dimension is, in itself, not a new claim. The importance of Cudworth's *EIM* in the history of ethical thought, and the ethical
arguments of *TISU* have long been recognised. In recent interpretations of
Cudworth's philosophy these have played an important role in rehabilitating Cudworth not only as a significant thinker in the history of philosophy,
but also as a means of rejecting the traditional caricature of the Cambridge Platonists as other-worldly and mystical thinkers.[20] In particular

[20] For instance see John Passmore, *Ralph Cudworth: An Interpretation*. Cambridge:
CUP, 1951; Stephen Darwall, *The British Moralists and the Internal 'Ought': 1640-1740*.
Cambridge: CUP, 1995; Frederick C. Beiser, *The Sovereignty of Reason: The defence of*

the interpretations of Passmore and Darwall have done much to unlock the meaning and depth within Cudworth unpublished works, in particular his freewill manuscripts. However, these interpretations have generally been made without reference to Cudworth's intellectual context. Consequently it has been common to find a-historical interpretations of Cudworth's thought. With reference to Cudworth's ethical thought this has led to what might best be described as a neo-Kantian reading of Cudworth. These accounts generally refer back to Arthur J. Lovejoy's 'Kant and the English Platonists.'[21] The basic premise of that paper is that the Cambridge Platonists, and Ralph Cudworth in particular, in some way anticipated the ethical thought of Kant. Although the similarities with Kant's thought were noted by Coleridge, this theory was not fully expounded until this point. Lovejoy claims that Kant's idealist reaction to the empiricism of Hume was 'entirely analogous' with Cudworth's reaction to the thought of Hobbes.[22] The major result of this reaction for Lovejoy is that Cudworth, in *TISU*, foreshadows Kant's Copernican revolution.[23] This line of argument is taken up in Darwall's work. There Darwall argues that Cudworth discoverd 'the path that led to Kant's view of morality as "laws of freedom."'[24] Darwall's argument paints Cudworth as a prophet for Kantian ethical philosophy, attributing to him the knowledge and acceptance of the Kantian distinctions between pure and practical reason. Cudworth is therefore credited by Darwall with the Kantian insight that 'ethics is possible only if pure reason can be practical.'[25] Accordingly, Darwall argues that Cudworth's philosophy contains within it 'the seeds of some of the most important and profound ideas in modern moral philosophy.'[26] Cudworth's role in Darwall's work is, therefore, to prepare the path for Kant. By viewing the Cudworth through this perspective, this account creates a false image in which Cudworth ceases to be historical figures in his own right, and merely a step on the road to Kant.

rationality in the early English Enlightenment. Princeton, NJ: Princeton University Press, 1996; G.A.J. Rogers, et al. eds, *The Cambridge Platonists in Philosophical Context – Politics, Metaphysics & Religion*. Dordrecht: Kluwer, 1997.

[21] Samuel Taylor Coleridge, *Coleridge on the Seventeenth century*, edited by Roberta Florence. Durham, NC: Duke University Press, 1955: 109; Arthur J. Lovejoy, 'Kant and the English Platonists,' in *Essays Philosophical and Psychological: In honour of William James by his colleagues at Columbia University*. New York: Longmans, Green & Co., 1908: 263-302.

[22] Lovejoy, 'English Platonists': 272; Darwall, *British Moralists*:109.

[23] Lovejoy, 'English Platonists': 271, 274.

[24] Darwall, *British Moralists*: 325.

[25] Darwall, *British Moralists*: 322, also 17.

[26] Darwall, *British Moralists*: 117.

Although there is much to agree with in this interpretation of Cudworth, it is not helpful when trying to reconstruct Cudworth's philosophy on it own terms. For this reason in this study Cudworth's ethical ideas will be read in the light of the Trinitarian theology of *TISU*. In particular I will argue that when Cudworth advocates the right use of reason in ethical and political matters he is implicitly arguing that man is engaging with something of the divine, and consequently participating in God's reasoned, divine nature. In doing so not only is it possible to deepen further our understanding of Cudworth's philosophy, but also present a more general account of the relationship between theological principles and ethical and political ideas in early-modern philosophy. Despite the great steps forward that have occurred in contextual studies of early-modern thought since the 1960s, the overtly theological aspect of much early-modern ideas has been side-stepped. The main reason for this is that theological ideas in these studies have been relegated to one of many competing contextual factors used to construct a certain pattern of ideas. In some cases it is possible to see how this has provided a fruitful avenue of enquiry. For all the advances made in contextual accounts in the history of ethical and political philosophy, however, I would argue that there remains a lacuna in the interpretation of religious thought in early-modern philosophy. With a thinker such as Cudworth it is not simply enough to acknowledge his belief in God, it is essential that this belief informed and defined all aspects of his work. So, as we shall see, whenever Cudworth advocates the use of reason he is not simply making a case for the primacy of one human faculty over another, but that reason is superior because it is God given, and given by God so man can, in some limited way, become more God-like. Whether we like it or not, thinkers in the past believed in God and, therefore, it is essential that if we are to understand their ideas on their own terms the profundity of the religious belief has to be accepted in the first instance. In this regard I have found myself drawn to developments in the history of science. John Hedley Brooke has argued against seeing science as a thing in opposition to, and naturally antagonistic to religion. Instead, he argues, we should take a much more inclusive approach to the understanding of the way in which religious belief influenced scientific enquiry. In this way the nature of a particular thinker's religious belief is not seen as in conflict with that part of his work which we can now recognise as 'scientific'. Rather, religious belief becomes an active influence on the intellectual process that historians seek to understand. This inclusive approach means that the intellectual historian must reconstruct not only the scientific arguments of a thinker, but also what the notion of 'science' meant to that thinker in the first place.[27] In this study I have found this conceptual model very helpful. For this reason I argue that it is not possible to separate our modern ideas of what is 'ethical' or 'political' from the theological world-view from which they were created. Historians of science have come to argue that early-modern 'science' was a developed directly out of the theological standpoint of those 'scientists'. In this same manner I argue that aspects of early-modern ethical and political philosophy should not be viewed not as a separate, secular, exercise, but as a working out of the underlying theological world-view of the philosopher in question. Consequently I argue throughout this work that there was no separation in Cudworth's mind between the theological and the ethical, rather ethical discussions were merely another means through which man came to express his understanding of God. In Cudworth's case these arguments, because of the explicit advocacy of reason in all things, are manifestations of his Trinitarian account of God.

The historiographical themes which are explored in this book provide the bridge between Cudworth and the use of his thought in the years after his death. In Chapter Six I examine the initial reception of Cudworth's writings. Two conclusions stand out. Firstly, confirming one of the central arguments of this book, Cudworth's definition of the Trinity became the means by which Cudworth was both received and defined in the years after his death. This may be simply because of the historical accident that debates on the Trinity flared in the years after his death. However, as I argue in Chapter Six, Cudworth was an unwitting participant in these debates whose theology provided impetus to these debates. Secondly, these debates allow us to establish a definitive intellectual link between Cudworth and the late seventeenth-century divines commonly remembered as the Latitudinarians. What is most instructive is that they do not simply view the Trinity as a doctrine but, like Cudworth, as a theological truth which defined all aspects of their lives, in particular their engagement with ethical and political matters.

This study provides one example of how an early-modern thinker constructed his ethical and political ideas in the theological world view in

---

[27] See for instance; John Hedley Brooke, *Science and Religion: Some Historical Perspectives.* Cambridge: CUP, 1991; John Henry, *The Scientific Revolution and the Origins of Modern Science.* Basingstoke: Palgrave, 2002; Francis Yates, *Giordono Bruno and the Hermetic Tradition.* London: Routledge and Kegan Paul: 1964. For a direct rejection of this conception of the history of science see Brian Vickers introduction to his edited collection *Occult and Scientific Mentalities in the Renaissance.* Cambridge: CUP, 1984.

which he existed. The problem though remains that these arguments, particularly the political ones, although interesting and perceptive, only exist in unpublished sources. What then is the use of reconstructing arguments which never found the form and expression that the author himself intended? With regards to Cudworth such an endeavour only helps deepen our understanding of this enigmatic figure in early-modern intellectual history. Certainly, although many of his explicit ethical and political arguments are found in his manuscripts, they are generally developments and explanations of ideas which exist in a lesser form in his published works. Therefore, this exercise, if nothing else, provides the first contextual study of Cudworth's theology and philosophy. In broader terms this study allows us to uncover the manner in which early-modern ethical and political ideas were conceived and constructed. In this way we are able to appreciate more fully the importance of religious ideas, as exemplified by Cudworth's concentration on the Trinity, on all aspects of early-modern intellectual endeavour. Finally, and most importantly, this study allows us to see something of the intellectual culture in which these ideas, many of which have relevance to our own contemporary ethical and political concerns, first developed. In particular Cudworth exemplifies an intellectual position and temper which sought to stand between the religious extremes of seventeenth-century English society and provide moderate, even liberal, answers to the problems of the day.

Defining an intellectual temper or culture, as this final point is, is a very difficult process. However, it is possible to find in the history of philosophy accounts which stress the importance of moderate English religious culture on the development of liberal thought. On a general level Edward Gibbon, in his *Decline and Fall of the Roman Empire*, describes a 'secret reformation,' in the reformed tradition based on a 'spirit of freedom and moderation.' Gibbon goes on to name the chief members of this liberal tradition as, 'the Arminianism of Holland, Grotius, Limborch, and Le Clerc; and in England Chillingworth, the Latitudinarians of Cambridge..., Tillotson, Clarke, Hoadley.'[28] Gibbon describes something of the moderate religious culture in which Cudworth lived. In theological

---

[28] Edward Gibbon, *The Decline and Fall of the Roman Empire*, 7 vols. London: Methuen & Co., 1906: VI:128, n.45. This free-thinking humanist tradition is described by the eighteenth century thinker Anthony Clarke who described a free-thinking tradition of Erasmus, Grotius, Chillingworth, Herbert, Wilkins, Whichcote, Cudworth, More, Tillotson, and Locke. Cited in Isabel Rivers, *Reason, Grace and, Sentiment: A Study of the Language of Religion and Ethics in England, 1660-1780*, 2 vols. Cambridge: CUP, 1991 & 2000: II:24. Also see Hugh Trevor-Roper, 'The Religious Origins of the Enlightenment,' in *Religion, the Reformation, and Social Change*. London: Macmillan, 1967: 206-220.

terms all these thinkers shared what could be termed as a 'Reformed universalism'; that is a concentration on the *sola gratia* of the Reformation, with a rejection of exclusivism of, particularly, the Calvinist doctrine of grace. In Cudworth life and writings this 'Reformed universalism' manifested itself in the Puritanism of his religious culture, mixed with his claim that by and through reason God's grace is manifested to all. By focusing on this shared religious and theological position it is possible to link the moderation and temper of Cudworth's theology and philosophy to the generation of liberal theologians, and philosophers, that followed him. Cudworth did not define this shared culture, which rejected doctrinal certainties — in Cudworth's case arbitrary authority — but Cudworth's writing does provide one of the fullest justifications for the virtues of reason and moderation as the most effective response to doctrinal certainty and arbitrary authority. The theology and philosophy of Ralph Cudworth is important not simply because it existed in, and helped define this culture, but because, in Cudworth, we have one of the earliest comprehensive philosophical systems to be defined in this moderate tradition of English thought. In Cudworth's writing this moderate, liberal temper was born out of Cudworth's initial intellectual development as a Puritan anti-Calvinist which underpinned Cudworth's thought till his death. It informed the development of his *Intellectual System*, and from this helped mould much of the characteristic liberal theology and philosophy of late-seventeenth and early-eighteenth century English thought.

CHAPTER ONE

THEOLOGY, POLITICS, AND CAMBRIDGE PLATONISM

The defining term of Ralph Cudworth's intellectual development was the religious culture of Puritanism. Puritanism is a notoriously difficult term to define. It first emerged in the sixteenth century as a term of abuse to describe those 'hotter sort of Protestants' who wished to see a completion of the English Reformation, particularly with regards to the simplification and purification of religious practice. Puritanism was, as John Spurr has pointed out, not a free standing movement, but one woven into the forms and structures of the English Church.[1] The central principles of Cambridge Platonism, therefore, grew out of the intellectual tapestry of English Puritanism, as is shown by their closeness to the central Puritan institutions within Cambridge, chiefly Emmanuel College. On questions of religious practise and observance Cudworth and his contemporaries remained true to these Puritan roots. They rejected ostentation in religious worship, and stressed that Christianity was, at its heart, a religion based on simple, definable principles. In this way many of the central intellectual themes of Cambridge Platonism can be recognised as Puritan in the first instance. The visible and liturgical manifestations of Puritanism were underscored by a deeper theological debate over whether salvation comes solely through the extraordinary action God's saving grace or through the realisation of God's grace in the observance of the sacraments. This fundamental division was to underline and the divisions between the 'Puritan' and 'Laudian' factions in the 1630s and 1640s.[2] When defined in these terms Cudworth and the Cambridge Platonists fall firmly with those who argued that salvation came through the working of God's grace alone.

Cudworth, and the Cambridge Platonists, fundamentally differed with other Puritans not on matters of religious practice, but in their understanding of how God's grace was transmitted to man. In particular, as we shall see below, Cudworth moved away from the Calvinist orthodoxy of

---

[1] John Spurr, *English Puritanism: 1605-1693*. Basingstoke: Macmillan, 1998: 1-7; Patrick Collinson, *English Puritanism*. London: The Historical Association, 1987.

[2] Jonathan D. Moore, *English Hypothetical Universalism: John Preston and the Softening of Reformed Theology*. Grand Rapids, MI: William Eerdmans Publishing, 2007: 226.

the majority of seventeenth-century Puritans, when he asserted that human reason provided the means through which man came not only to comprehend the nature of God's grace, but also freely accept or reject it. In this manner, although Cudworth remained culturally a Puritan, he did so whilst still rejecting the Calvinist theology of much of the English Church which taught that it was only by the action of God's will that man was saved. In Cudworth's thought this develops most clearly through the development of his 'intellectualist' theological position in opposition to what he perceived to be the arbitrary nature of the 'voluntarism' of contemporary Calvinism. By recognising the development of Cudworth's theology through the structure of an 'intellectualist' response to the 'voluntarism' of Calvinism, it is also possible understand why Cudworth, initially under the tutelage of Benjamin Whichcote, used Neoplatonic philosophy as his chief means of theological and philosophical expression.

Cudworth's intellectual development, and his rejection of Calvinism, should not be mistaken for an idle academic exercise, nor should his life within the University of Cambridge be mistaken for that of the cloistered and hidebound academic. By placing Cudworth's intellectual development within the religious and intellectual culture of English Puritanism we can see the way in which conflicts over theology existed within this culture not because they were philosophically dubious, but because they were perceived to be ethically dangerous. In the University of Cambridge arguments, which can seem to the modern eye overly technical and abstract, raged because of the profound ethical implications they had on the lives of those engaging in them. Therefore, we need to recognise not only the theological and philosophical ideas which influenced Cudworth's intellectual development, but also the ethical and even political conclusions that were drawn from those arguments. In this context theological debates on 'grace' and 'predestination' cannot be understood without reference to the political context within which they were drawn, particularly the build up to, and consequences of the English Civil War on the Puritan culture of the University of Cambridge.

Cudworth and anti-Calvinism

Cudworth's rejection of Calvinism has, at its heart, a rejection of the philosophical terms of Calvinist theology. Put most simply all of Cudworth's theology and philosophy derives from an intellectualist rejection of the voluntarism which characterised much of the Calvinist theology of seventeenth-century England. Voluntarism and intellectualism denote two fundamentally differing accounts of the nature of God. Voluntarism defines God's actions primarily as actions of will. As William Perkins, the leading Calvinist theologian of the generation preceding Cudworth put it: 'God's justice is that which he in all things willeth that which is just. God's justice is in word or deed.'[3] In contrast intellectualism defines divine actions in terms or reason or wisdom. Cudworth makes his position on this principle perfectly clear in *TISU* when we states that 'God's *Will* is *Ruled* by his *Justice*, and not his *Justice Ruled* by his *Will.*'[4] Cudworth's intellectualism, and through this his rejection of voluntarism, is characterised primarily through a rejection of the ethical, rather than purely metaphysical, problems of voluntarism. Cudworth rejected, what he viewed to be, the arbitrary nature of an ethical system governed only by will in favour of an ethical universe defined from the outset by the unchanging principles of God's wisdom and reason. To fully appreciate the form of Cudworth's reaction to Calvinism we need to place this reaction in the specific intellectual and theological culture of Cambridge in the early decades of the seventeenth century. Although Calvinism provided the dominant form of theological expression in the early decades of seventeenth-century England, in the Universities the orthodoxy of Calvinism was consistently questioned. In the literature on this subject it has been common to define the debates in terms of dichotomies such as Calvinist and anti-Calvinist, or Puritan and Anglican. However, in reality the picture was much more complex than this. In fact Jonathan D. Moore has recently, and persuasively argued that in early seventeenth-century England a 'Calvinist consensus' did not exist as a uniform expression of theological belief. Rather there existed a breadth of theological argument in the 'Puritan' model of salvation by grace alone, which all opposed the Laudian claims for the salvific efficacy of the Sacraments.[5] Although differences existed in this Puritan, or perhaps more accurately, Reformed position, this was not a development of constant change and opposition, but a process of debate which eventually brought about a softening of Reformed theology. Moore's work focuses on the role played by John Preston in this process, but one could just as well argue that Cudworth and the Cambridge Platonists, in their own way, played a role in the softening of English Reformed theology. This characterisation allows us to develop a more subtle account

---

[3] William Perkins, *The Works of William Perkins*, edited by Ian Breward. Appleford: The Sutton Courtney Press, 1970: 179.

[4] *TISU*: 897.

[5] Moore, *English Hypothetical Universalism*: 227.

of Cudworth as rejecting many of the specific claims of Calvinist theology, whilst still doing this within the compass of the Reformed tradition of which Calvinism was only one, if the most common, expression. For this reason if we are to understand Cudworth as an anti-Calvinist, it is important at this point to enumerate the different forms of anti-Calvinism to show more clearly the specific form that Cudworth's anti-Calvinism took.

Two forms of anti-Calvinism played a role in Cudworth's intellectual development. The first was the internal debate in the Reformed tradition between orthodox Calvinists and Arminianians which was a central part of the theological culture of the University in the early decades of the seventeenth century.[6] The second was the external imposition of Laudian reforms on religious practice in Cambridge during the 1630s, which were directed at Puritanism in general the theological position of Calvinism in particular. It has become common to term all anti-Calvinism as 'Arminianism.' However, Arminianism is, in reality, a specific Reformed theological response to Calvinism developed to by the Dutch theologian Jacobus Arminius. Arminius undermined the central tenet of orthodox Calvinism by asserting that although Christ died for the elect, the elected could freely accept or reject this salvific act. Arminius did not reject predestination, in fact his theology carries with it a very strong doctrine of predestination. However, in contrast to orthodox Calvinists such as William Perkins, Arminius made predestination subordinate to creation and the Fall.[7] Consequently, Arminius argued that although Christ died for all, God only saves those who have the moral fortitude to believe. Christ, therefore, acts as mediator not for the preordained with no regard for their action, but for the elect because they chose to 'repent and believe.' Although Arminianism is consistent with the belief that salvation is only open to those who have been preordained to be saved, it also implies that the power of grace can be resisted or accepted by human free choice. Human action, for Arminius, becomes integral to the process of salvation. Arminius' theology rejects of the 'particularism' of Calvinist justification by faith alone in favour of a two-fold justification of grace and human action.[8]

This form of anti-Calvinism first emerged in Cambridge University in the 1590s, most notably in a sermon preached in 1595 by William Barrat,

---

[6] H.C. Porter, *Reformation and Reaction in Tudor Cambridge*. Cambridge: CUP, 1958: 414-22.

[7] White, *Predestination*: 31.

[8] Moore, *English Hypothetical Universalism*: 43-44.

the then chaplain of Gonville and Caius College. In this sermon Barrat vehemently attacked the strict Calvinism being taught by some in Cambridge at the time. The chief influence on the sermon was probably the French Protestant Peter Baro who was then the Lady Margaret Professor of Divinity. Although publicly professing to be an orthodox Calvinist, Baro is thought to have held Arminian views in private.[9] The opposition to Barrat was led by Perkins.[10] So fierce was this opposition that Barrat was forced to recant his sermon. However, the controversy did not end in the confines of the University. The profession of anti-Calvinist sentiment in Cambridge led the then Archbishop of Canterbury, John Whitgift, to intervene to settle the doctrinal problems aroused by this controversy. The subsequent 'Lambeth Articles', published in November 1595, are the clearest statement of English Calvinist orthodoxy until the Westminster Confession of the 1640s.[11] These state clearly that 'God has predestined some men to life, and reprobated some to death.' The moving force of this election is not the 'perseverance…of good works, or of anything innate in the person of the predestined, but only the will and pleasure of God.' The Lambeth Articles conclude with the statement that '[i]t is not in the will or the power of each and every man to be saved.'[12] The immediate effect of these articles was simply to fire a warning shot across the bows of theologians such as Barrat and Baro who tried to deny the Calvinist orthodoxy of the day. The broader consequences of the Lambeth Articles was the codification and broad acceptance of Calvinist orthodoxy in the English Reformed tradition. This Arminian element, although important within the University, was largely silenced in England. It was not until the ascendancy of Archbishop Laud in the late 1620s that the Calvinist orthodoxy of the English Church was to be to significantly troubled.

Laud is normally referred to as an Arminian. It is, however, incorrect to see Laud's Arminianism as growing directly from the teachings of Arminius. T.M. Parker has argued that in English theology one can find a tradition of anti-Calvinism which is allied to, but not based entirely on, Arminian theology. Parker sees this tradition, exemplified by the actions

---

[9] Wallace, *Puritans*: 67.

[10] Breward, 'Perkins': 120.

[11] Nicholas Tyacke, *Anti-Calvinists: The Rise of Arminianism, c. 1590-1640*. Oxford: The Clarendon Press, 1987: 5.

[12] The best full-length discussion of this controversy is Porter, *Reformation and Reaction*. It is from this work (365-6) that the translations of the Lambeth Articles are taken. Also see, Tyacke, *Anti-Calvinists*: 29-31.

and reforms of Laud, growing from an increase in patristic scholarship in English Universities in the late-sixteenth and early-seventeenth centuries. The earliest exponent of this was Lancelot Andrewes who, on his death in 1626, Laud described as 'the great light of the Christian world.'[13] This interest in patristics can also be found in other anti-Calvinist thinkers of the time such as Thomas Jackson and William Buckeridge, both of whom found favour under the patronage of Laud.[14] There was some cross fertilisation of ideas between the theologians in the Netherlands and England who sought to reject the Calvinist theology. John Hales, later of the Great Tew circle, 'bade John Calvin goodnight' whilst observing the debates at the Synod of Dort in 1619. However, it is possible to see that, in Parker's words, 'English Arminianism was parallel to Armianism proper, not its product; it was not created by Arminius, nor did it follow him in detail.'[15] Even though Laud's own anti-Calvinism did not follow exactly the Arminian teachings of which he was accused, that does not mean that there was no theological consistency in his thought. In the past it has been popular to suggest that Laud's piety was a front for his political ambition. For instance, Hugh Trevor-Roper's influential account of Laud's life sees Laud's reforms as politically motivated by the wishes of Charles I and not by doctrinal conflicts with the Calvinist orthodoxy.[16] However, it is possible to find in Laud's early career a clear theological opposition to Calvinism. Whilst at Oxford Laud developed a defence of freewill, the interior nature of righteousness and the certainty of salvation.[17] As already stated, both Laud's anti-Calvinism and Arminianism proper centred on criticisms on the Calvinist doctrine of grace, and in

[13] Quoted in Nicholas Tyacke, 'Archbishop Laud,' in *The Early Stuart Church, 1603-1642*, edited by Kenneth Finchman. Basingstoke: Macmillan: 1993: 62.

[14] For Thomas Jackson see Sarah Hutton, 'Thomas Jackson, Oxford Platonist, and William Twisse, Aristotelian,' in *Journal of the History of Ideas*, 39 (1978): 635-52, in particular 638-41. For William Buckeridge see Tyacke, 'Archbishop Laud':56.

[15] T. Parker, '"Arminianism & Laudianism" in seventeenth century England,' in *Studies in Church History Vol. 1*, edited by C.W. Dugmore & Charles Duggan. London: Nelson, 1964: 29-30. Achsak Guibbory notes the complications distinguishing the different strands of seventeenth-century anti-Calvinism. Interestingly he distingquishes between 'Puritan' and 'Ceremonialist' tendencies instead of the traditional distinctions of 'Calvinist' and 'Arminian'. See *Ceremony and Community from Herbert to Milton: Literature, religion, and cultural conflict in seventeenth-century England*. Cambridge: CUP, 1998.

[16] For a critique or Trevor-Roper's biography of Laud see, Tyacke, 'Archbishop Laud': 51-3.

[17] Tyacke, 'Arminisim and English Culture', in *Britain and the Netherlands, Vol. 7 – Church & State since the Reformation*, edited by A.C. Duke & C.A. Tamse. The Hague: Martinus Nijhoff, 1981: 96.

particular the belief that it was the responsibility of man to freely accept the grace of God. Where Arminians differed was in the form that that free acceptance took. As we have seen above, Arminianism accepted the Reformed position that salvation could only come through the action of God's grace alone. Where they differed from Calvinists was in their belief that man could freely accept or reject God's grace. By contrast Laudianism focued on the sacraments as the agent of God's grace and so the means by which man is saved. This emphasis on the sacramental was peculiar to the English anti-Calvinism of Laudianism. Many of Laud's later hated reforms — altars moved to the east-end, use of communion rails etc. — had to do with the veneration and sacerdotal nature of communion within Laud's anti-Calvinistic theological system. As Nicholas Tyacke argues, 'it was no accident that during the Arminian ascendancy altars and fonts came to dominate Church interiors, for the two were logically connected, sacramental grace replacing the grace of predestination.'[18] What is clear, therefore, is that Laud's anti-Calvinism was as sincere as, but different in its form and temper from, the 'Reformed' anti-Calvinism of the Arminians.

With the ascendancy of Laud a systematic attack on those theologically opposed to him began. It is in these attacks that much of the confluence of the culture of Puritanism and the theology of Calvinism came about. Laud's theology, motivated as it was by an anti-Calvinism, promoted ceremonial and liturgical reforms which in turn attacked the religious culture of all Puritans, even if they themselves, like Cudworth and the Cambridge Platonists, opposed Calvinism for many of the same reasons as Laud. Laud's influence on the Universities was considerable both directly in Oxford, where he was elected Chancellor in 1630, and indirectly in Cambridge through the actions of intermediaries. This led to a systematic muzzling of Puritan interests within the University.

Despite this influence, some colleges and churches within Cambridge were able to resist Laud's reforms, most notably Emmanuel and Sidney Sussex Colleges, both of which were accused by Laud of being 'nurseries of Puritanism.'[19] What is of particular interest is that Cudworth and the Cambridge Platonists seem to have always remained connected to institutions that opposed, or at least resisted, Laud's reforms, most notably as students and fellows of Emmanuel but also by their connection with Holy Trinity Church. Holy Trinity was a centre of Puritanism in the City

---

[18] Tyacke, *Anti-Calvinists*: 176.
[19] Twigg, *University of Cambridge*: 38.

of Cambridge and often brought the displeasure of Laud.[20] Whichcote was appointed to the Sunday lectureship at Holy Trinity in 1636 at the height of Laud's influence in Cambridge. It is impossible to verify whether Whichcote's appointment was made with or without the blessing of the Laudians in Cambridge. It is possible to surmise, however, that Whichcote's conciliatory style may have been a nod to the dominance of the Laudians in Cambridge at the time. It may not be possible to go as far as Nicholas Tyacke in arguing that 'Calvinism had been silenced' in Cambridge by 1632.[21] It is, however, possible to see the Puritans, who included strict Calvinists as well as moderates such as the Cambridge Platonists, as very much on the defensive during this period. Although the Cambridge Platonists were not doctrinally Calvinist, their Puritan sympathies, especially in the face of Laud's reforms, placed them together with the strict Calvinists in opposing Laud during this period.

Cudworth and the Cambridge Platonists must, therefore, be understood as both anti-Calvinist in their theological outlook, and Puritan in their religious culture. In this way they were Puritan anti-Calvinists in keeping with the Arminian theology which had played a part in the theological life of Cambridge since the Barrat and Baro controversy of the 1590s. H.C. Porter has argued that this form of Puritan anti-Calvinism is marked out not simply a softening of the Reformed doctrine of grace, but also as a theological project which linked the recognition and acceptance of God's grace with the workings and faculties of human reason.[22] As we have seen the University of Cambridge in the early decades of the seventeenth century was home to an intellectual culture which openly questioned the orthodoxy of Calvinism. The intellectual development of Cudworth and the Cambridge Platonists is, therefore, not simply part of a rejection of Puritan Calvinism, but part of a broader religious culture of Puritanism. The importance of this existing Puritan intellectual culture in Cambridge in the seventeenth century also helps us understand how Cudworth, and the other Cambridge Platonists, not only turned to Neoplatonic thought in their rejection of Calvinism, but also did so initially from within Emmanuel College, one of the bastions of Puritan Cambridge.

---

[20] Twigg, *University of Cambridge*: 30.
[21] Tyacke, 'Archbishop Laud': 69. For a direct rejection of Tyacke's assertion see White, *Predestination*: 306.
[22] Porter, *Reformation and Reaction*: 416-429.

'The Emmanuel Platonists'

The term 'Cambridge Platonist' is an invention of modern scholarship. Although there is no doubt that there was a renaissance in Platonic philosophy in Cambridge beginning in the 1630s this was not a self-conscious school of thought as understood in the modern sense. For many the emergence of a group of Neoplatonic philosophers and theologians is seen almost as an aberration, a curious but largely insignificant development in the history of philosophy. Ernst Cassirier states that the Cambridge Platonists appeared 'to play no decisive part any phase' of the history of early-modern philosophy.[23] Certainly the general perception of seventeenth-century English philosophy is of the development, through the work of Bacon, Hobbes, and Locke, of the key principles and terms of empiricism. Consequently the adoption of Neoplatonic forms and modes of argument by the Cambridge Platonists certainly would appear to confirm the view of them as thinkers removed not only from the political, but also the philosophical concerns of the time. However, when placed in the Puritan intellectual culture of early seventeenth-century Cambridge, we can recognise Cudworth's use of Neoplatonism as an active response to this existing intellectual culture, rather than a self-conscious movement away from it. In particular the explicit use of Neoplatonic philosophy must be understood within two linked contexts. Firstly the tenets of Neoplatonism presented Cudworth and his contemporaries with a philosophical system which complimented the anti-Calvinism of their theology. In particular Cudworth's developed, through his Neoplatonism, a comprehensive intellectualism in opposition to the voluntarism of Calvinism. Secondly the use of Neoplatonism must be contrasted with the strictures and limits of the scholastic education which dominated Cambridge at the time. Scholasticism was not only criticised for being intellectually limiting, but also for provided the theoretical backdrop for much of the Calvinist theology of the early-seventeenth century.

Central to all aspects of Cudworth, and the Cambridge Platonists intellectual development is Emmanuel College. In fact so important is Emmanuel to the gensis of the Cambridge Platonists that John Tulloch termed Cudworth and his contemporaries the 'Emmanuel Platonists.' As has already been show, Emmanuel was at the heart of Puritan Cambridge. During the reign of James I, Emmanuel was criticised for failing both to have surplices worn in Chapel and to use the Book of Common Prayer. Most

---

[23] Cassirer, *Platonic Renaissance*: 1.

importantly, looking forward to Laud's reforms in the University, communion was taken sitting around a table, passing the sacraments from hand to hand. The chapel, which is now the Old Library in the college, was orientated north/south and remained unconsecrated. Emmanuel was, therefore, a great home to Puritanism understood in a more general sense. In fact two of the college's great masters from this period, Lawrence Chaderton and Richard Holdsworth, can be understood as Puritans who sought to distance themselves from the deterministic excesses of the Calvinism of their time.[24] Holdsworth as master actively discouraged his undergraduates from using Calvin as their sole or even their first source of Biblical interpretation.[25] That being said Emmanuel was also home to traditional Calvinist theologians, such as Anthony Tuckney, whose famous criticisms of Benjamin Whichcote will be discussed in Chapter Three. Emmanuel was, therefore, during this period definitely a Puritan institution, but, like much of Cambridge at this time, this does not automatically mean that the theological expression of this Puritanism was exclusively Calvinist in form.

On his matriculation in 1632 Cudworth, who we have seen was a child of Emmanuel, came under the tutorship of Benjamin Whichcote. Whichcote's influence on the young Cudworth and the other Cambridge Platonists cannot be stressed too much. Born in Stoke, Shropshire in 1609, Whichcote matriculated at Emmanuel in 1626 where he was initially tutored by Anthony Tuckney. He was elected to a fellowship in 1633 and appointed to the Sunday afternoon lectureship at Holy Trinity Church in 1636. Following his appointment as the Provost of King's by the Earl of Manchester, Whichcote acted as Vice-Chancellor in 1650-51, the year that his debate with Tuckney took place. He was removed from the Provostship of King's in 1660 by Royal order but, by accepting the Act of Uniformity, was appointed to St Anne's, Blackfriars. Later, in 1668, he was presented to the parish of St Lawrence Jewry becoming one of the leading members of the older generation of Latitudinarians counting amongst his regular congregation John Locke. Despite his removal to London, Whichcote always maintained a close affinity to Cambridge and in particular a close personal friendship with Ralph Cudworth, at whose house Whichcote died during a visit to Cambridge in 1683.[26] Perhaps

[24] Sarah Bendell, Christopher Brooke & Patrick Collinson, *A History of Emmanuel College, Cambridge*. Woodbridge: Boydell, 1999: 177, 224.
[25] Emmanuel College MS 48: 40.
[26] C.A. Patrides, ed. *The Cambridge Platonists*. London: Edward Arnold: xxix. The closeness of Whichcote and Cudworth's friendship is shown by Whichcote acting as security for Ralph Cudworth's youngest son Charles Cudworth's transit to work in India. Christ's College MS. Box 77: 'Letter of John C. Whitebrook to John Peile, May 26th 1902.'

because of Whichcote's geographical separation from Cambridge after 1660 it has become increasingly common for commentators to downplay and even deny a (Cambridge) Platonic element in his writings. In Whichcote's surviving work, posthumously collected sermons and aphorisms, one does not find the vast Platonic erudition that we find in Cudworth. Jon Parkin, in his recent work on Richard Cumberland, has argued that Whichcote was more a practical rational divine in the mould of the Latitudinarians than a 'cloistered' and esoteric thinker like Cudworth or More. Parkin argues that this is typified by his more common use of Aristotle than Plato in his sermons. This interpretation would seem strange for two reasons. Firstly, contemporary accounts never doubted Whichcote's use of Platonic theology. Gilbert Burnet, in his *History of my own time*, comments that it was Whichcote who had first encouraged the study of Plato and Plotinus in Cambridge.[27] Secondly, the non-Platonic reading of Whichcote relies too heavily on the surface, linguistic form of Whichcote's theology, examining whom he quotes, not how he uses them. It is true that Aristotle and many other non-Platonic philosophers are quoted by the Cambridge Platonists. Their use of these philosophers, however, has to be understood within the assumption of a broader Platonic framework.[28] Therefore, to downplay Whichcote's Platonism is completely to miss the essential Platonism of his intellectualist theology. Certainly, as shall be shown in more detail in Chapter Three, Whichcote's influence gave Cudworth not only the fundamental terms of his philosophical system, but also a bridge between the Puritan theology of *sola gratia* and the characteristic Cambridge Platonist philosophical endorsement of reason.

Whichcote's adoption of Platonism in his teaching needs to be understood against the context of the curriculum within which he was working and teaching The education which Cudworth would have received was, in the main, still dominated by the scholastic education which had defined the undergraduate curriculum of Cambridge since the mediaeval foundation of the colleges. One of the best sources showing the form this curriculum took is Richard Holdsworth's *Directions for a Student of the University*. This is not a direct transcript of a student education at the time but an idealised account of the form that that education might have taken.[29]

---

[27] Gilburt Burnet, *History of My own time*, 2 vols, edited by Osmund Airy. Oxford: The Clarendon Press, 1897-1900: I.331.

[28] Jon Parkin, *Science, Religion and Politics in Restoration England: Richard Cumberland's 'De Legibus Naturae'*. Woodbridge: Boydell, 1999: 76-7.

[29] For an account of the status and authorship of the *Directions* see John A. Trentmann, 'The Authorship of *Directions for a Student of the Universitie*' in *Transactions of the Cambridge Bibliographical Society*, 7 (1978): 170-83.

Central to *Directions* are the teaching of Aristotle. In fact it is possible to interpret the philosophical education that Holdsworth suggests for the four years of study as a preparation for the study of Aristotle's *Logic* at the end of it.[30] The final examination of this education came in the form of disputations. These were public examinations in which students had to defend or attack a set position using the forms of scholastic reasoning taught to them in the previous four years. Holdsworth was very keen to stress the importance of these disputations. They were not only needed to gain the degree, but would show the intellectual worth of the University when these students entered public life:

> Without those you will be bafeled in your disputes, digraced & vilified in Public examinations, laughed at in speeches & Declamations you will never dare so appear in any act of credit in the University.[31]

Cudworth would have received a basic education not dissimilar to that outlined by Holdsworth. However, during the seventeenth century the traditional scholastic curriculum at Cambridge was beginning to unravel. Holdsworth's desire to reform the curriculum, and Whichcote's innovations in the curriculum can be understood against a backdrop in which the scholasticism which had dominated Cambridge pedagogy was beginning to seem unsatisfactory.

In the broader context of seventeenth-century intellectual history many of the most interesting innovations in theology and philosophy can be traced, in part, to a reaction to the strictures of the scholastic education that most intellectuals received. Certainly Thomas Hobbes' antipathy to Aristotle, scholasticism, and University education is well known.[32] A similar reaction can be seen, if in a more muted form, in the development of Cudworth's theology and philosophy. In Cudworth's case the most important reason for this reaction was the central role that the scholastismc education played in the defining and justifying the arguments of Calvinist orthodoxy.[33] What characterises this reaction is not simply a

---

[30] William T. Costello, *The Scholastic Curriculum at Early Seventeenth century Cambridge*. Cambridge, MA: Harvard University Press, 1958: 14-5.

[31] Emmanuel College, MS.48: 22.

[32] For Hobbes' opposition to scholasticism see *Leviathan*: 385, 687-90, 708. Also see Martinich, *Hobbes – A Biography*. Cambridge: CUP, 1999: 8-18, 264-65.

[33] There is a long and continuing debate on the relationship between scholastic thought and the Reformed tradition. The traditional reading argues that the utilisation of scholastic forms of argument by the later generations of Reformers shows a break and development between the Reforming humanism of Luther and Calvin, and the 'Protestant Scholasticism' of late Reformers, in particular Theordore Beza. For a classic account of the 'Protestant Scholastic' argument see: Brian G. Armstrong, *Calvinism and the Amyrant Heresy: Protestant*

disagreement on theological principles, but a sense in which the strictures of scholasticism were limiting the ability of theological enquiry to conceive of both the enormity of the divine, but also the very real presence of God in every form of creation. As John Smith, one of Cudworth's pupils at Emmanuel, stated in a thinly veiled criticism of scholastic theology:

> To seek our divinity merely in books and writings, is to seek the living among the dead: we do but in vain seek God many times in these, where his truth too often is not so much enshrined as entoumbed: no; *intra te quare Deum* seek for God within thine owne soul;[34]

It is clear from this quote that as the heart of the 'Emmanuel Platonism' inaugurated by Whichcote was a rejection of not only the perceived limits and strictures of the scholastic curriculum, but also the use of scholasticism in the justification of the orthodoxy of seventeenth-century Calvinism.

'The Platonical Sauce'

It is clear that we gain a fuller picture of Cudworth's intellectual development, and that of the Cambridge Platonists in general, when it is placed within the broader intellectual culture of Puritan Cambridge. However, simply by characterising the Cambridge Platonists as reacting to the limits of Calvinism and scholasticism does not explain why this reaction took the form of what Ernst Cassirer termed a 'Platonic Renaissance in England'. Traditionally Cudworth's Neoplatonism has been contrasted with the developments in empirical philosophy which characterised seventeenth-century English philosophy, culminating with the publication of Locke's attack on innate ideas in his *Essay Concerning Human Understanding* in 1690. As a consequence the Neoplatonism of the Cambridge

---

Scholasticism and Humanism in Seventeenth century France. Madison, WI: University of Wisconsin Press, 1969: 136; and John S. Bray, *Theodore Beza's Doctrine of Predestination.* Nieuwkoop: B. De Graaf, 1975: 119. In recent years a revisionist position, largely driven by the work of Richard A. Muller, has argued that there is much greater continuity between the Reformers and the Reformed tradition both in matters of doctrine (orthodoxy) and matters of method (in particular scholasticism). Muller in particular has argued that scholasticism should not be viewed anachronistically as 'dry' and 'sterile' thinking, but a rigorous and logical method designed to uncover the truth of a proposition. Using an instrumental account of 'scholasticism' he, therefore, argues against the interpretation of 'Protestant Scholasticism' and argues instead for a unified and developing form to Reformed orthodoxy which used scholasticism as one of many forms of argument used by theologians in the Reformed tradition. See Muller, *Post-Reformation Reformed Dogmatics*: I:27-45.

[34] John Smith, *Selected Discourses*. London: 1821: 5.

Platonists has been viewed as esoteric and otherworldly in face of the practical and procedural virtues of empirical philosophy. This limited interpretation of the Cudworth's Neoplatonism can be overturned if we look to answer the question 'why did the Cambridge Platonists choose Neoplatonism'? No definitive reason is ever given for why Cudworth and his contemporaries drew so readily on Platonic sources. However, it is possible to argue that Platonism, and in particular the intellectualism implicit in Neoplatonism, presented an intellectual structure that complimented and strengthened the Puritan, anti-Calvinist, and Arminian sympathies of the Cambridge Platonists. If this theological context is established we can see how Cudworth was directly engaged with the intellectual and practical concerns of the seventeenth-century England.[35]

It is wrong to think that because Aristotle, rather than Plato, dominated the University curriculum, that Plato was entirely alien to seventeenth-century theology and philosophy. It is true that Platonic sources were far less common in England than in other countries on the continent. Only two Platonic texts, a Greek edition of the *Menexenus* and the pseudo-Platonic *Axiochus*, had been published in England by the beginning of the seventeenth century.[36] There had always been, however, since the sixteenth century writings of Erasmus, Jean Colet and Thomas More, a tradition of Platonic humanism within England. This was evident in the humanist foundations of St John's and of Christ's Colleges in Cambridge, and Corpus Christi College, Oxford. However, even in these foundations Plato remained an optional, not compulsory, element of the curriculum.[37] The prevalence of the study of Aristotle did not mean that there was necessarily no place for the study of Plato. The two thinkers were not seen as polar opposites, but as part of the same tradition of wisdom and learning.[38] Even among thinkers who championed the work of Aristotle a healthy respect for Plato can be found. One of the best examples of this is Richard Holdsworth's *Praelectiones Theologicae*. Holdsworth, who we have previously encountered advocating the importance of Aristotle in his *Directions for a Student of the University,* was a product of the humanism of St John's College, Cambridge. He first gave the *Praelectiones*

---

[35] Frederick Copleston, *A History of Philosophy*, 9 vols. London: Burns and Oates, 1946-1975: V.63.

[36] Sarah Hutton, 'Plato in the Tudor Academies' in *Sir Thomas Gresham and Gresham College: Studies in the Intellectual history of London in the sixteenth and seventeenth centuries*, edited by Francis Ames-Lewis. Aldershot: Ashgate, 1999: 107.

[37] Hutton, 'Plato in the Tudor Academies': 109-10.

[38] Charles B. Schmitt, *Aristotle and the Renaissance*. Cambridge, MA: Harvard University Press, 1983: 91-3, 103; Hutton, 'Plato in the Tudor Academies': 109.

Theologicae as lectures while he was Professor of Divinity at Gresham College in the 1630s. In these lectures references to Plato are frequent, using the common Neoplatonic epithet of '*divinissimus Plato.*'[39] There are also other clear examples of the use of Platonism in seventeenth-century scholarship that predates the Cambridge Platonists. Platonic works were readily, if not widely available in Cambridge libraries. There are over thirty instances of holdings of Plato in college libraries and private book collections in seventeenth century Cambridge. In addition there were also Neoplatonic sources in Cambridge collections in the seventeenth century, including an edition of Plotinus in Andrew Perne's vast book collection that found its way into Peterhouse library after his death in 1589.[40]

Far from its being anathema to seventeenth-century philosophy, there are explicit references to Platonic thought in the writings of philosophers and theologians of the period. Although not entirely positive, both Thomas Hobbes and Francis Bacon made references to Plato in their writings which assume knowledge of his work.[41] A more positive use of Platonic philosophy can be found in the writings of scholars educated in the humanist foundations mentioned above. At St John's in Cambridge Everard Digby used a wide range of sources from both the Aristotelian and Platonic traditions. Crucially he had not only a knowledge of Plato, but also the Neoplatonism of, amongst others, Plotinus, Proclus and Iamblichus.[42] However, the most important Platonist of the early-seventeenth century was Thomas Jackson. Jackson, born in 1579, was a student and later fellow of Corpus Christi College, Oxford. After a period as Vicar in Newcastle-upon-Tyne he was elected, under the sponsorship of Laud, as President of Corpus Christi, a position he held from 1630 till his death in 1640. In the early-seventeenth century the originality of Jackson's mind was marked by the manner in which he distanced himself from the scholasticism that characterised early-seventeenth century Reformed

---

[39] Richard Holdsworth, *Praelectiones Theologicae*, edited by Richard Pearson: London: 1661: 359, 57, 107, 203; Hutton, 'Plato in the Tudor Academies': 123.

[40] E.S. Leedham-Green, *Books in Cambridge Inventories*, 2 vols. Cambridge: CUP, 1986: I.448, 625-6, 629; II.419.

[41] For Hobbes' references to Plato's *Republic* see the conclusion to Book Two of *Leviathan*: 407. Bacon refers to Plato in *The Advancement of Learning* in *The Oxford Francis Bacon*, vol. 4, edited by Michael Kiernan: Oxford, The Clarendon Press, 2000: 83-84. Also see, G.A.J. Rogers, 'Locke, Plato, and Platonism' in *Platonism and the Origins of Modernity: Studies on Platonism and Early Modern Philosophy*, edited by Douglas Hedley and Sarah Hutton: Dordrecht, Springer, 2008: 194.

[42] Hutton, 'Plato in the Tudor Academies': 113

theology.[43] Jackson's theology constantly used Platonic imagery and distinctions leading to argue at times that there is an almost providential closeness between Christianity and Platonism. In his voluminous writings Jackson often cites the 'Divine' philosophy of Plato and Plotinus. Jackson also cites the myth of the 'Attic Moses' and the dissemination of revealed truth through ancient theology — the *prisca theologia* — as possible sources for the seeming closeness of Christianity and Platonism.[44] Jackson even goes so far as to argue that pagan Platonism written after the birth of Christ might have been influenced by the revealed truth of Christianity. In the case of Plotinus, Jackson argues that Plotinus, perhaps through contact with the works of Origen, had 'set forth stolen fragments of the food of life with the Platonical sauce.'[45]

There are clear biographical links between Jackson and the Cambridge Platonists. Jackson was friendly with Henry More's tutor Joseph Mede[46], and Jackson later published his correspondence with Henry More. Jackson's Platonism does differ from that of the Cambridge Platonists. In particular, his theology is based much more explicitly in the doctrines of the Church. This is shown by the fact that his works, although containing great Platonic learning, were primarily concerned with doctrinal Christian issues, rather than the more wide-ranging philosophical questions dealt with by Cudworth. Jackson also cautions against the dangers of too heavy a reliance on ancient wisdom, favouring primarily the revealed truth of Christianity. Despite this Jackson does share many affinities, both philologically and philosophically with the Cambridge Platonists. Jackson's theology, therefore, along with that of lesser figures such as Everard Digby, shows that there existed in the early-seventeenth century a small, yet significant tradition of Platonic thought in England.

The main sources for the Platonism outlined above, particularly those of Holdsworth, Digby, and Jackson, were the Platonic editions and writings of the Renaissance, Florintine Platonists of Marsilio Ficino and Pico della Mirandola. Because of the central role that the work of Plontinus, as well as Plato, played in Florentine this early-modern Platonic renaissance is more accurately a Neoplatonic Renaissance. In fact so strong is

---

[43] White, *Predestination*: 256-9. On Jackson's rejection of scholasticism see Jackson, *Works*: V.99.

[44] Jackson, *Works*: I.115, IV.404, V.27, VII.243.

[45] Jackson, *Works*: IV.404.

[46] See Jeffrey K. Jue, *Heaven upon Earth: Joseph Mede (1586-1638) and the Legacy of Millenarianism*. Dordrecht: Springer, 2006. For Mede's relationship with Jackson see 47-8; for Mede and the Cambridge Platonists see 37-64.

this influence of Plotinus on the on the Cambridge Platonists that Samuel Taylor Coleridge described them as not so much Platonists but 'more truly Plotinists.'[47] Although modern scholarship readily accepts the distinction between Platonism and Neoplatonism it is important to remember that this bifurcation only really developed in the nineteenth century. Since then it has become common to distinguish more clearly between the Neoplatonism of the Plotinian tradition and the authentic Plato of the dialogues and it has been routine to characterise the former as esoteric and implicitly mystical derivations of the original, more philosophically valid, Platonic sources.[48] This is nowhere more strongly seen when J.S. Mill argued that Neoplatonism was 'an aftergrowth of late date and little intrinsic value...a hybrid product of Greek and Oriental speculation, and its place in history is by the side of Gnosticism.'[49] Something of this later distinction between Platonism and Neoplatonism has almost certainly been imposed back on the Cambridge Platonists. It certainly is possible to identify some mystical and esoteric themes in the writings of the Cambridge Platonists, if not directly in those of Cudworth, certainly in Henry More's *Divine Dialogues* and John Smith's *Selected Discourses*. It would, though, be wrong to equate Cudworth's thought with the self-consciously esoteric thought of a later Neoplatonist such as Thomas Taylor.[50]

What is clear is that, placed within the broader theological context of seventeenth-century society, and the specific concerns presented by the culture the University of Cambridge at the time, Cudworth's Neoplatonism

---

[47] Coleridge, *Seventeenth Century*: 366.

[48] This distinction can be traced to Johann Jacob Brucker's *Critical History of Philosophy from the First beginnings of the World to our Times* in 1742-4, which was later popularised by Frederick Schleiermacher in his German translations of the Plato's *Dialogues* in 1804. The clearest account of this is E.N. Tigerstedt, *The Decline and Fall of the Neoplatonic interpretation of Plato*: Helsinki: Societas Scientiarum Fennica, 1974.

[49] J.S. Mill, *Dissertations and Discussions: Political, Philosophical and Historical*, 4 vols. London: Longmans, Green, Reader & Dyer, 1854-1875: III.276.

[50] For a critical assessment of Thomas Taylor's Neoplatonism see George Mills Harper, *The Neoplatonism of William Blake*. Chapel Hill, NC: The University of North Carolina Press, 1961. W.R. Inge argues persuasively that the traditional characterisation of Neoplatonism as esoteric and mystical is as much a linguistic as an intellectual distinction between transcendent idealism of Neoplatonism and the practical virtues of empiricism. In his *The Philosophy of Plotinus* Inge argues that the English language lacks the subtly to describe the transcendent themes in Neoplatonism. So where German can distinguish between the lower form of 'mystick' and the higher principle of 'mysticimus', in English both are subsumed into the more subjective term of 'mystical'. See W.R. Inge, *The Philosophy of Plotinus*. London: Longman's, Green & Co., 1918: I.1. Also John Rist, *Plotinus: The Road to reality*. Cambridge: CUP, 1967: 214; and R.C. Zaehner, *Mysticism: Sacred and Profane. An Inquiry into some Varieties of Praeternatural Experience*. Oxford: The Clarendon Press, 1957.

existed as an integral part of his practical intellectual project. As such it
is not only defined by, but also responds to, the specific practical and
political concerns of his day. It appears that Cudworth's Neoplatonism
developed very early in his university career. In a series of undated letters
sent by Cudworth to his orthodox Calvinist step-father John Stoughton,
probably written in 1638 or 1639, Cudworth refers to Neoplatonic thought
as central to his theological world view. Referring to Plato as 'that divine
Heathen', Cudworth equates the Platonic scale of being with the 'Jacob's
ladder of the Bible'. He argues that all knowledge, pagan or Christian,
should be used to bring man into a closer engagement with God and the
created world: 'I am perswaded all true knowledge, if our understanding
were right, would end in the Practicall Loving and closing with God.' Even
in these early letters we can see the manner in which Cudworth utilised
Neoplatonism. Crucially this adoption of Neoplatonism did not turn Cudworth away form the created world, but impelled man to come into a closer
'practical', ethical, and arguably political engagement with the world.[51]

Theology, politics, and Cambridge Platonism

By the end of the 1640s the intellectual themes which exist in Cudworth's
letters from the late 1630s became forged into the basic intellectual structure which remained with Cudworth throughout his life. The intellectual
factors that defined Cudworth's intellectual development is given greater
significance when they are related to the political chaos and instability of
the late 1630s and 1640s. As many commentators have noted, Cudworth
and the other Cambridge Platonists are notable in their absence from the
events of the English Civil War. In particular Cudworth's ability to pros-
per under the Parliamentary, Republican and Protectorate regimes, and
still maintain his place in Cambridge after the Restoration seems to show
something of his political quietism, 'standing aside' from the conflicts of
the time.[52] However, if the contemporary theological context is placed

---

[51] Undated letters from Ralph Cudworth to John Stoughton, in Thomas Solly, *The Will,
Human and Divine*. London: 1856: 288-99. In the first letter Cudworth discusses his
tutor's desire for him to apply for a Fellowship at Emmanuel. Cudworth implies that this
suggestion was made before he had taken his M.A. which would date the letters between
his graduation as B.A. in 1635 and M.A. in 1639. The discussion of the Fellowship, which
he was elected to in 1639, suggests that the letter was written in the latter part of this
period of post-graduate study.

[52] W.R. Inge, 'Introduction,' to Benjamin Whichcote, Moral and Religious Aphorisms.
London: Elkin Matthews, 1930: iii.

front and centre in an interpretation of Cudworth's work it is possible to overturn this caricature. The Civil War, more than any external event, shaped and defined Cudworth's intellectual destiny. It provided the circumstances for his swift promotion in the University. Following the Restoration the memory of Cudworth's elevation during the interregnum also provided the political capital for those who wished to undermine Cudworth's character, professional ability, and intellectual output. The importance of the political context of Restoration Cambridge on Cudworth, which will be discussed in greater detail in Chapter Two, had a defining effect on the form and composition of his *TISU*. As we shall come to see, for Cudworth the religious and social divisions created by the Civil War acted as a catalyst for the definition of his ethical and political ideas. In the context of the very real problems created by the Civil War Cudworth's ideas seem illusory at best. However, it is possible to find in Cudworth's whole body of work the development of ethical and political themes which, although not speaking directly to the issues of the Civil War, did seek to overcome the underlying premises on which the conflict was built. In particular Cudworth's advocacy for religious toleration, individual responsibility, and universally comprehensible ethical principles was a reply to the intolerance, division, and chaos created by the Civil War. This is not a slow and gradual development, but one which exists in his extant writings from the period of the Civil War, in particular his *First Sermon*, of 1647.

Cudworth, at the time of his invitation to preach to the House of Commons, had been appointed both master of Clare Hall and Regius Professor of Hebrew. In his *First Sermon* we can recognise the theological and themes outlined above which defined his thought. More importantly Cudworth's *First Sermon* shows how Cudworth argued that these intellectual principles could be used to respond to the ethical and political climate of the day. This sermon, therefore, provides a model through which we can see how Cudworth's development in the intellectual climate of seventeenth-century Cambridge informed his own ethical and political response to contemporary events. This model of theological insight informing practical action exists in all of Cudworth's writing, most importantly, as we shall see in later chapters, in his incomplete *Intellectual System*.

Cudworth, in his *First Sermon,* not only attacks the prevailing theological mood of the day, which he identifies with the Reformed orthodoxy of the Westminster Assembly, but also the divisive use to which religion had been put to tear the country apart through the extraordinary middle years of the 1640s. Cudworth links these two issues with a general attack on the dangers of what he terms 'self-love.' Although this is never clearly defined by Cudworth in the *First Sermon* it is clear that, by implication, Cudworth understands self-love in two ways. Firstly, it is the selfish, egotistical act of man following base emotions over higher intellectual principles. Secondly, and more importantly for the context of Cudworth's *First Sermon*, he uses self-love to attack the stale, legalistic interpretations of religion that made religion not something which reformed man, but something that merely confirmed man's own self-image and prejudices. Such a self-serving understanding of religion, Cudworth argues, fails to understand that man is, by his very creation, actively involved in the nature and reality of the divine. The most influential part of this religious legalism came, for Cudworth, in scholastic method employed by those who defended the Reformed orthodoxy of the Westminster Confession.[53] At the very beginning of the *First Sermon* Cudworth attacks those who write about religion as 'but a little *Book-craft*, a mere *paper-skill*.'[54] Cudworth argues that such thinkers fail because their bookish approach to theology can never bring man into a true participatory relationship with the divine. This scholasticism creates, in Cudworth's view, a prescriptive and legalistic ethical system that implicitly fails to appreciate the living, active nature of God's presence in the world. As Cudworth states, '[i]nke and paper can never make us Christians, can never beget a new nature, a living principle within us: can never form Christ, or any true notions of spirituall things in our hearts.'[55] Cudworth is dismissive of those who believe that knowledge or experience of salvation could ever be achieved by such means. It is, Cudworth argues, ridiculous 'to perswade our selves that we are certainly elected to everlasting happiness: before we see the image of God, in rightousnesse and true holinesse, shaped in our hearts.'[56]

The final clause of this quotation shows not only Cudworth's disquiet with much contemporary theology, but also the intellectualism he employed to oppose it. For Cudworth the English Reformed divines who created the Westminster Confession failed to recognise that man is, by nature, shaped not by logical arguments, but through the practical processes of

---

[53] For an account of the 'scholastic' defences of the Westminster Confession see Richard A. Muller, *After Calvin: Studies in the Development of a Theological Tradition*: Oxford, OUP, 2003.
[54] *First Sermon*: 91.
[55] *First Sermon*: 92.
[56] *First Sermon*: 94.

righteousness and holiness.[57] Man's relationship to God cannot be defined by the complications of scholastic logic but through the recognition of the divine principle in all men: 'Surely, the way to heaven that Christ hath taught us, is plain and easie, if we have but honest hearts: we need not many Criticismes, many School-distinctions, to come to a right understanding of it.'[58] To counter this perceived legalism Cudworth draws explicitly on his Neoplatonism to argue that the true principle of Christ is known because creation is defined by the wisdom, and not the will of God. Here Cudworth draws directly on Plato's *Euthyphro*, to link God's love not to an act of divine will, but to the constancy of God's wisdom, justice, and love in all things.[59] Comparing Plato's argument with 1 Jn. 4:10,[60] Cudworth equates the nature of man, the incarnation and the salvation of man to this central, intellectually understood, principle of divine love. For this reason Cudworth argues the principles of true theology are found, as the example of Christ taught man, in actions rather than in mere words. So Cudworth argues:

> The Gospel, that new Law which Christ delivered to the world, it is not merely a *Letter* without us, but a *quickening Spirit* within us. Cold Theorems and Maximes, dry and jejune Disputes, lean syllogistical reasonings, could never yet of themselves beget the least glympse of true heavenly light, the least sap of saving knowledge in any heart.[61]

Distinctions learnt from philosophy are important, but only as a means to confirm the truth already revealed to man in the example of Christ. In the example of Christ we have an example of the divine principle existing in all men. The implications of this are two-fold. Firstly all men owe their allegiance to God and are obliged to orientate themselves to the reasoned principles of the divine in all parts of creation. As Cudworth states, '*God was therefore incarnated and made man, that he might Deifie us*, that is…make us *partakers of the Divine nature*.'[62] Secondly by asserting something of the divine in all men, Cudworth asserts an implicit equality between all men as equal participants in the intellectual form of

---

[57] Richard Muller has correctly pointed out that the Westminster Confession is not, itself, a scholastic work. However he does argue that 'the method of the document itself is not scholastic, but the confession is certainly the product of English Reformed scholastic divines.' Muller, *Post-Reformation Reformed Dogmastics*: I:198.

[58] *First Sermon*: 96.

[59] *First Sermon*: 102.

[60] 'In this is love, not that we loved God but that he loved us and sent his son to be the expiation of our sins.'

[61] *First Sermon*: 92.

[62] *First Sermon*: 101.

divine creation. Therefore, Cudworth argues in his *First Sermon*, there is a double obligation on man, primarily to God as creator, and secondly to others as equal participants in the divine nature. Drawing directly on the experiences of the Civil War, Cudworth argues that men should not be pulled apart by conflict, but drawn together as free and equal participants in a human community defined by the intellect of the divine. As will be discussed more fully in Chapter Five, Cudworth envisaged this through a development of religious tolerance. In Cudworth's *First Sermon* it is possible to find not only the intellectual contexts which defined the development of his thought — particularly his anti-Calvinism and Platonic rejection of scholasticism — but also in a nascent form the central ethical and political principles of his mature philosophy. As with his *First Sermon*, Cudworth's mature intellectual project begins with a rejection of the perceived strictures of contemporary belief, what Cudworth styles as 'self-love' in his *First Sermon,* and what I will term arbitrary authority. By arbitrary authority I mean any system — be it theological, ethical, or political — which first rejects that the world is defined by eternal and immutable intellectual principles, and secondly denies that man has the freewill to live choose or decline the ethical norms hardwired into creation. All of Cudworth's theology and philosophy constantly returns to his rejection of arbitrary authority. As we shall see in the following chapters, Cudworth largest work, his *TISU*, sought to address the problem of arbitrary authority through a comprehensive defence of the reasoned form of creation. This is, however, not simply a loose defence of reason as such, but a thoroughgoing account of creation which has at its heart a God whose defining principle is reason. All things in creation are therefore defined by, ordered by, and related to one another by reason. Cudworth therefore not only attacks 'atheistic' systems such as Hobbism which appear to fulfil both the characteristics of arbitrary authority, but also 'theistic' systems like Calvinism which either suggest or have the potential to fulfil one or both of the qualities of arbitrary authority. What it characteristic about Cudworth's position is his linking of the comprehensive divine principle of reason to the Christian doctrine of the Trinity. The persons of the Trinity — the creator, redeemer, and sanctifier — provide for Cudworth not only a means through which man can come to comprehend the reasoned form of creation, but also man's place and responsibilities to God and to other men in creation. This Trinitarian project provides the *leitmotif* of Cudworth's *TISU* and will provide the subject matter for the next two chapters of this book.

CHAPTER TWO

THE TRUE INTELLECTUAL SYSTEM OF THE UNIVERSE I: CUDWORTH'S REJECTION OF ARBITRARY AUTHORITY

Cudworth's attack on arbitrary authority is found most fully in the first volume of his incomplete *Intellectual System*. All accounts of Cudworth's philosophy, even the most charitable, comment on the often wearisome length, and pedantic nature of Cudworth's longest published work. C.A. Patrides, in his well thumbed collection on the Cambridge Platonists, comments:

> Readers of the *System* have repeatedly attacked its "diffuse repetitions and enormous digressions," its "vast and unwieldy" size, its lack of "any graces of style." It has even been called "monstrously obese" — and who can demure?[1]

As a single text it runs to over 900 pages in the original edition and easily dwarfs in length all of Cudworth's other published works combined. It is work of staggering erudition, showing-off Cudworth's voluminous knowledge of ancient religions, philosophies, languages. A certain amount of lucidity was brought to the text through the footnotes to the Latin translation made by the German scholar Johann Lorenz Mosheim — a project of equal, if not greater erudition than Cudworth's original[2] — and the translation of Mosheim's notes and detailed index added in the 1845 English edition of the text made by John Harrison.[3] However, even with these aids there is the constant danger that one fails to see the wood for the trees. More precisely, that because of the historical and classical learning of the text something of the intellectual and philosophical worth of *TISU* is overlooked. For this reason it is instructive to examine something of the genesis of the text itself, to understand it not simply as a

---

[1] Patrides, *Cambridge Platonists*: ix.

[2] Ralph Cudworth, *Systema intellectuale huius universi,* translated by J.L. Mosheim. Jena: 1733. For a discussion of Mosheim's interpretation of Cudworth see Sarah Hutton, 'Classicism and Baroque – A Note on Mosheim's footnotes to Cudworth's 'The True Intellectual System of the Universe' in *Johann Lorenz Mosheim – Theologie im sannhungsfeld von Philosophie, Philologie und Geschichte, 1693-1755,* edited by Martin Mulsow. Weisbaden: Harrasowitz, 1997.

[3] Ralph Cudworth, *The True Intellectual System of the Universe*, 3 vols, edited by John Harrison. London: Thomas Tegg, 1845.

monolith, but as a text, as with Cudworth's early work, which was conceived and defined in the theological and intellectual context of seventeenth-
century England.

It is somehow fitting that a text which has brought so much trouble to
its readers should begin with an apology from the author. In the 'Preface
to the Reader' Cudworth states:

> Though, I confess, I have seldom taken any great pleasure, in reading other
> mens Apologies, yet must I at this time make some myself. First therefore,
> I acknowledge, that when I engag'd the Press, I intended onely a Discousre
> concerning Liberty and Necessity.[4]

Cudworth then goes on to explain that his original intention had developed into the current text which provided the groundwork for a later
text on freewill. Cudworth, therefore, intended *TISU* as one part of a
three volume work. The first volume was '*to Prove, That God is no meer
Arbitrary Will*; the second a 'Defence of Natural, Eternal, *and* Immutable
Justice, *or* Morality'; and the third showing that man has '*some Liberty,
or* Power *over our own* Actions.'[5] When we come to *TISU* we need to
recognise that it is an incomplete work. Although Cudworth is at pains
to stress that the work could stand alone, as a text it also '*needs beget an
Expectation, of the* Two *following* Treatises.' Therefore, when one comes
to deal with *TISU* it is important to recognise three key issues. Firstly one
must remember the proposed role that this volume was to take in Cudworth's
Intellectual System. As stated above, Cudworth intended the text to refute
any suggestion of arbitrariness in theology. From what we already know
about Cudworth's intellectual development, in particular his theological
rejection of Calvinism, we can read *TISU* as a continuation of Cudworth's
intellectualism which was discussed in the previous chapter. So much so
that it is possible to see that not only the philosophical arguments but also
the forms of argument used in *TISU*, particularly Cudworth's use of the
traditions of the *prisca theologia* — the ancient theology — exist as part
of unified intellectual project. Importantly for the reputation of *TISU*,
Cudworth's rejection of arbitrary authority extended from the potential
dangers of Calvinist theology to the very real threats presented by the authoritarianism Thomas Hobbes' philosophy. Secondly, it should be noted that
Cudworth's rejection of arbitrary authority in *TISU* is not simply a process of negation. Rather, as we shall see in Chapter Three, Cudworth's
attack on arbitrary authority provides the basis on which his Trinitarian

---

[4] *TISU*: iii.
[5] *TISU*: v-vi.

theology is built. Thirdly, although Cudworth stated that *TISU* could stand alone, it is important to recognise the relationship that it had to the rest of the unpublished *Intellectual System*. As we shall come to see in Chapters Four and Five, it is possible to reconstruct something of these later arguments from Cudworth's posthumously published works and unpublished manuscripts. Cudworth's rejection of arbitrary authority in *TISU* was not, therefore, an act of pedantic erudition, but part of a greater project. Cudworth's intention was not only to advocate the eternal and immutable moral laws and form of creation, but also the freewill of man to choose or deny these eternal and immutable moral norms. Cudworth's work therefore exists as both a polemical attack on any theological or philosophical system which denied one or both of the above qualities. *TISU*, therefore, not only presents the key to the understanding of Cudworth's ethical writings, but also acts an intellectual link between these mature works and the intellectual and ethical dilemmas that defined Cudworth's early life.

Restoration Cambridge and Cudworth's *Intellectual System*

By the time of the publication of *TISU* in 1678 Cudworth had been Master of Christ's for twenty-four years. Cudworth's livelihood was tied to his employment within the University of Cambridge. Cudworth, who did not enjoy the security of an independent income, had nearly been forced to quit to the University in the early 1650s because of a shortage of funds. In professional terms Cudworth benefited enormously from the political upheavals of the Civil War and interregnum. Between 1644 and 1654 he had gone from a respected fellow to being a leading member of the University with all the attached influence and financial security that that afforded Cudworth. At the Restoration Cudworth's position, and as consequence his financial stability, came under severe pressure, firstly through a campaign by Ralph Widdrington, a fellow of Christ's, and later through the actions of Bishop Humphrey Henchman.[6] The specifics of

---

[6] Cudworth's suspicion that opposition to his place at Cambridge was being orchestrated by Bishop Henchman is confirmed by a letter from Henchman to Richard Love dated 17 October, 1660 which is held in the Tanner manuscripts of the Bodleian Library. In this Henchman states that 'Dr Cudworth brought Clare-Hall into a ruinous condition, and then I have cause to feare that [he] may do that like at Christ College.' Henchman goes on to argue that the failures of a head of a college are based not on his economic management of a college which, he argues, can be delegated to a bursar, but on the moral leadership that the master gives to the college. Therefore Henchman's criticisms of

these campaigns, and Cudworth's reactions to them, will be discussed in Chapter Five, in relation to Cudworth's political utterances. However, in this context it is important to note the personal pressure that Cudworth was placed under in the 1660s had a direct bearing on the composition and production of *TISU*. At the Restoration most of the college heads who had been placed in their position by the Earl of Manchester in 1644 were removed, most notably Whichcote at King's, Worthington at Jesus, and Tuckney at Emmanuel. In contrast Cudworth's position was stronger than his colleagues because he had moved from his 'placed' position at Clare Hall to his 'elected' position at Christ's. Cudworth's stronger legal position at Christ's was also aided by the support he enjoyed from influential members of the court, most notably Heneage Finch and Archbishop Gilbert Sheldon. Despite strong opposition and the attempts to remove him from his position, the King, in 1660, confirmed Cudworth in his position as Master of Christ's.[7] In a series of letters which Cudworth wrote to his friend John Worthington in the 1660s it is clear that Cudworth recognised the help of those who had defended his position. In particular, he was searching for some means of thanking Archbishop Sheldon, to whom he owed his 'living and station.'[8]

It is into this very particular political context that Cudworth first conceived his *Intellectual System*. He had confided in Worthington his desire to dedicate a work to Sheldon to repay him for his support. Cudworth's intention was to write a work on natural ethics for this purpose. Although Cudworth does not state it, it seems clear that this work would not only publicly show his support to Sheldon, but also show how Cudworth's writings would not undermine the newly Restored monarchy. We can see something of his urgency in producing a work for Sheldon in the letters that Cudworth wrote to Worthington during this period. They detail a particularly fractious encounter Cudworth had with his fellow Cambridge Platonist, Henry More. In a letter dated January 1664/5 Cudworth confided in Worthington that he was 'struck into amaze' by the discovery that More, 'whom I have been entire friend to,' was also working on an intellectualist ethics. Cudworth claimed that More was perfectly aware that he had been working on this project, which had begun as sermons he had preached in the college chapel. More, writing in his defence to

---

Cudworth are not for his inexperience during his time at Clare, but because Cudworth's churchmanship was not in tune with the newly restored Anglican Church of which Henchman was a leading member. See Bod. MS Tanner 49: 32.

[7] Worthington, *Diary*: I.203.
[8] Worthington, *Diary*: II.135.

Worthington in May of the same year, claimed that he had intended to publish his work after Cudworth had published his.[9] For many the vehemence of Cudworth's reaction has been viewed as surprising. For instance Passmore stresses that the conflict is 'scarcely intelligible' and interprets it as Cudworth frustration at being usurped by his former pupil.[10] It is, however, possible to argue that there was more involved in this reaction than an academic spat over claims to intellectual property. The often fraught political context of Cambridge in the 1660s allows us to gain both a fuller understanding of this conflict, and also the political imperative that lay behind the project that would become the *Intellectual System*. Cudworth's clear anger at More was not that he was publishing on a similar area — this had never been, nor would it remain a problem for the Cambridge Platonists. Instead Cudworth feared that More, by publishing such a similar work (which he did with the publication of his *Enchiridion Ethicum* in 1666) would remove from Cudworth the chance to repay the debt to those on whose influence he relied. If this interpretation is correct one may then imagine Cudworth's increased anger when he discovered More's intention to dedicate his own ethical work to Sheldon, especially as Cudworth had already informed Sheldon of his intention to publish a work dedicated to him.[11]

We can identify the continued existence of this political imperative in Cudworth's project from its inception to the eventual publication of *TISU* in 1678. Cudworth had been given an 'Imprimatur' to publish his work by Gilbert Sheldon on 29 May 1671.[12] This leaves an unaccounted period of seven years between licensing and publication. It is tempting to suggest that the delay in publication was due to Cudworth's well documented reticence to publish, or his unwillingness to leave the final text.[13] However, Thomas Birch suggests that the delay was because the text 'met with great opposition from some of the Courtiers of King *Charles* II, who endeavoured to destroy the reputation of it, when it was first published.'[14] If this is true then it is clear that Cudworth's wider reputation remained stained by his close association with the Protectorate. There is no other evidence for the existence of this plot except for Birch's assertion. However, the

---

[9] Worthington, *Diary*: I.157-60, 172.

[10] Passmore, *Ralph Cudworth*: 16-8.

[11] Worthington, *Diary*: II.162, 166.

[12] *TISU*: xviii.

[13] On Worthington's attempts to encourage Cudworth to publish in the 1650s and 1660s see Worthington, *Diary*: I.271, II.61.

[14] Birch, 'Life': xiii.

fact that Cudworth dedicated the work to Heneage Finch, by this time
Lord Chancellor, shows that, as with his desire to dedicate a work to
Sheldon, Cudworth wished his work to gain the political cover afforded
by the public approval of his influential supporters.

Returning to Cudworth's position in the 1660s, it is clear from his letters to Worthington that, although stung by More's intervention, the political necessity of dedicating a work to Sheldon remained. Despite being
confirmed in his position Cudworth remained under attack from those who
opposed him both in Cambridge and at Court. As a consequence Cudworth, in 1664, published his *Second Sermon*. Cudworth was unsatisfied
with this work, but believed it the best he had to offer at the time.[15]
A close examination of the *Second Sermon*, particularly in this context
shows something of the political imperative which Cudworth wished to
bring to his work on natural ethics, which is also apparent in the rejection
of arbitrary authority in *TISU*. As a text it allows us to move from the
intentions of the *First Sermon*, which were discussed in the previous chapter, to the fuller expression of Cudworth's mature philosophical position.

The *Second Sermon* exists in the same Puritan intellectual culture
which formed the *First Sermon*. In the *Second Sermon* Cudworth, using
suggestively political language, lists three levels to describe how man can
ascend to a fully participatory relationship with God. The first level,
where Cudworth describes man as 'sin's freeman,' is the life driven and
defined by '*Carnal Liberty*, or Licentiousness.'[16] This position, Cudworth
claims, is taken by 'Epicureans, Antinomians and Enthusiasts.' Cudworth, in *TISU*, reserves this state for the absolute atheism of Thomas
Hobbes. The second level, which Cudworth terms as 'the bondsman to
the law and sin,' is the position mistakenly taken by many who claim to
live the religious life. Men in this position believe that the highest perfection of the Christian life is to exist within a legalistic relationship in
the world, whether this be following the rulings of organised religion or
the internal dictates of moral piety. Cudworth argues that, in this second
position, men fail to appreciate the active and living principle of Christ,
seeing the *forms* of religion as more important than the *role* of religion.
This is the position of the divine determinism Cudworth recognised in
seventeenth-century Calvinism. In this sermon we can, therefore, see an
early attempt by Cudworth to find a path between the two extremes
offered by the atheistic material determinism of Hobbism, and the divine

---

[15] Worthington, *Diary*: II.135.
[16] *Second Sermon*: 241, 239.

determinism of Calvinism. Both, for different reasons, presented versions of arbitrary authority, and both had to be undermined before it was possible to move to the final level of human existence. Here the true religious life could be found, Cudworth argues, by turning away from both the external and internal dictates of arbitrary codes and laws, to a true participation with the living principle of Christ. To become, what Cudworth terms, one of 'God's freemen' man has to accept the active principle of Christ over the passive acceptance of proscribed arbitrary codes.[17] It is clear from Cudworth's *Second Sermon* that his ethics would flesh out this theory of God's freeman. However, the problems inherent in the arbitrary codes of Hobbism and Calvinism had to be removed first. It appears, therefore, that it is from the specific historical context of 1660s Cambridge that Cudworth began to move towards the model of the *Intellectual System* and the composition of its first volume.

The '*Vanity* and *Ostentations*' of Cudworth's philosophical style

Cudworth's *TISU* is primarily a work concerned with opposing all forms of arbitrary authority, and primarily all philosophical arguments for atheism. As the continuation of the title states, *TISU* is a work 'Wherein, All the Reason and Philosophy of Atheism is Confuted; and Its Impossibility Demonstrated.' The main problem for the modern reader is that Cudworth approaches this project in the style of the Renaissance humanist, and not the seventeenth century rationalist. As a consequence it has become common for commentaries on the text to concentrate as much on the form as much the content of *TISU*. Many of these commentaries are complementary of the erudition of *TISU*. Thomas Birch, one of Cudworth's earliest biographers, commented the work penetrated 'the very darkest reaches of Antiquity to strip Atheism of all its Disguises & and drag up the lurking Monster to conviction.'[18] Such was the power and quality of the learning in *TISU* that John Locke, in his *Some Thoughts concerning Education*, suggests that:

> He that would look further back, and acquaint himself with the several Opinions of the Ancients, may consult Dr. *Cudworth's Intellectual System*; wherein that very learned Author hath with such Accurateness and Judgement collected and explained the Opinions of the Greek Philosophers, that

---

[17] *Second Sermon*: 241-4, 217.
[18] BL MS Additional 2497, 'Miscellaneous Papers of Thomas Birch': 93.

what Principles they built on, and what were the chief *Hypotheses,* that divided them, is better to be seen in him, than any where else that I know.[19]

The weight of learning in *TISU* has also been grist to the mill for many of Cudworth's strongest critics. John Turner, one of Cudworth's first opponents, saw *TISU* as, 'instead of being, as it calls itself, an *Universe*, is a *Chaos* of crude and indigested *Notions*; and *Abyss* of bottomless *Vanity* and *Ostentations.*'[20] This form of criticism has continued into the twentieth century where the formless and unsystematic nature of much of Cudworth's argument has been judged to be 'intolerably verbose' and 'monstrously obese.'[21] Cassirer was correct in pointing out that Cudworth's style did differ from the clarity offered by more 'modern' seventeenth-century philosophers such as Bacon, Hobbes, Descartes and Montaigne. That being said, Cudworth was remembered by his contemporaries as much for being a philosopher, as he was for his encyclopaedic style.[22] However, so dominant are the stylistic aspects of *TISU* that they need to be accounted for for two reasons before the content of the argument is analysed. Firstly, as already stated the style of *TISU* has, in some way, served to mask the content of the text. Although it is a text attacking atheism, it is not a text which is entirely negative in form. Cudworth attacks, what I describe as, the dangers of arbitrary authority not simply as a negative argument, but also as a means of defining the parameters of the positive aspects of his own theology and philosophy. Therefore, the dismissal of atheism needs to be dealt with before his Trinitarian theology (discussed in full in the next chapter of this study) can be understood in any meaningful way. Secondly, the text needs to be understood within the wider historical and intellectual context in which Cudworth was working. The text was, as Cudworth himself stated, only the first of three projected volumes. Although the remaining volumes never appeared in print, the existence of the ethical and eventually political ideas in Cudworth's unpublished manuscripts means that *TISU* should be viewed as a text preparing the ground for these later ideas. As we have seen both

---

[19] John Locke, *Some Thoughts Concerning Education*, ed. John W. & Jean S. Yolton. Oxford: The Clarendon Press, 1989: 248.

[20] John Turner, *A Discourse concerning the Messias ... To which is prefixed a large Preface asserting and explaining the Doctrine of the Blessed Trinity against the late writer of the Intellectual System.* London, 1685: xxi.

[21] Quoted in Mintz, *Hunting of Leviathan*: 96.

[22] For praise of Cudworth the philosopher see for instance David Hume, *Enquiries Concerning Human Understanding and Concerning the Principles of Morals*, edited by L.A. Selby-Bigge & P.H. Niddich. Oxford: The Clarendon Press, 1975: 73. Also see Hutton 'Classicism and Baroque': 211-2.

in this chapter and the last, Cudworth's intellectual development and early writings were intimately linked to his own situation and to the wider political context. Therefore, if Cudworth's work is to be allowed to speak on its own terms, it is essential that *TISU*, despite its many problems, be understood in the wider intellectual and historical culture of Cudworth's life and work.

The best way to approach *TISU* is, as Cassirer suggests, to view it as a work in the humanist traditions of the fifteenth and sixteenth centuries.[23] The humanism of the text not only explains its style but also the philosophical form and assumptions that lie behind it. Cudworth's work is one in the tradition of the *prisca theologia* or ancient theology. The Christian version of his tradition has its roots in the early Church where the alleged writings of 'ancient theologians,' such as Hermes Trismegistus, Zoroaster and Orpheus, Pythagoras, Plato, Moses, Noah and even Adam, were used to convert the pagans.[24] Much of the content of *TISU* can be explained by Cudworth's use of the *prisca theologia*. One of the fundamental assumptions of the *prisca theologia* is that all existing ancient theological and philosophical traditions were, to a lesser or greater extent, preparations for the authentic revelation of Christ. The ideals of the *prisca theologia*, particularly its syncreticism (the amalgamation of different religious and theological schools of thought), appealed to Cudworth. As an intellectualist Cudworth argued for the primacy of divine wisdom. It is, therefore, logical for him to argue that all forms of human knowledge display something of the wisdom of the divine, not just those which were exclusively Christian. So broad, for Cudworth, was the truth held in this syncretic tradition that he goes so far as to argue, in his *Discourse on the True Nature of the Lord's Supper*, that '[a]ll great Errours have ever been intermingled with some Truth.'[25]

Although it is possible to recognise the important role that the *prisca theologia* played in Cudworth's project, it has to be acknowledged that Cudworth was working in this tradition during a time when many of the central texts of the ancient theology were coming under increased scrutiny and attack. During the late-sixteenth and early-seventeenth centuries

[23] Cassirer, *The Platonic Renaissance*: 43.

[24] See: D.P. Walker, *The Ancient Theology: Studies in Christian Platonism from the Fifteenth to the Eighteenth Century*. London: Duckworth, 1972: 1-2; also D.W. Dockrill, 'The heritage of Patristic Platonism in Seventeenth-century English Philosophical Theology,' in *The Cambridge Platonists in Philosophical Context*, ed Rogers, et al. Dordrecht: Kluwer, 1997.

[25] Ralph Cudworth, *A Discourse concerning the true notion of the Lord's supper*. London: 1670: 1.

many of the texts central to the *prisca theologia* came to be recognised as Christian forgeries. The best examples of this are the writings of the Neoplatonic Pseudo-Dionysius the Areopagite, the cabalistic Hermes Trismegistus, and the Neo-Stoic apocryphal letters between St Paul and Seneca. The apocryphal Pauline letters were proved to be forgeries by Erasmus and, in 1614, Isaac Casaubon proved that the texts attributed to Hermes Trismegistus were forgeries.[26] Francis Yates has argued that Casuabon's discovery, as much through the method of analysis he employed as through his conclusion, marked one of the great water-sheds between the Renaissance and the early-modern. Certainly the limited use of the *prisca theologia* by Cudworth and the other Cambridge Platonists after Casaubon's writings is one of the factors that has caused them to appear to be viewed as out of step with their contemporaries. Cudworth accepted Casaubon's theories on the falsity of the Hermetic texts. However, while accepting the Hermetic texts to have been Christian forgeries, Cudworth does argue that these forgeries might have been based, in some small part, on true Hermetic sources.[27] Despite this coded acceptance of something of the Hermetic tradition, Cudworth always backs up his claims with additional references to less dubious sources, usually references to Neoplatonic and Patristic texts.[28] Even though Cudworth is not as uncritical in his uses of these sources as many of his forbears, the manner with which he analyses these ideas places him firmly in a tradition of Renaissance humanism. In the preface to *TISU* Cudworth make the explicit claim that his work appeals to 'Philology and Antiquity'.[29] It is easy to see how Cudworth's style appeals to antiquity; however, it is the philological form of Cudworth's argument that does the most to underpin his philosophical assumptions. Cudworth assumes there to be a unified philosophical system which can be uncovered by man. Cudworth also assumes that this unified system relies on a single, common philosophical vocabulary. By understanding this assumption we can understand the heavy burden of quotation and reference in *TISU*, the text at times simply listing the occasions where various thinkers have deployed the same terminology. This philological style is in stark contrast to the critical analysis of language that underpinned Casaubon's critiques of Hermetic texts, a contrast which is stressed in Mosheim's later criticisms of Cudworth's style.[30]

---

[26] Yates, *Giordano Bruno*: 398-400.
[27] *TISU*: 287, 713-4.
[28] Yates, *Giordano Bruno*: 427-30.
[29] *TISU*: xvii.
[30] Yates, *Giordano Bruno*: 400. Hutton, 'Classicism and Baroque': 225-6.

However, once the justification for Cudworth's erudition is understood, it becomes easier to come to terms with the theological and philosophical arguments of *TISU*.

Cudworth and Hobbes

As we have seen, it is possible to tie the form and argument of Cudworth's *TISU* to the rejection of Calvinism which defined Cudworth's intellectual development. His rejection of Calvinism provided Cudworth with the intellectual tools to meet his greatest foe, Thomas Hobbes, straight on. It has become common to view Cudworth, particularly in his opposition to 'atheism', as the anti-Hobbes. John Passmore, in his classic study of Cudworth states emphatically that:

> Hobbes' influence is...a pervasive one, but in a direction almost entirely negative. Hobbes is never far long out of Cudworth's mind, but among the multitude of references to that 'atheist politician' (never once mentioned by name — like the Devil) not one is unreservedly favourable.[31]

Passmore's characterisation of Cudworth's distaste for Hobbes is, of course, correct. However, this quote, and like many others, over emphasises the importance of Hobbes on the development of Cudworth's philosophy. On one hand the constant linking of Cudworth's name with Hobbes is understandable. In the history of philosophy placing Cudworth in the orbit of a canonical thinker such as Hobbes, even if only in a negative light, gives places and purpose to his writings. However, this approach can lead to a limiting and overly simplistic understanding of Cudworth and certainly does not help us understand him on his own terms.

It has become common to assume, as with Passmore's account above, that Hobbes was Cudworth's constant and sole intellectual adversary. As we have already seen, however, the themes of Cudworth's intellectualism and Neoplatonism were present in Cudworth's thought as early as the late 1630s. In addition, as Frederick Beiser has shown, the chronology of Cudworth's intellectual development would seem to suggest that many of Cudworth's arguments, which are commonly viewed as being defined in opposition to Hobbes alone, were used by Cudworth before he would have been able to engage fully with Hobbes' work. In particular, Cudworth's B.D. disputations of 1644 show that Cudworth's defence of

---

[31] Passmore, *Ralph Cudworth*: 11.

'eternal and immutable morality' was present before he could have read
Hobbes.[32] Beiser argues correctly that the arguments that Cudworth used
against Hobbes were in fact a modification of arguments he had first developed against Calvinism. Beiser concludes rhetorically, '[w]hat, indeed, was
the God of Hobbes but the God of Calvin spelt out in material terms?'[33]

The reason why Cudworth was able to deploy the same arguments
against Hobbism as he was against Calvinism is that, for Cudworth,
Hobbes' philosophy was cut from the same voluntarist cloth as Calvinism. Cudworth approached Hobbes in the first instance as an extreme
proponent of the voluntarism that he encountered and opposed in orthodox Calvinism. As A.P. Martnich has pointed out, many of Hobbes' first
critics were anti-Calvinists, most notably Clarendon, Bramhall and, of
course, the Cambridge Platonists.[34] Many of the early critiques of Hobbes
were explicit in their equating of Hobbes to Calvinism. Thomas Pierce,
who would later become Dean of Salisbury, claimed in 1658 that 'Mr
Hobbs…is as able a *Calvinist* (as to these points) as their party hath lately
had.'[35] The voluntarist element in Hobbes' thought remained central to
criticisms of his philosophy into the early eighteenth century. Leibniz,
for instance, utilised the dilemma of *The Euthyphro*, which Cudworth
used in his *First Sermon*, in his criticism of Hobbes' ethical theory.[36]

The source of the voluntarism in Hobbes' philosophy comes from his
use and, to an extent, secularisation of the salvific structure of Calvinist
theology. Hobbes certainly grew up within the strict Calvinist orthodoxy.
Hobbes' father, although not the most pious of men, was an ordained
minister who followed the Calvinist orthodoxy of the Elizabethan and
Jacobean Church. Hobbes also received an orthodox Calvinist education as an undergraduate at Magdalen Hall, Oxford.[37] Hobbes in his own

---

[32] The most telling evidence of this is that Cudworth defended the principle of an
eternal and immutable morality in his Cudworth's B.D. disputations in 1644, see 'Memoirs
of Ralph Cudworth': 24-38. The *Bibliotheca Cudworthiana,* published by Edward Millington in 1691 to advertise the sale of Cudworth's book collection, list several works by
Hobbes. The earliest philosophical work is a 1647 Dutch edition of Hobbes' *Elements of
the Law.* Edward Millington, *Bibliotheca Cudworthiana.* London: 1691.

[33] Beiser, *Sovereignty of Reason*: 147-8.

[34] A.P. Martinich, *The Two Gods of Leviathan: Thomas Hobbes on Religion and Politics.* Cambridge: CUP, 1992: 33.

[35] Thomas Pierce, Αυτοκατακρισις, *or Self-Condemnation.* London: 1658: 138.

[36] See Goldie, Mark, 'The Reception of Hobbes,' in *The Cambridge History of Political Thought, 1450-1700,* edited by J.H. Burns, with the assistance of Mark Goldie. Cambridge: CUP, 1991. The fullest discussion of Hobbes' relationship to voluntarist theology
is Noel Malcolm, 'Thomas Hobbes and Voluntarist Theology', Ph.D. Thesis, University
of Cambridge: 1982.

[37] Martinich, *The Two Gods of Leviathan*: 64; Martinich, *Hobbes*: 1-18.

writings expressed an admiration for Calvin and other Calvinist writers, most notably William Perkins.[38] Despite these biographical influences, the nature and extent of Hobbes' religious belief remains an extremely contentious issue. The problem in interpreting this religious belief comes, I believe, as a consequence of the extreme negative theology that runs through all of Hobbes' philosophy. Much of this ambiguity comes from Hobbes' professed belief that philosophy should not seek to discuss the nature of God, as Hobbes clearly states: 'We ought not to dispute of God's nature, he is no fit subject of our philosophy.'[39] Much time and effort has been spent discussing the sincerity of Hobbes' religious faith, and this quote often been cited by those who wish to deny the sincerity of Hobbes' religious belief. However, it could just as well be read, in the light of the Calvinist orthodoxy of the day, as an attack on the efficacy of natural theology against revealed theology; a position that Hobbes shares with Calvin.[40] In a similar vein to Calvin, Hobbes argues that all the human mind can know that God exists, '[f]or there is but one Name to signifie our Conception of his Nature, and that is, I AM: and but one Name of his relation to us, and that is *God.*'[41] From his reason alone man is able to conceive of God, but only recognise his utter insignificance in the face of God. As a consequence Hobbes argues that it is not for humans to understand God, only to honour him.[42] As J.G.A. Pocock has argued, 'Hobbes's God is one of whom we can know by reason only that he must exist and must be all-powerful. His nature is incomprehensible, and anything we say about it is no more than language designed to honour his power.'[43] Hobbes uses his negative theology to reinforce his pessimistic view of human nature. For Hobbes the account of the natural man is

---

[38] Thomas Hobbes, 'Of Liberty and Necessity,' in *Hobbes and Bramhall on Liberty and Necessity*, edited by Vere Chappell. Cambridge: CUP, 1999: 70, 80. Also see Martinich, *Two Gods*: 3.

[39] Hobbes 'Of Liberty and Necessity': 42.

[40] Calvin's disquiet with natural theology comes out most clearly in the early chapters of his *Institutes*. There he argues that although the natural mind can know something of the divine because of the fallen nature of man this knowledge is limited to an understanding of God as creator and a recognition of the ordering of the Universe through the creative power of God. Beyond this the human mind can only come to know God in the forms that God gives directly to man, primarily through the words of scripture: see *Institutes*, I.i-vi. For a detailed account of Calvin's account of natural theology see Helm, *John Calvin's Ideas*: 209-245.

[41] *Leviathan*: 403.

[42] *Leviathan*: 99.

[43] J.G.A. Pocock, 'Time, History, and Eschatology,' in *Politics, Language, and Time: Essays on Political Thought and History*. Chicago: The University of Chicago Press, 1960: 185.

therefore not simply a useful rhetorical tool to justify absolutism and the rule of the Leviathan, but also the political working out of the fallen state of man which, although not identical to, is certainly related to the fallen man of Calvinist theology.

Hobbes also follows Calvin in arguing that redemption and salvation is found exclusively through the will of God.[44] The means by which this is achieved is where Hobbes primarily differs from Calvin. Both accept that a satisfactory authority is required to bring man into communion with God. For Cudworth there is a similarity in this structure as both rely on a single, possibility arbitrary, act of authority. However, where Calvin argues that the will of God can only be known by man through the power of grace and his accommodation to mankind in scripture, Hobbes argues that God's will is mediated to man through the correct form of the civil sovereign.[45] For Cudworth the potential problems of the voluntarism of Calvinist theology are made real in the ethical and political consequences of Hobbes' voluntarist philosophy. Hobbes, as a voluntarist, argues that justice is created exclusively by an act of will. However, where Calvinism places this right solely in the free actions of God's will, Hobbes allows justice to be created by the will of the earthly, civil sovereign. This claim is then given theological credence by Hobbes' argument that the sovereign is the true heir of the kingship of Christ. The Leviathan, therefore, becomes for Hobbes the image and mirror of the kingship of Christ. Although Hobbes' argument in this respect differs from that of Calvin, his interpretation of the person of Christ still remains loyal to Calvinism. Hobbes interprets the office of Christ as three-fold: Redeemer, Pastor and Eternal King. This three-fold distinction follows Calvin's interpretation of Christ as Prophet, King and Priest.[46] For Hobbes, the most important of these was the office of 'Eternal King.' Hobbes argues that the only source of God's law can be through one sovereign, '[o]ut of which we may conclude, that whosoever in a Christian Commonwealth holdeth the place of Moses, is the sole Messenger of God, and Interpreter of his Commandments.'[47] Once this relationship is established, the voluntarist nature of Hobbes' ethical theory becomes clear. Salvation is only available to those who adhere to the will of the sovereign, who is, for Hobbes, the only arbiter of God's will: 'All that is NECESSARY *to Salvation*, is contained in two Vertues, *Faith in Christ*, and *Obedience*

---

[44] Martinich, *Two Gods*: 67.
[45] *Leviathan*: 415.
[46] *Leviathan*: 512; *Institutes*: II.xv. Also see Martinich, *Two Gods*: 294.
[47] *Leviathan*: 504.

to Laws.'[48] Sin is, therefore, synonymous in Hobbes' eyes with the breaking of the laws ordained by the civil sovereign, which is 'not only showing contempt of the legislator, but also the will of God.'[49] Consequently law is, for Hobbes, not dependent on a pre-existent naturally occurring notion of justice; rather, Hobbes' voluntarism is clearest when he argues that justice is created by the will and power of the sovereign alone.

Even when Hobbes' voluntarism is clearly established Beiser's assertion that Hobbes and Calvin where synonymous in Cudworth's mind is only partially correct. Central to *TISU* is a rejection of all forms of voluntarism. Therefore, to an extent, both Calvinism and Hobbism could be criticised as unacceptable forms of arbitrary authority. However, as we have seen in the *Second Sermon*, by the time he was composing *TISU* Cudworth had marked Hobbism and Calvinism as two linked but different problems. Both could, for Cudworth, be rightly criticised as opening the door to arbitrary authority. However, where Calvinism merely presented the potential for arbitrary authority, Hobbism promoted this danger as a reality. Importantly Cudworth's rejection of both Calvinism and Hobbism was not simply a rejection of the perceived arbitrary nature of these systems, but also the ethical implications of both systems. Therefore, although Hobbes may have presented a more thorough going philosophical version of the voluntarism Cudworth had earlier opposed in Calvinism, the differing ethical implications of Hobbism and Calvinism required different responses from Cudworth. To revert to the language of the *Second Sermon* the life of both 'Sin's Freeman' and 'God's Bondsman' had to be rejected before the life of 'God's Freeman' could be asserted. As a consequence, Cudworth's criticisms of the philosophical basis of, and ethical implications of Hobbism differ from his criticisms of Calvinism in many fundamental ways. For Cudworth both Calvinism and Hobbism failed to recognise the eternal and immutable principles of the divine in all things. However, Calvinism could be partially supported because it allowed for the origin of the world in the mind of God, even if that God was misconceived. Hobbes, by contrast, borrowed the structures of Calvinism, but built his philosophy on what, for Cudworth, was the unacceptable materialist doctrine of 'matter in motion'. So grave were the errors of Hobbes' absolute atheism that it was to the refutation of those that Cudworth first turned.

---

[48] *Leviathan*: 610.
[49] *Leviathan*: 335.

Cudworth's attack on 'absolute atheism'

For Cudworth atheism was not simply a rejection of the existence of God, it was a refusal to accept the role of God as the sole determining and judging factor in the world.[50] For this reason any form of false theology opened itself up to the dangers of atheism. Cudworth's rejection of atheism is broken into three sections. The first is 'Absolute Atheism,' typified by the revival of Epicurean philosophy by Thomas Hobbes.[51] The second is what he terms 'Immoral Theism,' which allows for religion but no understanding of natural justice. The third is a form of Theism which, although it allows for God and natural justice, does not allow for this to be achieved through liberty but from necessity. These final two can be subsumed into Cudworth's general critique of divine determinism.[52] Before Cudworth's own philosophical system could be constructed he argues that these different forms of atheism had to be thoroughly rejected, beginning with the most serious, absolute atheism. Cudworth's attacks on absolute atheism in *TISU* are designed to discredit any arguments which suggest that the world is founded on anything other than theistic principles. As we shall see in Chapter Three, Cudworth, throughout *TISU*, defines this theism in Trinitarian terms. Consequently it is possible to understand Cudworth's criticisms of atheism as not only arguments to justify his theism, but also arguments that confirm his understanding of God as Trinity. In *TISU* Cudworth mainly concentrates his attacks on thinkers who he defines as 'atomical fatalists.'[53] Cudworth accuses these thinkers of believing that the universe was created by merely the random motion of atoms: the world, and all that was in it, is, in essence, the sum of parts of a cosmic random motion. Cudworth rejects this view out of hand because, he argues, atomic fatalists remove the possibility that there is a guiding, incorporeal principle within the world. Cudworth argues that these thinkers assert matter, or 'extended bulk,' as the founding principle

---

[50] John Redwood, *Reason, Ridicule and Religion: The Age of Enlightenment in England, 1660-1750.* London: Thames and Hudson: 30.

[51] Although Cudworth never names Hobbes in the *TISU* his criticisms of Epicurius and Democitus are clearly thinly veiled criticisms of Hobbes' philosophy and so it will be assumed that an attack on either of these two is implicitly an attack on Hobbes.

[52] *TISU*: iv.

[53] Cudworth uses the term 'fatalist' where modern philosophical vernacular would use 'determinist'. Although these terms have in recent literature been distinguished for Cudworth they retained one shared characteristic: the actions of man are controlled by something other than his own free choice. For this reason, although the terms carry with them different meanings in different contexts, both terms will be assumed to mean the same thing with reference to Cudworth's thought and will therefore be used interchangeably.

of the Universe. The world could, therefore, only be understood in terms of the mechanical relations of one body to another.

Cudworth sees this philosophy as a perversion of the ancient and respectable theistic tradition of atomic philosophy founded by the Phoenician philosopher Moschus. Far from being implicitly atheistic, he argues that the true atomism of Moschus is founded on, and logically reliant upon, theism. It is this form of atomism which Cudworth states influenced Hellenistic thought, in particular Pythagoras, and from there the writings of Plato and Aristotle.[54] Cudworth argues that this tradition, in its correct theological form, had been resurrected in Cartesianism.[55] Cudworth's argument here, prioritising mind over matter, shows his reliance on the Cartesian distinction between the substance of the mind as thinking, *res cogitans*, and the substance of the body as extended, *res extensa*. The atomism resurrected by Cartesian rationalism creates, for Cudworth, an acceptable means of understanding the world, because it based on the logical dictum *'de nihilo nihil, in nihilum nil posse reverti'* (nothing can come from nothing or go to nothing). Cudworth interprets this argument as meaning that because nothing can come from nothing the something that it comes from must be superior in form and status than matter. By presenting an implicit hierarchy of causes Cudworth's theology and philosophy consistently argues that a material act must be, in some manner, preceded by an intellectual cause. The external world is, therefore, for Cudworth merely a confirmation of the existence of

---

[54] *TISU*: 3-18.

[55] *TISU*: 174, Cudworth also makes this observation in *EIM*: 151. *FM*.4979: 144. *FM*.4980: 221. It is important to note here the important role that Cudworth and the Cambridge Platonists played in the dissemination and criticism of Cartesian philosophy in England, a fact which is often overlooked because of the overt Neoplatonism of their philosophy. However, interestingly Cudworth's daughter Damaris Masham described her father's intellectual circle as 'my friends, the Cartesians, and the Platonists;' see: Locke, *Correspondence*: 882. Also one of the earliest defences of the Cambridge Platonists which focused particularly on their use of the *'New Philosophy'*, see: S.[imon] P.[atrick], *A brief account of the new sect of Latitude-men together with some reflections upon the New Philosophy*. London: 1662. Most importantly, Henry More published his correspondence with Descartes, see: Henry More, *A Collection of Several Writings of Dr Henry More* 2. vols. London: 1662: 1.53-133. For the interaction of the Cambridge Platonists with Cartesian philosophy see: M. Baldi, 'Cudworth versus Descartes: Platonism et sens commun dans la critique de *Meditations*,' in *The Cambridge Platonists in Philosophical Context* edited by G.A.J. Rogers et al. Dordrecht: Kluwer, 1997; G.A.J. Rogers, 'Descartes and the English,' in *The Light of Nature: Essays in the History and Philosophy of Science presented to A.C. Crombie*, edited by J.D. North and J.J. Roche. Dordrecht: Kluwer, 1985; Danton B. Sailor, 'Cudworth and Descartes,' in *The Journal of the History of Ideas*, 23 (1962): 133-40; J.E. Saveson, 'Differing Reactions to Descartes among the Cambridge Platonists,' in *The Journal of the History of Ideas*, 21 (1960): 560-67.

intellectual principles which cause and form the observable motion of atoms.[56] For Cudworth this philosophical, even scientific, understanding of the world always leads us back to the theological: to '*loudly to declare, that the World was made by God.*'[57]

Cudworth argues that atomical atheism perverts the central dictum of atomism by suggesting, not that 'nothing could come from nothing', but that 'nothing [materially] could be raised from nothing or reduced to nothing.' Consequently Cudworth accuses these thinkers of making matter, or 'bulk' the founding principle of all creation. He argues:

> And indeed it was really one and the self-same Form of Atheism, which both these entertained, they derived all things alike, from *Dead* and *Stupid Matter Fortuitously Moved,* the Difference between them being only this, that they managed it two different ways; *Anaximander* in the way of *Qualities* and *Forms*, which is the more Vulgar and Obvious kind of Atheism; but *Democritus* in the way of *Atoms* and *Figures*, which seems to be a more learned kind of Atheism.[58]

By making matter the only substance within creation, Cudworth argues that atomical atheists have removed the first cause from the world and in this way removed the philosophical understanding of God from creation.[59] By this logic all of creation is derived from chance, or what Cudworth terms 'fortuitous motion.' The basic premise of this argument, he states, removes the necessity of God from creation and therefore denies the central premise that God's intellect is the defining principle of creation.[60]

Although there exists in many of these atomical atheists a residual theism this is, Cudworth argues, merely a poor mask for atheism. God is used by these thinkers in two ways, both of which lead to atheism. Firstly, some of these materialist philosophers suggest that a purely materialist understanding of the world is acceptable because God's perfection and freedom cannot be limited by the mundane matters of the world. Material atomism is used by these thinkers as a means of explaining the organisation of the world without recourse to the divine. So Cudworth argues, Epicurus had sought to free God from '*Benefits and Employments*, and doing nothing at all.'[61] This conception of the divine is an impossibility for Cudworth because it would mean denying God as the defining principle

[56] *TISU*: 30.
[57] *TISU*: 197.
[58] *TISU*:130.
[59] *FM.*4979: 153.b; *FM.*4980: 252.
[60] *TISU*: 61, 75.
[61] *TISU*: 64.

of all reality. This form of atheism, he thinks, can easily be dispatched by the observation of the surrounding world. It is, he argues, nonsense to assert that the entire world can be understood as simply the actions of local, mechanical motion because if nothing comes from nothing, then logically there must be a primary principle which was the source of this motion. Genuine atomism recognises this principle to be God. Cudworth argues, therefore, it is only possible to explain the organisation of an atomistic universe if an active intellectual principle is understood to exist prior to passive matter. Things of beauty in the world, using his example, a silver cup, are not made by the random movement of the atoms in silver. Rather these mundane, passive atoms are moved and influenced by the active principle of the workman crafting the silver into the cup. Such is the form and nature of the world that it is impossible to understand the form of passive corporeal objects without the influence of an active, incorporeal substance on them. In this way the whole world can be understood in the framework of the influence of active incorporeal principles on passive matter.[62] The logical impossibility of the material atheist argument for Cudworth, therefore, makes the belief in an incorporeal divine power acting prior to the material world the only logical explanation. Cudworth's use of the argument of the 'non-inferiority of causes', given teeth by his adoption of the Cartesian definition of substance, provides a reasonable argument through which 'atomic atheists' could be refuted. Reason, Cudworth argues, tells us that absolute atheism is incorrect because the world cannot be controlled by material principles alone, but by 'the Attributes of another kind of Substance distinct from Body.'[63] Atheistic systems can be discounted because, Cudworth argues, they reject the existence and superiority of incorporeal intellectual principles, making them.[64] The argument that Cudworth deploys against Hobbes provides, as we shall see in the following chapter, one of the defining principles of Cudworth's definition of God as Trinity. Consequently Cudworth, through his critique of the premises of atheism, is able to create an explanation of the created world which implicitly assumes not only the presence of God, but also the active influence of him in it.

Cudworth's rejection of Hobbes' materialism carries with it an ethical dimension. In his unpublished manuscripts Cudworth is able to develop more fully the ethical implications of the arbitrary form of material atheism.

---

[62] *TISU*: 28.
[63] *TISU*: 50.
[64] *TISU*: 417.

In particular Cudworth moves from an attack on the logical absurdities of the Hobbist account of the created universe to an attack on Hobbes' denial of freewill. Cudworth goes about this task, as in *TISU*, by attacking what he sees as the contradictions implicit in Hobbes' materialism. Hobbes argues that reality can only be explained by the competing physical forces in the world. Freewill is, therefore, denied by Hobbes because man has always been necessarily determined by the external physical forces that played against him. Freedom can, therefore, only ever be understood, in Hobbist terms, as the absence of an external physical impediment.[65] Although man can refuse to follow this external impediment, so strong are external forces that man's basic human instincts would necessarily lead to him following these external forces. To justify this position Hobbes' used his famous example of the man in the sinking boat:

> Feare and Liberty are consistent; as when a man throweth his goods into the Sea for *feare* the ship should sink, he doth it nevertheless very willingly, and may refuse to doe it if he will:[66]

One could, Hobbes argues, pay lip service to the idea of freewill; however, so strong are the external determining factors in the world that freewill can never exist in any tangible or effective form. Cudworth reasons that Hobbes' argument is limited because the Hobbist man is *only* defined by his relationship to the external world. Because of the physical imperative in Hobbes' thesis, Cudworth asserts that Hobbes creates two levels in his argument for necessity over freewill. Firstly, Hobbes asserts the crude notion of random physical motion that we have already examined. Secondly, because this material reality is the only one that Hobbes allows, the physical imperative of his materialism is transformed by Hobbes into a philosophical system of necessary certainty.[67] Such an argument, Cudworth argues, diminishes God as redundant in the world and diminishes man, making him nothing more than the sum of the external causes acting upon him.[68] Returning to the terminology of Cudworth's *Second Sermon*, this is the realm of 'Sin's freeman.' According to Cudworth the only reality open to the Hobbist man are the hedonistic temptations of the physical world. This system, Cudworth argues can be discounted on two grounds. Firstly, as with his criticisms in *TISU*, Hobbes' materialism makes inanimate, material form the founding principle of

---

[65] *Leviathan*: 189. Hobbes 'Of Liberty and Necessity': 38.
[66] *Leviathan*: 286.
[67] *FM*.4980: 274.
[68] *FM*.4980: 224.

reality. This, Cudworth states, is nonsense as it contradicts the law of the non-inferiority of causes.[69] Linked to this is Cudworth's second criticism, which is that it is not only impossible to account for the existence of the world, but also impossible for man to have an intellectual comprehension of the existence of a world which is, in Cudworth's terms, created by 'the stupid coincidence of matter.'[70] Implicit in both these arguments is Cudworth's assumption that intellectual forces are superior, and therefore prior to, material causes. Consequently, Cudworth argues that not only is it impossible to account for the form and nature of the world in material terms alone, but that it is contradictory to make an intellectual interpretation of the world which denies the existence of the incorporeal, intellectual substance that allows one to come to that conclusion. Hobbist determinism can, therefore, be dismissed as a further perversion of a fundamentally flawed philosophical system.

Cudworth also criticises the manner in which mechanical atheists use God as a means of hiding the reality of their atheism. This argument is central to Cudworth's attack on the philosophy of Hobbes. He argues that theology is used by Hobbes as a veneer of respectability, allowing him to 'walk abroad in the masquerade of theism.' God, instead of being the source and principle of goodness and love within the world, becomes a political principle justifying acts which were anathema to the implicit goodness and wisdom of the divine. So Cudworth argues that, in Hobbes' thought, God is:

> a meer *Figment* or *Invention* of *Politicians*, to promote their own Ends, and keep men in Obedience and Subjection under them, then would they doubtless have so framed and contrived it, as that it should have been every way *Flexible* and *Compliant*: namely by perswading the world, that whatsoever was Commanded by themselves, was agreeable to the *Divine Will*, and whatever was Forbidden by their Laws, was displeasing to God Almighty, and would be punished by him:[71]

Cudworth argues that God is only used by Hobbes to legitimise the arbitrary and absolutist state he is advocating. This form of state fails for two reasons. Firstly, as already stated, it is built on a false, and even feigned, conception of the divine. Secondly, it fails, Cudworth argues, because the defining principles of the Hobbist states is the arbitrary will of the civil sovereign. This criticism of Hobbes, as we shall see in Chapter Five, provides Cudworth with one of his most pertinent political arguments;

---

[69] *FM*.4982: 51.
[70] *FM*.4979: 187.
[71] *TISU*: 698.

that the central purpose of human society is not merely the maintenance of order and stability, but the creation of an effective community of ethically responsible individuals. Consequently, Cudworth argues, that Hobbes only believes in a God who rules over the world:

> no otherwise, than by and in these Civil Sovereigns, as his Vicegerents; and the only *Prophets* and *Interpreters* of his will to men. So that the *Civil Law* of every *Country*, and the *Arbitrary Will of Sovereigns*, should be acknowledged to be the only *Measure* of *Just* and Unjust (these being nothing *Naturally* such) the only *Rule of Conscience and Religion*. For from Religion thus modelled, *Civil Sovereigns* might think to have an *Absolute Power*, or an *Infinite Right*, of Doing or Commanding whatsoever they pleased, without exception, *nothing* being *Unlawful* to them, and their Subjects being always *Obliged, in Conscience*, without the least Scruple to Obey.[72]

Hobbes' philosophy, Cudworth argues, completely de-couples man from any notion of individual moral responsibility by placing the arbitrary figure of the civil sovereign between the justice of God's wisdom and man's ability to discover that individually. Cudworth, by rejecting Hobbes' voluntarist conception of the political nature of man, implicitly argues that the political nature of man is not an artificial creation, but something that flows unmediated from the reason and wisdom of God. For this reason, as we shall come on to see, Cudworth's conception of the political individual is intimately linked with his theological, and particularly Trinitarian, understanding of creation.

The contrast between Cudworth and Hobbes on this matter is typified by their differing views on the creation of the political realm. Hobbes, in this area, follows much of the style and form of republican writers during the middle years of the seventeenth century. Writers such as John Milton and James Harrington alluded to the Old Testament creation story, and in particular, to creation as the imposition of order on chaos, as a metaphor for the imposition of order by the Godly republic on the chaos of the inter-regnum.[73] We can identify this political metaphor, although in a less explicitly 'republican' form, in Hobbes' assertion that civil society

[72] *TISU*: 698, Cudworth here is clearly alluding to the arguments used by Hobbes in *Leviathan* where the political legitimacy of the civil sovereign is equated to the legitimacy God gave Old Testament Kings to be his representatives on earth. For instance: 'Again, he is to be King then, no otherwise than as subordinate, or Vicesegerent of God the Father, as Moses was in the wildernesse; and as the High Priests were before the reign of Saul: and as the Kings were after it.' *Leviathan*: 518.

[73] David Norbrook, *Writing in the English Republic: Poetry, Rhetoric and Politics, 1627-1660*. Cambridge, CUP, 1999: 330, 400, 470-2. For Cudworth's account of creation see J.-L. Breteau, 'Chaos and Order in Cudworth's Thought' in *Platonism and the Origins of Modernity*, edited by Sarah Hutton and Douglas Hedley. Dordrecht: Springer, 2007.

developed out of the natural chaos of the state of nature.[74] In contrast, we find Cudworth explicitly rejecting the idea of creation as the imposition of order on chaos. The idea of there being chaos would, after all, deny that the intellect and wisdom of God was the eternal founding principle of all creation. In *TISU* Cudworth deploys the idea of chaos as a foil for his own version of creation as part of the perpetual out-flowing love of the divine. In all these cases the idea of a chaotic world was contrasted with the true, reasoned principle of divine love in creation. Just as the chaotic nature of atomical atheism cannot create beauty in the world, neither can it create a politically just society.[75] Political justice and order in society are, for Cudworth, not brought about by the imposition of a single will on society, as in Hobbes, rather they grow naturally through a collective understanding of the reasoned form and structure of society. By rejecting Hobbes' mechanical explanation for the order of the world, Cudworth implicitly suggests that man's political position is understood not by force, but by the consensual appreciation of the divine principle in creation. This participatory relationship lies at the heart of the political principles in Cudworth's writings.

Cudworth's rejection of 'divine determinism'

Once Cudworth had despatched the arbitrary authority of absolute atheism he was able to turn his attention to the different, but no less pressing dangers of 'divine determinism', which Cudworth identified in aspects of seventeenth-century Calvinism. The difference, Cudworth argues, between Calvin and Hobbes comes not in the form the determinism takes, or the ends it brings about, but the initial source of that determinism. Cudworth begins *TISU* with a discussion of the distinction between divine and material determinism. Prior to the material determinism of Hobbes, Cudworth argues, there exist two forms of divine determinist. Firstly, there are those who argue that God's will determines all things and actions. Secondly, there are those who argue that God created a framework in the world from which a set of causes inevitably and unavoidably run. The problem that Cudworth faced was that, unlike material determinism, he could not deny the theological basis of these divinely ordained systems. As we have seen, Cudworth rejects material determinism because

---

[74] *Leviathan*: 183-201.
[75] *TISU*: 79-80, 121-2.

at its hearts is a rejection of the principle of the non-inferiority of causes. The logical consequence of Cudworth's rejection of absolute atheism was the assertion that the universe was created by the higher intellectual powers of God, and that this was a creation *ex nihilo*, from nothing. With the systems of divine determinism both these basic theological premises were fulfilled. In *TISU* Cudworth's attention is drawn to, and remains focused largely on, the weaknesses of material atheism. It is therefore in Cudworth's manuscripts, rather than *TISU*, where the logical problems of the arbitrary authority of divine determinism are discussed at length.

As already stated, Cudworth argues that there is a fundamental distinction between the arbitrary codes of material determinism and the potentially arbitrary codes of divine determinism. In the second section of *FM*.4982, Cudworth neatly sums this distinction up when he asserts that the material determinism of Hobbes has no 'decrees' at all, in contrast to the divine determinism of Calvinism which is entirely dependent on divine 'decrees'. The difference, therefore, is that Hobbist determinism is defined by external physical forces, whereas Calvinist determinism is defined by definite acts of God's will.[76] Hobbes can, therefore, be discounted, in Cudworth's mind, because of the logical absurdities in his argument. Calvinism and divine determinism in all its forms, by contrast, is a more acute problem for Cudworth. Calvinism grasps the essential truth of reality, that God is the animating and active force in the Universe. However, instead of allowing the divine to exist as the all-encompassing intellect, Cudworth argues that divine determinists limit God to a being defined by the arbitrary power of volition and, as a consequence, potentially driven by passion and power. For Cudworth the failure of divine determinism is that it limits God by failing to appreciate that the defining characteristic of God is the power and breadth of his intellect rather than the limitless power of his will. This misunderstanding of the true nature of the form of divine action, Cudworth argues, is not unique to the voluntarism of seventeenth-century Calvinism, but a recurring problem in all religion.[77] Both in *TISU* and later in his manuscripts Cudworth suggests that the divine determinism of Calvinism mirrors in some way the determinism of Stoicism. However, Cudworth never makes this claim as strongly as he does when comparing Hobbes to Epicurus.[78]

---

[76] *FM*.4982: II.63.
[77] *FM*.4979: 72.
[78] There is clear evidence both that Calvin was influenced by Stoic ideas, and that early-modern thinkers clearly identified the links between Stoic 'Fate' and Calvinist

As with Cudworth's criticisms of Hobbes, the danger presented by the arbitrary authority of divine determinism is not simply that it is philosophically incoherent, but that it is ethically dangerous. There is, for Cudworth, a threefold problem highlighted by theistic determinism. Firstly, and most importantly, it degrades God. Cudworth argues that Calvinists, in particular, by defining God in terms of will and power, seek to understand and describe God in what are essentially human terms. To define God in terms of power and will is to define God in the manner that humans judge themselves. Instead, he argues that God should be defined in terms of goodness and wisdom, which in their purest form always remain beyond the grasp of man, but which are still recognisable by man through his reason.[79] Secondly, divine determinists open up the possibility that men exist merely as chattels for the will of God. By making man determined in all things Cudworth argues that men are viewed as little more than 'little devils,' unable to have anything more than a mechanical, and consequently involuntary, relationship to the world.[80] Thirdly divine determinism creates the possibility that God is the author of evil which, Cudworth argues, completely undermines the basis of morality. If God is the author of evil, by virtue of his all-powerful will, then morality cannot exist because the equitable judgement by God of all men on death, what Cudworth terms 'distributive justice,'[81] could not occur. Such is the power of this determinism that man cannot be expected to make

---

'Predestination. In his manuscripts Cudworth alludes to the link between the two systems. However it appears that for Cudworth there were too many fundamental differences between the two systems to make the link with any certainty, and so he never makes the comparison as strongly as he does between Hobbism and Epicureanism. For Cudworth on the links between Stoicism and Calvinism see: *FM* 4980: 38, *FM* 4982: 60. For the relationship between Stoicism and early-modern thought see; William Bouwsma, 'The Two Faces of Humanism. Stoicism and Augustianism in Renaissance Thought,' in *Itinerium Italicum: The Profile of the Italian Renaissance in the mirror of its European Transformations* edited by Heiko A. Oberman and Thomas A. Brady Jr. Leiden: Brill, 1975. For Calvin's specific distinction between Stoic Fate and Divine Providence see: *Institutes*: I.xxvi.8-9. For the relationship between Calvinism and Stoicism see: William Bouwsma, *John Calvin*. Oxford: OUP, 1988: 91-2, 134-135; and Reid Barbour, *English Epicures and Stoics: Ancient Legacies in Early Stuart Culture*. Amhurst, MA: University of Massachusetts Press, 1998: 121, 242. Paul Helm has recently argued that Calvin's determinism is qualitatively different from Stoic Fate, and that Calvin actively rejects Fate in his account of Providence. See: Helm, *John Calvin's Ideas*: 104-5.

[79] *FM*.4979: 91; *FM*.4980: 193, 297.

[80] *FM*.4980: 139.

[81] *TISU*: v-vi. The accusation that God is the author of evil is common for determinism. For recent study of early modern accounts of this problem see Oliver Crisp, *Jonathan Edwards and the metaphysics of sin*. Aldershot: Ashgate, 2005.

even the most mundane decisions, let alone take any level of moral responsibility. As Cudworth bluntly argues in *FM*.4980:

> This is ye very condition of those y[t] hypocrtically pretending y[e] Fall of Adam & originall Sin & y[e] inability of depraved nature to any supernaturall Good y[e] confessing of w[ch] alone they think to be a propitiatory Sacrifice & highly grateful to y[e] Allmighty in y[e] meantime slothfully neglect to use y[t] Power w[ch] really they have, w[ch] is all one in this blunt language of the y[e] Stoick, as if a man having hands should not use y[m] to blow or wipe his nose but sit still expecting y[t] God by miracles should do that office for him.[82]

For Cudworth any system of divine determinism not only degrades God and man but makes an equitable system of ethics impossible. As Cudworth argues:

> For we say agn y[t] if God be nothing but Arbitrary Self-will indetermined by any immutable [form] of Justice & holinesse, he is all y[e] worst y[t] is or can be in y[e] Devill armed wth irresistable power or omnipotence & this is to confound Heaven & Earth & Hell togethr, Good & Evill, Holinesse & wickednesse or w[ch] is all one to destroy all morality & differences of Good & Evill, by making y[e] nature of God devoid of all Morality.[83]

Although thoroughgoing, Cudworth's attack on divine determinism is not particularly searching or deep, rehearsing as it does many of the standard criticisms of deterministic theological systems such as Calvinism. However, the role of Cudworth's attack both in *TISU* and in his manuscripts is as much rhetorical and polemical as it is theological or philosophical. It is clear that Cudworth has both theological and ethical qualms with any theory which either advocated or suggested determinism. The 'polemical' nature of this argument is shown by the interchangeable way in which Cudworth uses the terminology of 'determinism' and 'fatalism'. Cudworth's project paints all deterministic systems in as negative light to make his intellectualism appear as attractive as possible. As a consequence, according to Cudworth, for an equitable system of morality to exist the specific moral norms, which are only found in the wisdom and intellect of the divine, must be not only eternal and immutable in their form (a quality which Cudworth thinks is impossible for Hobbism, but certainly acceptable to Calvinism), but also identifiable freely by all men (a quality which he argues is anathema to both Hobbism or Calvinism). For this to be possible Cudworth's system of morality assumes, contrary to all versions of determinism that he understands, the complete freewill of the individual

---

[82] *FM*.4980: 38.
[83] *FM*.4980: 316.

moral actor. For Cudworth an account of freewill is impossible whilst human agency is restricted by the narrow view of humanity in creation built on the limiting foundations of determinism. Cudworth is in agreement with divine determinism in believing God to be active in an essentially atomistic world. The problem for Cudworth is, therefore, how one can account for human agency whilst still accepting the atomistic form of creation.

The ethical dilemma of arbitrary authority, as much as the fundamental philosophical problems created by it, offered the major intellectual dilemma which Cudworth worked through in the remainder of his mature thought. The themes which drove this project forward did not differ in any meaningful way from the intellectual aspirations that have already been identified in this and the first chapter of this study. It is important to recognise that *TISU* is the product of the same intellectual culture and traditions that fashioned Cudworth's early writings. In particular the ethical dimension of those early texts which, as we have seen, are identifiable in the Cudworth's rejection of arbitrary authority in *TISU*, help us to understand how Cudworth would have progressed from the completed first part into the incomplete second and third parts. Cudworth's intention was to account for human and agency and distributive justice within the compass of what he saw as a theologically sound world view. This endeavour, rather than simply the rejection of atheism as such, was in fact the main purpose of *TISU* as the first volume of the *Intellectual System*. The basis of Cudworth's world view, as shall be shown fully in the next chapter, came from his intellectualist understanding of the divine, and his explicit definition of God as Trinity. The themes of Cudworth's intellectualism and Trinitarianism imbue all of Cudworth's ethical writings, and these writings are made more comprehensible when placed within this theological and philosophical context. However, as we shall see in the following chapters, Cudworth's advocacy for the Trinity was not, like his attack on arbitrary authority, merely an end in itself. Rather this task was undertaken by Cudworth in *TISU* to define and prepare the ground for his ethical, and eventually political, understanding of the individual as 'God's freeman.'

CHAPTER THREE

THE TRUE INTELLECTUAL SYSTEM OF THE UNIVERSE II:
THE TRINITY AND REASON

Cudworth's *TISU* may be best remembered as a broad-side against atheism, however its main aim was not simply to discredit atheism, but to provide a strong defence of God, not simply as a creative being, but in terms of the Christian doctrine of the Trinity. Cudworth's account of the Trinity dominates the pages and argument of *TISU* and defines not only Cudworth's theism, but also provides the impetus for the practical reason of his ethical and political ideas. The intellectual origins of Cudworth's Trinitarianism are complex. In seventeenth-century theological debate the Trinity came under consistent attack. Although this is nothing new in debates on the Trinity, the debates engendered by the anti-Trinitarian heresy of Socinianism provided the theological context for Cudworth's Trinitarianism. However, as we shall see, the threat of Socinianism was nothing new. The founders of the religious movement which took their names, Laelius and Faustus Socinus died in 1562 and 1604 respectively. In fact, as we shall see, the threat of Socinianism merely helped highlight a deeper problem facing theological discussion in the seventeenth century, that of how to reconcile doctrine (in the case of Trinity the traditional language of three persons of one substance) with the increasingly scientific and clearly defined language of the 'new philosophy' of the seventeenth-century. As we shall see, Cudworth's account of the Trinity steps into this debate by seeking to provide a middle ground which explains the Trinity in orthodox terms, whilst using the philosophical language of the seventeenth century, in particular that inaugurated by the writings of Descartes.

Cudworth's approach to the specifically theological debates on the Trinity was to reorientate the terms of the debate. Where the orthodoxy of the Reformed tradition had been to maintain the essentially Calvinist position stressing the role of the persons of the Trinity in the economy of salvation *ad extra* — the so-called economic Trinity — Cudworth adopted the alternative position which focused on how the persons of the Trinity related to one another *ad intra* — the so-called immanent Trinity. The theological terms 'economic' and 'immanent' with reference to the Trinity were most famously presented by Karl Rahner in his short text,

The Trinity.[1] In this text Rahner famously asserts his 'Rule' that these differing accounts of the Trinity did not pertain to different versions of the Trinity, rather that they were differing accounts, from differing standpoints, of the Trinity: 'the "economic" Trinity is the "immanent" Trinity, and the "immanent" Trinity is the "economic"'.[2] In this survey of seventeenth-century Trinitarian theology this rule will largely be accepted. In the face of the threat of Socinianism the aim of Cudworth was not to prove the efficacy of his account against the Calvinist 'economic' account, rather he argued that his 'immanent' account provided a more effective, but no less sound, response the immediate threats of seventeenth-century anti-Trinitarianism.

By beginning with how God exists as Trinity *ad intra*, rather than the economic account *ad extra*, Cudworth presents a departure from the standard account of the Trinity presented in the seventeenth century.[3] Cudworth's aim here is to present an account of the Trinity which is not only theological sound, but also philosophically coherent. As we shall see, Cudworth argues that the Trinity is at the heart of all sound forms of theism, Pagan and Christian alike. Drawing on what he argues are intimations of the Trinity in ancient Pagan theology, particularly Platonism, Cudworth provides what he argues is a reasoned account of the Trinity which is made perfect by the historical fact of the incarnation of the *Logos* as Jesus Christ. Cudworth's argument here is not simply to present a defence of Christian orthodoxy, but stress the centrality of the Trinity to all things. As we shall see, Cudworth does this by arguing that not only is the Trinity reasonable, but that in some qualified sense, true reason is manifested in the Trinity. In particular, Cudworth argues that the theological truth of the Trinity correctly understood led to the philosophical realisation that, 'our *Faculties* of *Reason and Understanding* are not *False and Imposturous*, but *Rightly Made*.'[4] Cudworth's account of the Trinity therefore stretches beyond the context of theological debate to provide the basis for his account of human reason. By linking reason

---

[1] Karl Rahner, *The Trinity*, translated by Joseph Donceel. London: Burns & Oates, 1970.

[2] Rahner, *The Trinity*: 22. The efficacy of 'Rahner's Rule' has recently been called into question by Randal Rauser in his essay 'Rahner's Rule: An Emporer without Clothes?' *International Journal of Systematic Theology*, 7 (2005): 81-94.

[3] It is interesting to note here that so pervasive if the 'economic' account of the Trinity to seventeenth-century theology that the best survey of that debate, Philip Dixon's *Nice and Hot Disputes*, only mentions the Rahner's distinction in passing. See: Philip Dixon, *Nice and Hot Disputes: The doctrine of the Trinity in the Seventeenth Century*. London: T&T Clark, 2003. On the economic and immanent Trinity: 8, 190, 192.

[4] *TISU*: 717.

with the Trinity, and the incarnation of the *Logos* in particular, Cudworth's Trinitarianism links God's grace and man's reason by relating reason explicitly to the manifestation of that grace. For Cudworth this grace is freely and unconditionally given by the triune God to all men. It is the choice and responsibility given to man whether to accept and responsibly use this reasonable power. Cudworth's account of the Trinity, therefore, bridges the gap between his own attack on arbitrary power and his defence of the ethical responsibility of man. As Cudworth argues in one of his manuscripts, 'Self Love is so strong y^t reason...[is] ye only principle y^t can control it.'[5] The Trinity, therefore, stands as the defining term of not only Cudworth's theology but also his practical philosophy.

The Trinity in seventeenth-century theology

As we have seen, it would be wrong to see theology in seventeenth-century England as exclusively Calvinist. However, Calvin's theology did provide the backbone to the orthodox Trinitarianism of the time. Calvin's doctrine of the Trinity, as with all his theology, begins with his voluntarist doctrine of God, what Thomas Torrance describes as the 'sheer Godness of God.'[6] Calvin's doctrine of the Trinity builds on the central premise of his theology, that man, in his fallen and incomplete state, can only conceive of God as he condescends to reveal himself to man. God's self-revelation to man, for Calvin, is comprehended by man through the soteriological workings of God in creation. Calvin's theology constantly seeks to distance man from theological speculation, and so argues that we know God as Trinity not through delving into the mystery of the Trinity, but by knowing God in his self-revelation to the world. As a consequence Calvin follows Augustine's arguments from book five of *De Trinitate*, that man knows God as Trinity through the different workings of God in the different persons of the Trinity.[7] Man can, therefore, only know God *ad extra*, which in turn reflects the tri-unity of God *ad intra*. This unity is revealed to man through the relational unity of the persons of the Trinity, that is that the Father is only Father because his relation to the Son, and the Son is only the Son because his relation to

---

[5] *FM* 4983: 22

[6] Thomas F. Torrance, 'Calvin's Doctrine of the Trinity' in *Calvin Theological Review*, 25 (1990): 165-193: 165.

[7] *Institutes*: I.13.19.

the Father. But because of the limited mind of man this immanent unity will always be hidden from human eyes.[8]

The strength of Calvin's account is that it limits man's knowledge of the Trinity to those aspects of the Trinity which are revealed to man. This sidesteps the basic arithmetic dilemma that three into one will not go. God reveals himself to man through the workings of the three persons of the Trinity, but the form that the unity these persons takes is hidden from and beyond the capacities of the human mind. As Calvin states it is better to 'rest contented with the relation as taught by him, than get bewildered in vain speculation by subtle prying into a sublime mystery.'[9] The second strength of the economic Trinity is that by stressing the workings of the persons of the Trinity in creation it becomes simpler to reconcile the doctrine of the Trinity to the thin biblical evidence for the Trinity. So Christ's assertion in the Gospel of John that 'I go to the Father; for the Father is greater than I', which would seem to undermine the doctrine of the Trinity, can be explained as a clause explaining the soteriological role of Christ in the economy of salvation; as Christ states earlier in the same Gospel narrative, 'no-one comes to the Father except through me.'[10]

In the seventeenth century the greatest threat to the Reformed orthodoxy on the Trinity came from the Unitarian heresy of Socinianism. Socinians argued that the Trinity was shown to be untenable when scripture was exposed to rational enquiry. This belief was based on, what Richard Muller has described as, 'a radical a-traditional version of the Renaissance *ad fontes* and the Reformer's *sola Scriptura*.'[11] This led to two important characteristics to the anti-Trinitarianism of the Socinians. Firstly, in keeping with most anti-Trinitarian heresies, the Socinians stressed the lack of biblical evidence for the orthodox, creedal definition of God as both three and one. However, unlike the ancient heresy of Arianism, the strictly linguistic interpretation of scripture presented by the Socinians interpreted the person of Christ as a divine human, rather than God, or the first derivation of God. This account of the person of Christ leads us to the second, more radical, characteristic of Socinianism; their strict definition of the substance of God as a single, indivisible,

---

[8] *Institutes*: 1.13.19. See also, Philip Walker Butin, *Revelation, Redemption, and Response: Calvin's Trinitarian Understanding of the Divine-Human Relationship*. Oxford: OUP, 1985; and Torrance, 'Calvin's Doctrine of the Trinity'. On the Augustinian understanding of the 'Relational Unity' of the Trinity, see Lacugna, *God for Us*: 10; and David Brown, *The Divine Trinity*. London: Duckworth, 1985.

[9] *Institutes*: 1.13.19.

[10] Jn.14: 7-8 & 28.

[11] Muller, *Post-Reformation Reformed Dogmatics*: IV:75.

intelligent substance. This allowed them to assert, to use the English derivation of Socinianism, both the Unitarian form of God, and the singularity of the person of Jesus Christ as a divinely inspired human. This focus on the substance of God comes out most clearly in the founding statement of Socinian belief, the *Racovian Catechism* of 1605:

> the essence of God is one, not in kind but in number. Wherefore it cannot, in any way, contain a plurality of persons, since a person is nothing else than an individual intelligent essence. Wherever, then, there exist three numerical persons, there must necessarily, in like manner, be reckoned three individual essences; for in the same sense in which it is affirmed that there is one numerical essence, it must be held that there is also one numerical person.'[12]

Socinianism can, therefore, be understood not simply in theological terms as a Christian heresy, but also in a broader intellectual context in which the very language of 'God' was being stretched by the developments of sixteenth- and seventeenth-century philosophy. Whereas in mediaeval thought the term essence had referred both to the individuality of the thing, and the quiddity, the 'whatness' of the thing, the seventeenth century saw a greater demarcation stressing substance in a more exclusively individual sense, away from the more general sense of the essence and nature of the thing. The radical Socinian stress on the individual nature of God and of Jesus Christ, therefore, belies a deeper crisis concerning the technical language and understanding of the Trinity in the seventeenth century. As we shall see below much of Cudworth's account of the Trinity engages with this debate not so much as a direct rebuttal or response to the orthodox, Socinian, or even Hobbist account of the Trinity, but to find a way of using the philosophical terminology of the new philosophy whilst not undermining the orthodox understanding of God as Trinity.[13]

One of the main consequences of the Socinian threat was that it engendered a theological panic over the 'spectre of Socinianism' which found its way into all theology. Many of the leading orthodox theologians of the Reformed tradition in seventeenth-century England saw Socinianism as the greatest error of the age and one to which all heresies tended.[14] As a consequence 'Socinianism' became a term of abuse not simply for those who followed the teaching of Laelius and Faustus Socinus, but anyone whose ideas could be thought to tend in that direction. As we have seen many of the problems highlighted by Socinianism derived

---

[12] *The Racovian Catechism*, translated by Thomas Rees. London: 1818: 33.
[13] Muller, *Post-Reformation Reformed Dogmatics*: IV: 74-80, 94-103.
[14] Muller, *Post-Reformation Reformed Dogmatics*: III:130.

from the change in the philosophical lexicon during the seventeenth century. This link between philosophy and heresy meant that the charge of 'Socinianism' was often given to those who sought to explicitly employ reason in doctrinal questions: it is, therefore, no surprise that many of the Cambridge Platonists were tarred with the brush of Socinianism simply because of their explicit use of reason in matters of religion. At the heart of these accusations lies an irony that Socinianism, although often viewed as a form of weak rationalism, was in fact rigidly and dogmatically biblical. The accusation of reason leading to heresy was, therefore, not a direct consequence of Socinianism, but a by-product of the spectre of Socinianism.

We find something of these accusations of Socinianism in Anthony Tuckney's criticisms of Cudworth's mentor, Benjamin Whichcote. In 1651 Tuckney, who was Master of Emmanuel and who had been Whichcote's tutor at Emmanuel in the 1630s, wrote to Whichcote warning him of what he thought were the potential errors of his introduction of reason into questions of religion. Whichcote, who at the time was Provost of King's College Cambridge, replied to this letter setting in course correspondence which gives a fascinating insight into the relationship of the Cambridge Platonists to the Reformed orthodoxy of the time.[15] In his letters Tuckney seeks to admonish Whichcote for his overuse of reason in his theology, and so warn him away from the potential heresies that it lead to. Stressing his own orthodoxy from the outset, Tuckney states that:

> I had rather, by reason of my adaering to the truth, that CALVINE maintained; men shoulde call mee a Calvinist: than by reason of eyther and indifference, or by propending to somthing that Socinians, or Arminians hold; men, though unjustlie and in sinfullie should besmeare mee with their appellation.[16]

By contrast Tuckney argues that Whichcote, by moving away from the safety of the Reformed tradition was opening himself up to heresy particularly in his over-reliance on non-Biblical pagan sources.

> Those ... Philosophers, and other Heathens, made fairer candidates for Heaven; than the scriptures seeme to allowe of: and They, in their virtues, preferred before Christians, overtaken with weaknesses — A kinde of a Moral Divinitie minted; onlie with a little tincture of Christ added: nay, a Platonique faith united to God.[17]

---

[15] Tuckney was not only Master of Emmanuel, but also a leading member of the Westminster Assembly. See Patrick Collinson, 'Anthony Tuckney (1599-1670)', *Oxford Dictionary of National Biography*: Oxford, OUP: 2004.

[16] *Letters*: 79.

[17] *Letters*: 39.

Tuckney sees in Whichcote's 'Platonique faith' something incompatible with his own understanding of God. He complains that Whichcote's undue respect for the ability and faculties of men are too easily being used as a screen for heresy. Chief of these heresies in Tuckney's mind was the heresy of Socinianism. His accusations of heresy centre on two linked factors in Whichcote writings: first his Platonism, which can lead to Arianism, and second his use of reason, which opens the door to Socinianism. In Tuckney's attacks we encounter for the first time the accusations of anti-Trinitarian heresy which were laid at the door of the Cambridge Platonists with increasing regularity through the remaining decades of the seventeenth century. With reference to Cudworth's account of the Trinity Tuckney's attacks on Whichcote are particularly instructive. Firstly they bring up the narrow historical argument as to whether Platonism was at the heart of the heresy of Arianism, a question which, as shall be shown below, particularly exercised Cudworth. Secondly, Tuckney's constant allusions to reason and Socinianism highlight again the dilemma facing seventeenth-century theology of how to find a theological language which allowed one to both accept contemporary developments in philosophy, whilst also remaining doctrinally sound.

In the case of Cudworth's account of the Trinity the broader philosophical context which affected seventeenth-century debates on the Trinity was made even more stark by the Trinitarian utterances of Cudworth's bet noire, Thomas Hobbes. Although Hobbes' account of the Trinity does not feature explicitly in Cudworth's Trinitarianism it is possible to argue that Hobbes' idiosyncratic reworking of the Calvinist 'economic' conception of the Trinity provided an impetus for Cudworth to favour an 'immanent' account. As has already been stated, by the time Cudworth was working on his account of the Trinity in *TISU*, probably at somepoint in the 1660s, the threat of Socinianism was well established. After all the *Racovian Catechism* was first published in 1605, and the term 'Socinian' was so current in contemporary debate that it had developed into a term of abuse for any thinker who strayed from the orthodox and conservative high ground. The terms of the debate therefore did not change a great deal through most of the seventeenth century. A case in point is John Owen's *A Brief Declaration and Vindication of the Doctrine of the Trinity* published in 1676, two years before *TISU*. In this Owen states 'each Person having the Understanding, the Will, the Power of God, becomes a distinct Principle of operation; and yet all their actings *ad extra* being the actings of God, they are *undivided*, and are all the works of one, of the self same

God.'[18] In fact most of the defences of the Trinity published before 1678, the publication date of *TISU*, maintain that the Trinity can only be known by man *ad extra*, through its revealed qualities in the world. However, in one of these accounts of the Trinity, that presented by Thomas Hobbes, we find a version of the economic Trinity perverted in such a manner as to make, in Cudworth's view, this traditional orthodoxy untenable.

As shown in the previous chapter, Cudworth interpreted much of Hobbes' philosophy as a development of the structure and forms of Calvinist theology. This link to Calvinism is also true of Hobbes' definition of the economy of the Trinity. Recent work by George Wright has shown the centrality of Trinitarian issues to Hobbes' work, particularly in the extensive appendix to the Latin *Leviathan*.[19] Wright's work, along with that of A.P. Martinich, has shown the important relationship that exists between the traditional structures of Calvinist theology, and the theological arguments deployed by Hobbes. In *Leviathan* Hobbes presents a version of the Trinity which follows those which we have already encountered in the Calvinist economic Trinity. For Hobbes the persons of the Trinity disclose themselves to man through their revealed qualities in human history. Hobbes argues that the persons of the Trinity represent different qualities of God in different material examples. So the persons of the Trinity are — corresponding to Hobbes' description of the Body Politic — artificial persons 'owned by those they represent.'[20] Whereas in the political arena this ownership is in consenting members of the body politic, in the Trinity the persons represent the different characteristics of God. So, Hobbes argues, God-the-Father is represented by Moses the Lawgiver; God-the-Son is represented by Jesus of Nazareth, and God-the-Spirit is represented by the Apostles. As Hobbes' argues; 'they are Persons, that is, they have their names from Representing; which could not be, till divers men had Represented God's Person in ruling, or in directing, or in directing under him.'[21] Hobbes argues that this form of the Trinity allows for the maintenance of the unity of God, whilst allowing for a differentiation in the persons of the Trinity. Hobbes asserts that he is able to do this because the unity

---

[18] John Owen, *A Brief Declaration and Vindication of the Doctrine of the Trinity: As also of the Person and Sanctification of Christ.* London: 1676: 78.

[19] George Wright, *Religion, Politics, and Thomas Hobbes.* Dordrecht: Springer, 2006. Also see the recent discussion on the topic see the recent debate between Edwin M. Curley, 'Calvin and Hobbes, or Hobbes as an orthodox Christian,' in *The Journal of the History of Philosophy*, 34 (1996): 257-71, published with a reply by A.P. Martinich on 272-84, and Curley's reply to his reply on 285-87.

[20] *Leviathan*: 218.

[21] *Leviathan*: 524.

comes, as in the political arena, in the unity of the represented, the one true God, not the representatives, the persons of the Trinity.[22]

Where Hobbes differs from other accounts of the economic Trinity is in his account of the substance of the Trinity. Unlike the Reformed ortho- doxy of a theologian such as John Owen, Hobbes is unwilling to argue that the substance of God is somehow beyond the comprehension of man. For Hobbes substance is substance, and that substance is material and corporeal. As he famously states in Chapter Thirty-four of *Leviathan*:

> substance and body signify the same thing; and therefore substance incor- poreal are words which, when they are joined together, destroy one another, as if a man should say, an incorporeal body.[23]

Hobbes' account of substance, therefore, draws him towards an account of the Trinity, beginning with the historical, substantial, occurrences of the persons of the Trinity, and then showing how these distinct substances present a unity in the 'representation' of the one God.

> In this Trinity on Earth the Unity is not...of the same substance, though they give the same testimony: But the Trinity of Heaven, the Persons are the persons of the one and the same God, though Represented in three dif- ferent times and occasions.[24]

Hobbes argues that the persons of the Trinity lead us to our knowledge and understanding of the unified nature of God. For Cudworth, Hobbes' account of the Trinity is dangerous for two reasons: firstly, it is based on a flawed understanding of substance, and secondly that this definition of substance leads to an account of the Trinity which fundamentally undermines any sound conception of God. Cudworth's response to this theological context is to re-orientate his conception of the Trinity around an understanding of the substance of the Trinity, and so the Trinity *ad intra*. This, he argues, would use new philosophical definitions of sub- stance to present a doctrinally sound account of the tri-unity of God.

Cudworth's account of the Trinity

Cudworth's account of the tri-unity of God in *TISU* follows the same method which was outlined in the previous chapter. Although presenting a positive theological account of the Trinity, Cudworth embeds this

[22] Martinich, *Two Gods*: 206.
[23] *Leviathan*: 289.
[24] *Leviathan*: 524.

account in the historically minded form of his method. In particular Cudworth seeks to show that not only is his account of the Trinity theological
sound, but that this is the conception of the Trinity which has existed, to
a lesser or greater extent, in all past forms of sound theism. Cudworth's
argument for the existence of a divinely inspired thread of reason in
creation allows us to understand a key element of Cudworth's method.
By arguing that the true form of God can be found in all elements of
creation, Cudworth argues that anyone who lives in that creation can
know, if only in a hidden form, something of the truth of the divine. This
means that, although the truth of God is confirmed and consummated in
the revelation of Christ, something of the truth of God's existence was
known and available to the pre-Christian pagan world. The best example
of this, Cudworth argues, is St Paul's sermon from the Areopagus to the
unknown God.[25] This recognition by Paul of the essential monotheism in
Hellenistic religion shows, for Cudworth, in keeping with his adherence
to the *prisca theologia*, that pagan religion, far from being anathema
to Christianity, could hold a kernel of truth in it, even if God was wor-
shipped and understood incorrectly. As a consequence, Cudworth argues
that it is worthwhile studying Pagan theology because those elements
which 'followed the free *Sentiments* and Dictates of their own Minds,'
could provide metaphysical insights that not only clarified Christian
teaching, but gave it historical and philosophical verification.[26] In *TISU*
Cudworth is particularly keen to show those Pagan traditions which had
anticipated something of the Trinitarian form of God. Following this
schema, Cudworth identifies Trinities in Egyptian and Roman theology.[27]
Such is the power of this tradition in pagan and even Jewish theology
that he argues that Trinitarianism can be understood as one of the central
tenets of the Cabala. It is in the supposed Trinities of the Cabala that
Cudworth found the most authentic anticipations of the Christian tradition.[28] Cudworth's defence of the Trinity utilises his belief that central
truths about the nature of reality, in particular the Trinity, have always
been identifiable in differing forms throughout history, describing this as
'the Cabala of the Trinity.'[29]

[25] *TISU*: 474-5. Also see Acts.17:16-34.

[26] *TISU*: 627.

[27] *TISU*: 328, 453, 491.

[28] *TISU*: 546, 557, 570. This claim must be tempered by the knowledge that many of
these Cabalistic sources, in particular the Orphic and Hermetic traditions, were almost
certainly Christian forgeries.

[29] *TISU*: 552.

In making this argument Cudworth's language is of interest. Cudworth does not always speak of the Trinity as revealed 'persons'. Such language suggests the more exclusively 'Christian' explanation of the Trinity *ad extra*. Instead Cudworth often chooses to describe the persons of the Trinity as 'expressions' of God's nature. This then allows for, in some limited sense, the recognition of these expressions by non-Christian theological traditions. Cudworth's Trinitarianism, however, always assumes the primacy of the Christian Trinity. The first person, the Father, expresses himself as the creator who is necessarily 'self-existent, and the cause of all things.'[30] The second person, the *Logos*, is expressed in the embodiment of the perfection of the first person in a moment in time; the person of Jesus Christ as *Logos*. The third person, the Spirit, is this perfect mind expressed throughout history, the imprint of the true God seen dimly by the Pagans and recognisable by us in the order and reasonableness of creation. Cudworth argues that all the pagan Trinitarian systems uncover a central truth about God: that there is one God, but that that God 'expresses' himself to the world in different forms.[31] This sense of the differing expressions of the divine is what Cudworth argues exists in Pagan Trinities, but remains only half formed as it lacks the historical certainty given to the Christian Trinity by the person of Jesus Christ. Even without this certainty, Cudworth argues, pagan theologians were able to comprehend that God, as a perfect being, does not require knowledge of himself. Therefore the principle of reason which allows man to recognise and confirm the existence of the divine must, Cudworth argues, be derived from a separate expression of the divine. Cudworth defines this distinction through the terminology of the 'intellect' of God — 'necessarily self-existent, and the cause of all things' — and the 'understanding' of God — the means by which this perfection is expressed to the world and so the means by which the world can know God.[32] At one point Cudworth equates this principle directly with 'love' stating that the reciprocity provided for in the expression of the 'understanding' of God exists because, '*God is Love*, [which] seems to warrant this much to us, that *Love* in

[30] *TISU*: 633.

[31] Leslie Armour, in a recent paper, has rightly shown the importance of the term 'expression' — over the traditional language of 'hypostasis' or 'persona' — for Cudworth in describing the form of the different persons of the Trinity. See Leslie Armour, 'Trinity, Community and Love: Cudworth's Platonism and the Idea of God' in *Platonism and the Origins of the Modernity: Studies on Platonism and Early Modern Philosophy*, edited by Douglas Hedley and Sarah Hutton. Dordrecht: Springer, 2008: 113. For Cudworth's use of this terminology see *FM*.4983: 20.

[32] *TISU*: 633; Armour, 'Trinity, Community and Love': 127.

some rightly Qualified sense, is *God.*'[33] Cudworth argues that this truth, which is fully revealed in scripture through the Passion of Christ as the full embodiment of love, is also fully reasonable and so available in traditions of philosophy which knew nothing of Christ, but still knew something, if only imperfectly, of the true form of the divine.[34]

Unsurprisingly for Cudworth the fullest pagan definition of this distinction is in the writings of Plotinus, and it is from Plotinus that he develops his language of the intellect and understanding form of God. In *Ennead* III.8, 'On the nature and contemplation of the one,' Plotinus makes the distinction between the intellect of 'the One' and the means of participating in that intellect. Essentially that distinction is between the still source of all creation, the intellect of the divine, and the active principle of participation, the understanding of the divine. Plotinus uses the metaphor of the divine as a spring or fountain to show how the active principles which come from it differ from the still source of this action:

> think of a spring which has no other origin, but gives the whole of itself to rivers, and is not used up by the rivers but remains of itself at rest, but the rivers that rise from it, before each of them flows in a different direction, remain for a while all together, though each of them knows, in a way, the direction in which it is going to let the stream flow.[35]

This action does not diminish the intellect of the divine which is an inexhaustible source. In turn it draws all things to it and reinforces the power and integrity of intellect through the participatory power of the understanding. As Plotinus argues, 'For all things…are not an origin, but they came from an origin, and this is no more all things, or one of them.'[36] Cudworth goes on to argue that many of these pagan systems, although imperfect were able to move beyond the recognition of intellect and understanding to posit a third expression of the divine as an active, perceptive power. This three-fold nature becomes, for Cudworth, the essential structure that informs Trinitarian thought in Pagan theology and Platonism in particular.

Cudworth use of the Plotinian distinction between intellect and understanding draws him naturally towards an immanent account of the Trinity *ad intra*, as God appears to himself. Cudworth argues that the active principle of understanding, which brings man to recognition of the divine in the first instance, must, logically, be the second expression of the

---

[33] *TISU*: 123.
[34] *TISU*: 204.
[35] *Enneads*: 3.8.10.
[36] *Enneads*: 3.8.9.

divine. This distinction, Cudworth argues, exists because understanding must be viewed in terms of multiplicity and therefore has to be secondary to the singular intellect of the One. For man to appreciate the intellect of the divine, the means of that appreciation, knowledge and understanding cannot be the highest good in itself, but must be drawn from and reliant upon on a single principle prior to it.[37] As Cudworth states:

> Now whatever this Chiefest Good be, which is a Perfection Superiour to Knowledge and Understanding; that Philosopher resolves that it must needs be First and Principally in God who is therefore called by him,...*The very Idea and Essence of Good*.[38]

Cudworth argues that this appreciation of the difference between intellect and understanding is not corrosive of the idea of one true God, or derivative from it. It is the existence of this reasonable principle of understanding, uniting all creation to the divine that becomes the key term that Cudworth uses to assert the Trinity as the true, united form of God.

Cudworth stresses the existence of pagan Trinities not to undermine the efficacy, or remove the uniqueness of the Christian Trinity, but rather to stress the inevitability and perfection of the true mystery of the Christian Trinity. Cudworth, drawing on his syncretic method, defends the Platonic interpretation of the Trinity by linking the Platonic and Christian Trinities through their shared heritage in, what Cudworth termed, the 'Mosaic Cabala', the shared heritage of Christian and Hellenistic theology in the ancient theology of the Jews and Egyptians. Despite this influence, Cudworth argues that the Hellenistic form of this tradition inevitably became corrupt. The clarity and coherence of the Mosaic Cabala is identifiable in Plato and Plotinus, but in later Neoplatonic thinkers the tradition became perverted. Cudworth asserts that one finds the authentic culmination of the Mosaic Cabala not in the Platonic tradition but in the revelation of Christ as *Logos*.

With this qualification in mind, it is worthwhile examining how, for Cudworth, the Platonic Trinity both anticipates and differs from the Christian Trinity. Cudworth is clear that it is the Platonic Trinity which is the most sophisticated of the Pagan systems in this respect.[39] It is not, Cudworth claims, because the Platonic system is peculiar in having a Trinitarian structure; such a system is a logical part of true monotheism. Rather it is that, although taking an adulterated path, Platonism is based

---

[37] *TISU*: 584-5.
[38] *TISU*: 204.
[39] *TISU*: 558.

on the same theological and philosophical tradition as Christianity. As Cudworth argues:

> This is therefore that *Platonic Trinity*, which we oppose to the *Christian*, not as if *Plato's* own *Trinity* in the very Essential Constitutions thereof, were quite a Different Thing from the *Christian*; itself in all probability having been first derived from a *Divine* or *Mosaick Cabala*.[40]

For this reason the Platonic Trinity describes with more depth and subtlety than any other pagan source the complex relationship between the different persons of the Trinity, and is to be respected above all the others. In particular, unlike other monotheistic traditions, the Platonic tradition comes closest to the Christian in appreciating the immediacy of the relationship between the first and second persons of the Trinity.[41]

However, in seventeenth-century debates on the Trinity it had become common to equate both the Trinity, and heresies on the Trinity, with the muddling of Christianity with Hellenistic, and particularly Platonic, metaphysics. To defend the Christian Trinity from the accusation that it was an Hellenistic perversion Cudworth seeks to place some distance between the Christian and Platonic Trinities. He argues that the Christian Trinity can be found entirely within Scripture which is 'the only true Rule and Measure of this *Divine Cabala* of the *Trinity*.'[42]

Cudworth argues that, outside the Judeo-Christian tradition, the 'Cabala of the Trinity' is found in its fullest form in the 'Platonic Trinity.' He views this as incomplete compared to the Christian Trinity, but finds in the philosophical distinctions that allow for it the most coherent explanation of the Trinitarian form of the divine. Cudworth's defence of the Trinity along Platonic grounds also carries with it a second motive. By explicitly basing his defence of the Trinity in Platonism Cudworth places himself between two opposing theological criticisms of Platonic philosophy. The first, from orthodox Christian theology, was that Platonism inevitably leads to the anti-Trinitarian heresy of Arianism.[43] The second, and directly contrasting criticism of Platonism, came from Socinians who argued that the Trinity was a theological perversion of the truth of the new covenant

[40] *TISU*: 557.
[41] *TISU*: 407-8.
[42] *TISU*: 550.
[43] Sarah Hutton, 'Neoplatonic roots of Arianism Ralph Cudworth and Theophilus Gale,' in *Socinianism and its Role in the Culture of XVI-th to XVIII-th Centuries* edited by L. Szczucki and Z. Ogonowski. Warsaw: PWN – Polish Scientific Publisher, 1983: 143. Also see Maurice Wiles, *The Archetypal Heresy: Arianism through the Centuries*. Oxford: The Clarendon Press, 1996: 66.

brought about by the dangerous mixing of Christianity with Hellenistic thought.[44] To counter this first accusation Cudworth defends the Platonic Trinity from the suggestion that it errs towards Arianism by stressing the philosophical coherence of the true Platonic Trinity. However, to counter the Socinian attacks on the Trinity Cudworth argues that the Platonic Trinity is theoretically coherent but philosophically corruptible. As a consequence Cudworth argues that although a reasoned account of the Trinity can be found in Platonic thought, the Trinity is only fully manifested in the revelation of Christ. This final claim leads to problems in the examination of Cudworth's Trinitarianism because, as Sarah Hutton has argued, 'it relies heavily on the very Platonists on whose accounts of the trinity he casts doubt.'[45]

Despite Cudworth's often contradictory use of Platonism in his Trinitarianism the fundamental tenor of his account is that, despite its virtues, in fundamental areas the Platonic Trinity is corrupt.[46] This corruption is, Cudworth argues, found in the subordination that inevitably occurs when explaining the relationships between the different persons of the Trinity. Although in its purest form, Cudworth argues, the Platonic Trinity grasps the relational unity at the heart of the Trinity, because this is built on philosophical presuppositions, rather than the confidence given by the revelation of the historical person of Jesus Christ, such a system is open to corruption. In particular, by stressing too vigorously the supreme nature of the first person, the second and third persons become diminished by association. So Cudworth states:

> if it be considered in *Visibles*, then will the *Second Hypostasis*, be resembled to the *Image* of a *Face* in a Glass, and the *Third* to the *Image* of that *Image* Reflected in another Glass, which depend upon the *Original Face*, and have a *Gradual Abatement* of the vigour thereof.[47]

Thus, Cudworth suggests, there is in some Platonic philosophy a danger of destroying the great strength of the Platonic Trinity, namely the relational unity of the persons of the Trinity, by concentrating too clearly on the first person above the others. By alluding to St Paul's metaphor of man's appreciation of God only 'through a glass darkly,' Cudworth here seems to suggest that this dangerous tendency of some Platonists to diminish

---

[44] McLachlan, *Socinianism*, pp. 8-20.
[45] Hutton, 'Neoplatonic roots of Arianism': 140-1; D.W. Dockrill, 'The Authority of the Fathers in the Great Trinitarian Debates of the Sixteen Nineties,' in *Studia Patristica*, 18 (1990): 335-47: 340.
[46] *TISU*: 558.
[47] *TISU*: 581.

not only the second and third persons of the Trinity, but also the integrity of their theology. As he vehemently argues:

> Shall we say that the *First Hypostasis* or *Person*, in the *Platonic Trinity*, (if not the *Christian* also) is...*Senseless* and *Irrational*, and altogether devoid of *Mind* and *Understanding*? Or would not this be to introduce a certain kind of *Mysterious Atheism* and under pretence of Magnifying and Advancing the Supreme Deity, Monstrously to Degrade the Same?[48]

For Cudworth there are two logical dangers created by the corruptions of pseudo-Platonic thinkers. Firstly, they undermined the relational unity of the Trinity, making the separation of intellect and understanding merely the first step in a hierarchy of Gods, thus opening the door to the hierarchies of Arianism and Polytheism.[49] Secondly, and more dangerously, such readings suggest that the second and third persons, rather than being expressions of the divine are, in fact, separate, created creatures, thus opening the door to the monarchalism of Sabellianism. So Cudworth argues:

> Wherefore we conclude, that this ancient *Cabala of the Trinity*, was *Depraved* and *Adulterated* by those Platonists and Pythagoreans, who made either the *World* itself, or else...*an Informing Soul of the World*, to be the *Third Hypostasis* thereof, they Mingling *Created* and *Uncreated Beings* together, in that which themselves notwithstanding call a *Trinity* of *Causes* and of *Principles*.[50]

Cudworth argues that it is these pseudo-Platonic theories, rather than the true Platonic Trinity, that gave birth to the heresies of Sabellianism and Arianism. Cudworth does not indicate clearly which thinkers are to blame for this decline in the Platonic tradition. Certainly Cudworth sees this as an adulteration made after Plato and places the blame at the feet of, what he loosely describes as, 'Juniour Platonists.' He does at one point suggest that the chief culprits might have been Proclus and Iamblichus. This claim is, however, undermined by Cudworth's earlier use of Proclus and Iamblichus to defend the integrity of the true Platonic Trinity.[51]

Cudworth's solution to this dilemma is, characteristically, to argue that the solution lies in a middle position between the two extremes of Arianism and Sabellianism. The excesses of Arianism and Sabellianism are only solved by the revelation of the new covenant which brought into the light the true Trinitarian dynamics of God's life.[52] Cudworth's argument

---

[48] *TISU*: 585.
[49] *TISU*: 570.
[50] *TISU*: 552.
[51] *TISU*: 625. On Proclus compare, for instance *TISU*: 626 & 557.
[52] *TISU*: 555.

here follows the syncretic form of the whole of *TISU* by defining his definition of the Trinity against ancient heresies which mirrored contemporary attacks on the Trinity, namely the 'Arianism' of the Socinians and the 'Sabellianism' of Hobbes. Cudworth argues that the form of metaphysical deduction he was using against his contemporary enemies was the same as that used by the Nicene fathers, 'who not withstanding made not *Plato* but the Scripture, together with Reason deducing natural Consequences there from, their Foundation.'[53] The Church fathers used Platonic thought not to pervert scripture, but to confirm its revelation. For this reason Cudworth argues that the Christian Trinity is a more authentic understanding of the intellectual form of the divine. In this way he asserts that the revelation of Christ perfectly unlocks the implicitly reasonable form of the divine, and is, therefore, by implication, more reasonable than the pagan account the Trinity. Consequently Cudworth is able to argue that:

> the *Christian Trinity* though there be very much of *Mystery* in it, yet is there nothing at all of *plain Contradiction* to the Undoubted Principles of human Reason, that is, of *Impossibility* to be found therein,...[it is]...much more agreeable to Reason, than that *Platonick* or *Pseudo-Platonick Trinity*.[54]

Cudworth argues that what the revelation of Christ gives the Christian Trinity a pure understanding of the embodiment of divine which not only reflects on the first person, but also exists, un-created, with the first person in the unity of God. His interpretation of this peculiar Christian relationship rests heavily on his understanding of the prologue to the Gospel of John, in particular the various clauses defining the *Logos*. Crucially, he argues that John gave the firm assurance of Christ as existing in the form of the Godhead from eternity; 'the λογος or *Word* be said to have been, *With God* (this is *God* the *Father*) and also itself to *Be God* (that is not a *Creature*) yet is it no where called *Another* or *Second God*.'[55] In the person of Christ Cudworth finds the concrete historical affirmation of the philosophical principle of understanding which is only suggested by the Platonic Trinity. Cudworth, again drawing on John's Gospel, affirms this point by arguing that, 'the word was made flesh, *we look upon this Word even in Flesh as God*.'[56]

Cudworth's interpretation of the Church Fathers' use of a Christianised Platonism also leads Cudworth to the problem, which as we have seen is

---

[53] *TISU*: 579.
[54] *TISU*: 560.
[55] *TISU*: 550.
[56] *TISU*: 631.

a particular mark of sevteenth-century Trinitarian theology, of how to account for the persons of the Trinity as 'being of one substance.' As we have already seen in seventeenth-century theology the spectre of Socinianism, and the explicit challenge of Hobbism, revolved around changing understandings of what was meant by substance. This problem was more acute in Cudworth's conception of the Trinity because of his focus on the Trinity *ad intra*. In the traditional economic account of the Trinity it was possible to hold to this definition because man could know the substantial economic form of the different persons of the Trinity and still assert the shared essence of the three persons in the Trinity. Because Cudworth chose to talk of the Trinity in immanent terms primarily he was required to deal more explicitly with what he understood as the substantial or *homoousian* relationship of the persons of the Trinity. To do this Cudworth turns again to the writings of Descartes, in particular Descartes' definition of substance in his *Principles of Philosophy*.[57] As we saw in the last chapter, Cudworth adopts the Cartesian distinction between *res cogitens* and *res extensa* in his rejection of Hobbist materialism. Cudworth's account of the substance of the Trinity can be read as an extension of this discussion. As with his criticism of 'atomistic atheism' Cudworth rejects the materialism of Hobbes' Trinity because the extended, divisible, and unthinking form of material substance could not provide the substance of an omniscient creator God. In doing this Cudworth asserts the primacy of indivisible thinking substance over material substance as the true substance of God. Cudworth's language is, though, softer that the Cartesian distinction of 'thinking' and 'extended' substance, choosing instead to describe God using the more Plotinian language of 'intelligible' or 'sensible' substance. Because the 'intelligent' form of the divine is not 'extended' it is, by implication, indivisible. It is this quality in particular which Cudworth focuses on to allow him to define God as a single unified undivided substance who still expresses himself in the form of three distinct persons.

Although based on the contemporary distinctions of Cartesianism, Cudworth argues that the dualism he employs is the same as the dualism of Platonism. Cudworth makes this claim for several reasons. Firstly, as we have seen before, Cudworth constantly refuses to accept the existence of philosophical innovation, therefore the dualism of Descartes can never be 'new' only a resurrection of an ancient system or principle. Secondly Cudworth's historical claim allows him to argue that this definition of

---

[57] Descartes, *Works* : I.241.

homoousious cohered with that used by the Nicene Fathers. Cudworth argues that the Nicene Fathers, in particular Athanasius, drew on the same metaphysics, which Cudworth argues had been resurrected by Cartesian dualism, in their definition of the *homoousian* form of the Trinity. Cudworth argues that the Fathers used *homousious* to mean a single undivided thinking substance which allowed the individual persons or expressions 'not a *sameness* of singular and Numerical, but of Common or *universal Essence* only; that is, the *Generical* or *specifical Essence of the Godhead*; that the *son* was not a *Creature* but truly and properly *God*.'[58] This reasoned form of this account of the Trinity is, for Cudworth, not only more reasonable than those he encountered in the seventeenth century (in that it cohered to philosophical account of substance), but also doctrinally sound.

Despite his claims to orthodoxy, Cudworth's account of the Trinity remains problematic. In particular Cudworth's immanent account opens him to the problem which he lays at the door of the Platonic Trinity, that of subordination. Cudworth's account of the Trinity never conclusively explains the co-eternity of the *Logos* of the Trinity with the *Father*. The suggestion always remains, despite his many protestations to the contrary, that the second person is not simply as an emanation, but a created by-product of the first person. This suggestion led many of Cudworth's earliest critics to accuse him of pseudo-Arianism.[59] The potential problem of the 'subordination' of the second person to the first is a recurring problem in all his theology. This problem is evident in his early writings. Cudworth, through all his work, argues for the active nature of the divine. In his *First Sermon* this is evident when he states of Christ, '*God was therefore incarnated and made man, that he might Deifie us*, that is… make us *partakers of the Divine nature*.'[60] In his *Second Sermon* he puts more detail into this assertion. Throughout the *Second Sermon* Christ is understood by Cudworth to be acting as mediator between man and God, the principle by which God is represented to man. In this sermon we already find Cudworth arguing that this mediating role of Christ exists in the Plotinian division of the source of the Trinity, in the intellect of the *Father* and the understanding of the divine in the person of Christ as *Logos*. His explanation of this relationship between the first and second persons brings him close to suggestions of anti-Trinitarianism. Christ is,

[58] *TISU*: 608.
[59] Wiles, *Archetypal Heresy*: 68.
[60] *First Sermon*: 101.

in his language, a being that is 'hypostatically united to the Divinity,' however, the mediating nature of the kingdom of Christ made it historically subsequent to the *Father*. Cudworth, by stressing the mediating power of the Christ, could be seen to be suggesting that Christ was created by the Father, thus opening Cudworth up to accusations of anti-Trinitarianism.[61]

In *TISU*, Cudworth's argument for the relationship of the first and second persons of the Trinity remains the same as his assertion in the *Second Sermon*. However, the form the argument takes changes. This change comes about, I would argue, to counter possible accusations that the 'Christocentric' argument of the *Second Sermon* is anti-Trinitarian. In the light of Cudworth's *Second Sermon* G.R.Cragg's assertion that, 'to Cudworth the Incarnation signifies not so much the word made flesh in an historical sense as the eternal incarnation of the Logos,'[62] would appear to be only partly correct. Certainly in *TISU* we find the Trinity discussed almost exclusively in Logocentric terms. Cudworth takes this line in the *TISU* to move himself away from the theological problems of describing the Trinity using the historical person of Christ, to a philosophical discussion over the relationship of the *Logos* to the founding principle of the *Father*. It is in this context that Cudworth's language of 'expression' becomes most useful. God, as Cudworth states, is the eternal and immutable fountain of all things. God then expresses himself to his creation in three distinct, but related forms. The dilemma presented by, and never fully explicated in, Cudworth's account of the Trinity is whether the first person is the primary form of God, or merely the first expression of a plural union. Leslie Armour has recently argued forcefully that although problematic, Cudworth's Trinitarianism can be interpreted as both orthodox, and reasonable, as long as 'the Trinity... becomes a model of a community of equals.' The failure of the Platonic Trinity, Armour argues, is that the stress on the unity of the Godhead promotes the first person and diminished the second two. However, the soteriological importance of the second two persons to the Christian tradition allows for a plurality of persons, or expressions, in the unity of God.[63]

---

[61] *Second Sermon*: 199-202.
[62] G.R. Cragg, *From Puritanism to the Age of Reason: A Study of changes in Religious thought within the Church of England, 1660-1700*. Cambridge: CUP, 1950: 56.
[63] Armour, 'Trinity, Community and Love': 113-129.

Logos, reason, and 'the candle of the Lord'

Cudworth's Trinitarianism, although in places problematic, presents a 'reasonable' account of the Trinity. The implicit reasonableness of this account means that Cudworth's advocacy of reason in his more explicitly philosophical writings can be linked to the reasonable, intellectual, structure of God as Trinity. The primacy of reason is, therefore, not simply a philosophical distinction, but also a theological one. For Cudworth, God is a being of perfect reason and so all human action which uses reason correctly has something of the divine about it. In these terms it is possible to argue that Cudworth's movement from the language of 'Christ' to the language of '*Logos*' between his *Sermons* and *TISU* has as much to do with a change in philosophical and theological emphasis as it does with problems of doctrine. As we have already seen, Cudworth, in his *First Sermon* argues that '*God was therefore incarnated and made man, that he might Deifie us*, that is…make us *partakers of the Divine nature.*'[64] In light of the detailed Trinitarian theology of *TISU* it is possible to argue that the incarnation presented the consumation of the reasonable form of creation, so that, to paraphrase, God was incarnated that he might make us reasonable, that is partakers of Divine reason. In making this claim one has to be careful not to be seen to be falling into the rationalistic heresy of Deism where God is equated to a loose understanding of rationality alone. For Cudworth, who actively opposed Deism in his manuscripts, the reason presented to man in the incarnation of the *Logos* is the expression of a God who is not only identifiable, but also actively involved in that creation. As we shall see in the ensuing chapters it is the fact of this embodied reason that leads Cudworth's own work directly from theological to ethical questions. Before we turn to those ethical questions we can see in Cudworth's treatment of exclusively theological discussions, particularly his discussions of the 'proofs' of God in *TISU*, the move Cudworth makes from his theological to his philosophical understanding of human reason.

Cudworth's discussion of the 'proof' of the existence of God comes out most clearly in his lengthy discussion of Descartes ontological proof. From what we have already seen of Cudworth's intellectualist theology it will come as no surprise to see that he was drawn to an account of God's existence which was derived from *a priori* principles alone. This proof is found most clearly in the fifth meditation of Descartes'

---

[64] *First Sermon*: 101.

Meditations on First Philosophy.[65] Here Descartes argues that one can, without recourse to other external stimuli, conceive of the existence of God. By recognising the divine by intellectual means alone Descartes argues forcefully not only that God could exist but that God necessarily does exist. He defends this claim by asserting that if God exists he must, by definition, be perfect. The intellectual conception of a perfect principle cannot, however, simply be created from nothing in the imperfect mind of man because it is impossible for the imperfect human mind to create something that is perfect, something which is superior to itself. Consequently the only source of this perfect idea must be a perfect being that has independent existence from the mind of man. As only God can be perfect it necessarily follows, Descartes argues, that God exists.[66]

Cudworth accepts the starting premise of Descartes' proof, that the existence of God can be inferred from intellectual principles alone. What Cudworth rejects in Descartes' fifth meditation are the methodological assumptions Descartes makes to justify his conclusion. It is possible, Cudworth argues, to account for not only the existence of the divine but also the form the divine takes as Trinity if Descartes' methodological limitations can be overcome. Cudworth's criticism of Descartes initially follow the criticisms of Descartes' earliest critics, Gassendi and Arnauld, by pointing to the essential circularity of the argument that Descartes employs. For Cudworth the circularity in Descartes' argument is a direct result of Descartes' use of sceptical rationality in his proof. Such a sceptical method necessarily brings human faculties into doubt. However, the knowledge of the existence of God is, in ontological terms, founded exclusively on the supposition of his faculties, faculties which in Cartesian terms, because of sceptical rationality, can only be truly reliable if the existence of God is assumed. As Cudworth puts it:

> For to say, that the *Truth* of our *Understanding Faculties*, is put out of all Doubt and Question, as soon as ever we are assured of the *Existence of a God Essentially Good*, who therefore cannot deceive; whilst this Existence of God, is in the mean time it self no otherwise proved than by our

[65] The term 'the ontological proof' was not one used by Descartes, or by Anselm of Canterbury the founder of this argument. It was coined by Kant, in his *Critique of Pure Reason*, to describe a proof of the existence of God from a priori principles alone. See John Cottingham, *A Descartes Dictionary*. Oxford: Blackwell, 1993: 137. For an excellent overview of the ontological proof see, Jonathan Barnes, *The Ontological Argument*. London: Macmillan, 1972; Graham Oppy, *Ontological Arguments and Belief in God*, Cambridge: CUP, 1996; Charles Hartshorne, *Anselm's Discovery: A Re-Examination of the Ontological Proof for God's Existence*, Lasalle, IL: Open Court, 1965.
[66] Descartes, *Works*: I.181-4.

Understanding Faculties...this I say is plainly to move round in a *Circle*; and to prove nothing at all.[67]

The weakness in Descartes' argument, Cudworth argues, is a logical one. By asserting that reason can doubt the existence of all things, Cudworth argues that Descartes can only effectively make claims with certainty if the divine is first presupposed. As a consequence, the existence of God cannot be known with any certainty because this conclusion is based on a method which itself relies on God to create that certainty. Consequently, Cudworth argues that Descartes' proof relies on the '*Firmness* and *Solidity*, of such *Thin* and *Subtle Cobwebs*.'[68]

Cudworth's solution to this dilemma is to reassert the true, divine form of reason which we have seen Cudworth develop in his Trintarianism. Descartes comes to his conclusion by using his reason to doubt all other possible explanations, leaving the existence of God to be the only possible conclusion. In his argument the necessary existence of God is not verified because of a positive conclusion, but because after a process of sceptical deduction God remains as the only possible explanation. Cudworth takes issue with this argument, because Descartes is implicitly assuming that the faculty of reason can, in principle, deny everything, even the existence of God. What is needed, Cudworth argues, is not simply an *a priori* assertion of God's existence, but a confirmation that the means by which that supposition is made automatically leads to God; that reason in its correct form has something of the divine about it. Such an argument is outlined in Descartes' ontological proof, but is impossible to verify, as the form of reason that Descartes employs is sceptical in form. Cudworth asserts that the reasoning faculty man uses to acknowledge the existence of God is not Descartes' sceptical human reason, but the *Logocentric* account of reason confirmed in the Trinity.

To modern eyes Cudworth's presupposition of the Trinity in his 'proof' of the existence of God would seem antithetical. However, it should be remembered here that 'proofs' of the existence of God were not posited as simple logical questions to suggest the viability of a particular issue: does it successfully *prove* the existence of God. Rather proofs should be read more in terms of the scholastic *viae* or paths through which reason is guided by faith to the understanding of certain divine attributes.[69]

---

[67] *TISU*: 717. Also see John Redwood, *Reason, Ridicule and Religion*: 55; M. Baldi, 'Cudworth versus Descartes': 174.

[68] *TISU*: 725.

[69] Muller, *Post-Reformation Reformed Dogmatics*: III:26-48.

Cudworth's attack on Descartes ontological proof is, therefore, an attack on a use of human reason which has become perverted away from its essential form; that is the understanding and recognition of God. Cudworth found philosophical confirmation of his idea of the divine source of human reason in the Platonic tradition, in particular drawing on Plato's argument for the pre-existence of knowledge in the *Meno*. In this dialogue Socrates argues that by showing that a mathematical principle can be drawn out of the mind of an uneducated slave-boy, one can establish the existence of pre-existing intellectual principles in the mind.[70] This premise relies on one key philosophical principle, that of the non-inferiority of causes which we have already encountered Cudworth using against Thomas Hobbes, that something cannot be caused by something that is inferior in nature to it. Using this argument Cudworth argues that the ability of man to know God through reason proves the sources of those ideas in the divine:

> The Humane Mind therefore hath a *Power* of framing *Ideas* and *Conceptions*, not only of what Actually Is, but also of things which never were, nor perhaps will be, they being only *Possible* to be. But when from our *Conceptions*, we conclude of something, that though they are Not, yet they are Possible to be; since nothing that Is not, can be *Possible* to be, unless there be something Actually in Being, which hath sufficient Power to produce it; we do Implicitly suppose, the *Existence* of a *God* or *Omnipotent Being* thereby, which can make whatsoever is *Conceivable*, though it yet be not, to Exist.[71]

The human faculty of reason, therefore, is drawn directly from the superior intellectual principles that place these same principles in the mind of man in the first instance. The only logical source of these principles is the intellect of the divine. It is because of the divine source of man's reason that Cudworth argues it is possible for man to appreciate the intellectual '*Paradigm* or *Platform*, according to which this *Sensible World* was made.'[72] The ability of man to know of God's existence by man's reason is confirmed, Cudworth claims, by the recognition that the reasoned means of understanding must have their source in the intellect of the divine. He argues that man, by recognising that reason has its source in the divine, can first verify the existence of God, something which he accepts Descartes' method unable to do. This philosophical supposition

[70] Plato, *Meno*, translated by W.K.C. Guthrie in *The Collected Dialogues of Plato*, ed. Edith Hamilton and Huntington Cairns. Princeton, NJ: Princeton University Press, 1961: 81b-86b.
[71] *TISU*: 732.
[72] *TISU*: 734.

is then given historical and theological teeth by the recognition of Jesus Christ, the *Logos*, as the perfect expression and embodiment of the reasonableness of God.

Cudworth's engagement with Descartes sceptical rationality in his discussion of the ontological proof points us both to the fundamentally Trinitarian form of Cudworth's theological and philosophical position, and also to the implicitly active, and so ethical, form of Cudworth's conception of reasoned action. As stated in Chapter One of this book, Cudworth's theological heritage is drawn directly from the Reformed tradition in English theology. However, his own theology developed against Calvinism, whilst remaining true to the central terms of the Reformation. The fundamental 'Reformed' belief that runs through all of Cudworth's theology, is that it is God's grace, rather than the sacraments or the structure of the Church, which inform God's fundamental relationship and engagement with creation. Cudworth's rejection of Calvinism is, therefore, not a rejection of grace, but that that grace can not be manifested through the explicit and possibly arbitrary will of the God of Calvinist theology. The question of the true manifestation of God's grace defines all the debates that the Cambridge Platonists engaged in with 'orthodox' members of the Reformed tradition. Benjamin Whichcote, in his correspondence with Anthony Tuckney, picks up on this very point when he argues that through reason 'Christ is able to be acknowledged, as the principle of grace *in* us.' In Whichcote's theology reason becomes the principle in all men that brings man towards God. As Whichcote concludes his correspondence with Tuckney:

> Now that Christ is more known and freelie professed, let him also be inwardlie felt, and secretlie understood; as a principle of divine life within us, as well as a saviour without us.[73]

Whichcote argues that, through reason, all can develop their Christ-like potential. Reason, therefore, exists for Whichcote as evidence of the God's grace in the world. This is most eloquently put forward in Whichcote's oft-quoted dictum, that 'the spirit of man is the candle of the Lord'. Whichcote argues that 'the candle of the Lord', human reason, is not a shallow or empty principle, but a sign of God's grace placed in man.[74]

Cudworth's Trinitarianism can be read as a fuller theological development of Whichcote's link of reason and reasonableness to grace. Both Cudworth and Whichcote argue that reason is given to man by God as a

---

[73] *Letters*: 126.
[74] *Letters*: 112.

means by which we can come to know God more clearly. As Whichcote states in his sermon on *The Use of Reason in Matters of Religion*, '[i]f Reason did not apprehend God; Religion could not be learn'd.'[75] In this manner they both accept the central 'Reformed' belief of *sola gratia*. Where they fundamentally diverge from the orthodoxy of Reformed theology is in equating human reason directly with the grace of God.

As we have seen above, Cudworth argues, with reference to his definition of God's grace, that the biblical truth that '*God is Love*, seems to warrant this much to us, that *Love* in some rightly Qualified sense, is *God*.'[76] Consequently, with Cudworth's Trinitarianism in mind, it is possible to argue that, to paraphrase again: 'God is reasonable and so in some rightly qualified sense, reasonableness is Godlike'. The key qualification here is 'in some rightly qualified sense'. Human reason is not, Cudworth argues, an end in itself, the well meaning errors of Descartes' ontological proof are evidence enough of this. Rather reason is the gift of God's grace which has to be used and understood with care. Whichcote's metaphor of the Candle of the Lord is instructive here. The divine light in all men is not a shining beacon, but a dim, flickering, and fragile candle light. If its light is sometimes dimmed, or only perceived 'through a glass darkly,' it still remains as a reflection of the light of Christ and consequently the means by which man can reconcile himself to the divine. In Cudworth's thought the link of grace to reason provides the means by which man can move towards God. God in his gift of reason to all men provides not only with the means of coming to know God, but also the freedom to choose whether to accept or decline this loving gift of grace. Cudworth's account of human reason again stresses to us his Reformed nature, but also reminds us of his Arminianism, arguing that man has the choice whether or not to accept the freely given grace of God. In this way Cudworth's account of human reason implicitly draws his theology into practical questions of ethics and politics because the question is not the theological one of who has received the grace of God and how, but the ethical one of what man is going to do with the grace of God now he has it?

---

[75] Benjamin Whichcote, 'The Use of Reason in Matters of Religion,' in *The Cambridge Platonists*, edited by C.A. Patrides. London: Edward Arnold, 1967: 47. Also see *Letters*, p. 44. Robert Greene has argued that the use of the metaphor of 'light' is not unique to Whichcote in the seventeenth century. However where Whichcote always equates light, the Candle of the Lord, with the intellectual principle of the divine reason, Calvinist uses of the metaphor generally equates it with the revealed word of God. See Robert A. Greene, 'Whichcote, the Candle of the Lord, and Synderesis,' in *The Journal of the History of Ideas*, 52 (1991): 617-44: 621.

[76] *TISU*: 123.

Chapter Four

PROVIDENCE AND FREEWILL

The first volume of Cudworth's *Intellectual System* offers not only a rejection of arbitrary authority, but also a comprehensive theological and philosophical system to replace it. As has already been argued, even with a contextual reading of Cudworth's *TISU* it is, arguably, too easy to read it as a stand alone volume rather than as part of the wider *Intellectual System* it was intended to begin. However, we know that Cudworth planned the remaining two volumes of this project, and in his unpublished manuscripts and posthumously published works we have the sketches which allow us to reconstruct what the arguments of the missing volumes of the *TISU* might have looked like. Before we look at the specifics of Cudworth's ethical and political ideas it is necessary to explore how Cudworth moves from the theological insights of *TISU* to the practical philosophy of his posthumously published writings, primarily his *EIM*, which will be discussed at greater length in the next chapter. The central problem facing Cudworth is how to reconcile his comprehensive theological account of God with his philosophical desire to explain the freewill of man. This is, of course, not a new problem. In fact William Hasker, in his book *God, Time, and Knowledge*, has argued that 'whenever theistic belief encounters or engenders a tradition of philosophical reflection, questions will arise about the relation between divine knowledge and power and human freedom.'[1] In the Christian tradition the two principles of divine omniscience and human freedom would seem to constantly be puling against one another. For instance in the Book of Psalms we have the direct affirmation of the omniscience of God: 'Even before a word is on my tongue, lo, O Lord, though knowest it altogether.'[2] However, elsewhere in scripture there are countless examples of seemingly freely willed actions which provoke a reaction from God.

In the Christian tradition the general approach to this dilemma has been to combine God's providential knowledge and freewill. From the writings of Augustine through to the Reformed orthodoxy of the seventeenth

---

[1] Hasker, William, *God, Time, and Knowledge*. Ithaca, NY: Cornell University Press, 1989: 1.

[2] Ps. 139:4.

century this 'compatibilism', in various guises, marked the orthodox theology of Christianity. This chapter will, through a brief discussion of the compatibilism of William Perkins, the leading Puritan theologian of the generation preceding Cudworth, outline the theological context in debates on providence and freewill in which Cudworth was working. In particular this will be used to show the subtlety of Cudworth's own Neoplatonic account of the 'harmony' of providence, marked not only by his well known theory of the 'Plastic Nature of Reality', but also his theory of 'Moveable Providence' which is sketched in his manuscripts. Cudworth's unpublished manuscripts on freewill, which are now held in the manuscript collection of the British Library, were probably works in progress, never intended for the eyes of more than a handful of Cudworth's closest intellectual allies. They were probably written after *TISU*, sometime during the 1670s and even 1680s.[3] The manuscripts can, in part, be read as initial sketches for the second and third parts of his projected *Intellectual System*. They are, however, also affected by contemporary debates, in particular the well known debate between Bishop Bramhall and Thomas Hobbes. Cudworth's manuscripts, although acknowledging Hobbes and Bramhall, were not written in answer to that debate. Rather they should be viewed as Cudworth's contribution to the wider seventeenth-century debate on freewill and necessity of which the Hobbes/Bramhall debate were also a part.[4] Consequently in these disorganised and often rambling manuscripts we can begin to put flesh on the bones of the moral and political principles which Cudworth only begins to hint at in *TISU*.

In these manuscripts Cudworth constantly circles around the problem of providence and freewill. In particular Cudworth tries to provide an account of God's foreknowledge and human freewill in such a manner as not to diminish freewill. Although problems remain in Cudworth's account of providence, caused primarily by the lack of a systematic discussion of his theory, it does provide the theological basis for his broader philosophical account of his practical philosophy. What is interesting is that this discussion does not simply provide a coherent understanding of how human freewill could exist in a universe controlled by the providential mind of God, but also the terms and constraints that play on the individual moral actor. Again, like Cudworth's Trinitarianism, a slippage occurs between the theological discussion of divine knowledge and the

---

[3] See Appendix on the dating and ordering of Cudworth's freewill manuscripts.

[4] On Cudworth on Hobbes and Bramhall see: *FM*.4979: 148, 148b, 152; *FM*.4980: 160, 199, 274, 276. On the Hobbes/Bramhall debate see *Hobbes and Bramhall on Liberty and Necessity*, ed. Vere Chappell. Cambridge: CUP, 1999.

practical implications of this in the realm of ethical action. Cudworth's intention is, therefore, not simply to account coherently for the providential actions of his Trinitarian God, but also to assert how the individual exists '*throughout the whole World*' of God's creation.

Providence and freewill in seventeenth-century theology

In the Reformed orthodoxy of Calvin's theology the solution to the problem of providence and freewill was to begin with the omniscience of God, and then understand the form and nature of human action in this providential plan. Central to Calvin's account is a continual stress on the limitations of human knowledge in the face of divine knowledge. As we have seen previously, Calvin does allow for a limited level of natural theological knowledge. However, this only allows man to recognise the 'epistemic gap' that exists between the quality of divine omniscience and human knowledge.[5] To give some definition to the principle of omniscience Reformed theologians took on the Scholastic distinction between *scientia simplicus intelligentiae seu necessaria* and *scientia voluntaria seu libera* or God's 'natural' knowledge and God's 'free' knowledge. The first term defines the omniscience of God, the knowledge of all things that God *naturally* has because he is omniscient. In this form of knowledge all things, except divine essence, are possibilities, not actualities. This is contrasted with God's 'free' knowledge which rests on the absolutely free actions of God's will. God's free knowledge then explains how God's omniscience becomes defined into the providential action of his omnipresence where the possibilities known by his natural knowledge are actualised by the free action of his will. This knowledge is definite not because God's knowledge is restricted to certain necessary events, but because it refers to actualities of God's will.[6]

Although this distinction was not taken on unreservedly by theologians of Reformed orthodoxy, it did define the debate. This can be shown by a brief examination of the compatibilism of William Perkins, the leading English theologian of the generation prior to Cudworth. In his posthumously published sermon *A Treatise of God's Free Grace and Man's Freewill* Perkins, like Calvin, allies himself with Augustine; playing the role of orthodox compatibilist in the face of the perceived heretical Pelagian

---

[5] *Institutes*: 1.i-v; Helm, *John Calvin's Ideas*: 182; Muller, *Post-Reformation Reformed Dogmatics*, III:392.

[6] Muller, *Post-Reformation Reformed Dogmatics*, III:411-412.

libertarianism of Roman Catholicism.[7] For Perkins all things are defined
and created by the will of God. God's will is not dependent on anything
except its own nature, and is completely free in all things that it does:

> in God's will there is a *Soveraigntie*, that is, an absolute power, whereby he
> is Lord of all the actions that he willeth, willing himselfe without dependence
> from any, without impediment or controlement, what he will, when he will,
> and however he will.[8]

In this account of the will of God Perkins rests clearly on the distinction
between God's natural and free knowledge. As we have seen, Perkins
argues that God's will is supreme, however, that does not mean that God
is tied to a predetermined chain of future events. Rather that God knows
naturally all things that are, and could be, and that once he has willed
something to happen it necessarily will. As he states in his sermon:

> there is in God, a knowledge of thinges that possibly may bee, though they
> never be: and this knowledge goes before God's decree. Yet the divine
> knowledge of things that certainly shall be, followes the will and determina-
> tion of God.[9]

This stress on the sovereignty of God's will imbues all of Perkins'
account of God's relationship to the created world. For Perkins nothing
can come into existence without being expressly willed by God. Most
importantly, all human actions are controlled, defined, and predetermined
by the will of God. However, this is not to say that the plan of history has
been mapped out by God allowing him to retreat from creation. Rather
that the omnipresence of an omnipotent God means that all actions are
acts of his will, and consequently foreseen by God; as Perkins states:

> God's foreknowledge depends on his will. Not because God foresees things
> to come, therefore they come to passe: but because according to God's will,
> they are to come to passe, therefore he foresees them.[10]

All parts of creation, including men, owe their allegiance and existence
to God and no act is explicable except with reference to the preordained
will of God.

Perkins breaks his understanding of the working of the human will into
five categories: the action of the mind; deliberation of the different

---

[7] William Perkins, *The Works of that famous and worthie Minister of Christ... M.W. Perkins: gathered into one volume and newly corrected according to his owne copies.*
London: 1605: 867, 883.
  [8] Perkins, *Works*: 873.
  [9] Perkins, *Works*: 873.
  [10] Perkins, *Works*: 873.

means; determination of what shall be done; election of the will to accept or refuse this determination; and finally the action of the will. In this typography the mind of man acts with complete freedom in the definition of the first three of these characteristics. However, these are all redundant without the power of election, and the will refuse or reject the prior actions of deliberation and determination. The actions of man are, therefore, defined not by the mechanisms of the will alone, but by the 'liberty' of the will to act. To stress the distinctness of human liberty Perkins deploys a dichotomy between what he terms the 'liberty of will' and the 'liberty of grace' to stress the perpetual reliance of human action on the will and grace of God.[11]

Liberty of will is, for Perkins, the basic mechanism of human action, what Perkins defines as 'freedom from all compulsion and constraint.'[12] All human actions are, therefore, defined in their most basic form through this mechanism of free action. As Perkins' typography of the human will outlined above shows, all human action is defined by the process of free choice, what he describes as the liberty to 'will, nil, or suspend.'[13] However, this liberty of will is of no use without the power of man to put these willed intentions into practice. For this reason Perkins argues that although the will is free from all compulsion and constraint, it is not free from necessity. As the will of God defines all actions in creation the necessary power that man has to fulfil, or not, the intentions of the liberty of will, depend entirely on the predetermined will of God that this will should, or should not occur. To illustrate this definition of the compatibilism of liberty and necessity Perkins uses the example of a patient who may wish to be better, but is completely reliant on the actions and will of the doctor for this recovery to take place:

> We are to God as the sicke man to his keeper, who saith, Take me up, and I will rise: hold me, and I will stand. In regard of this our frailtie, it is the best for us to deny ourselves, and by faith to depend on the providence and mercy of God.[14]

Perkins argument here stresses that man cannot bring about his own salvation, only the predetermined will of God can decide if man is saved or not. This theory of double predestination (of both the elect and reprobate) is characteristic of the Calvinism that Perkins helped define and popularise.

[11] Perkins, *Works*: 877-8.
[12] Perkins, *Works*: 872.
[13] Perkins, *Works*: 879.
[14] Perkins, *Works*: 879.

In the seventeenth century this traditional account of God's knowledge was countered by the writings of the Spanish theologian Luis de Molina. Molina's theory of divine knowledge, commonly known as Molinism, asserted the existence of a third, or middle form of divine knowledge between the indeterminate form of God's natural knowledge, and the determinate form of his free knowledge. Molina argued that in this middle knowledge God does not know the determinate acts, but only contingent acts that could occur given the free actions of man. As God knows all the possible choices that man could make he knows what all these contingent acts are, but not whether they are determinate. This determination depends on the free choice of man. The Molinist account of divine knowledge found its way into the Reformed tradition providing the philosophical basis for the Arminian account of predestination. In particular it provided an account of divine omniscience in which human freedom was also explicable in something other than the limited terms of Calvinist compatibilism.[15] The great limitation of Molinism, and arguably also with Arminianism, is that the principle of middle knowledge makes God's free knowledge of determinate actions dependent on the actions of man. The omniscience of God is, therefore, limited. This limitation of God's omniscience is apparent in certain Socinian accounts of divine providence which adopted the Molinist position to allow for the 'uncertain' nature of all future knowledge. Richard Muller has gone so far as to argue that 'the Socinians press the Molinist formula toward a logically stable form by degrading divine omniscience.'[16] Certainly the Molinist account of providence met with opposition in both Catholic and Reformed theology in the seventeenth century. In particular these debates show that any comprehensive account of divine action which also sought to account for an equitable system of freewill, such as Cudworth's, would have to deal with the vast and complex theological debate engendered by the Molinist, and latterly Arminian, accounts of providence and freewill.

The harmony of providence

As we have seen in the previous chapters, it is possible to cast Cudworth's theology as broadly Reformed in temperament, and Arminian in content. Although there is not direct evidence of Cudworth engaging with

---

[15] Muller, *Post-Reformation Reformed Dogmatics*: III:417-8; Eef Dekker, 'Was Arminius a Molinist?' in *The Sixteenth Dentury Journal*, 27 (1996): 337-352.
[16] Muller, *Post-Reformation Reformed Dogmatics*: III: 419.

the work of Molina, it is unthinkable that a thinker of Cudworth's erudition, and particularly his known engagement with Arminian theology, would not been aware of the controversy engendered by Molinism. In particular, as Cudworth's account of providence is developed below it is important to retain the central dilemma of a theological defence of freewill: how do we allow for a realistic account of human freewill without diminishing our understanding of divine omniscience? Cudworth's own account of providence is developed in a three-fold manner. The primary principle of providence, Cudworth argues, is that of the harmony of creation, where all parts benefit and complement all other parts. Under this comprehensive account of the harmony of creation Cudworth asserts two secondary principles. The first are the providential laws 'woven into the constitution of all things'. These are the laws which provide for the order of creation and the basic needs of man. This part of Cudworth's account of providence is defined by his 'Plastic Nature of Reality.' Alongside the providential form of Plastic Nature Cudworth stresses a second level of providential action that Cudworth terms 'Moveable Providence', which fills the 'gaps and chinks in creation'. One limitation which always exists in discussing Cudworth's theory of providence is that 'Moveable Providence' is only developed in any meaningful form in his manuscripts. Cudworth's theory of Moveable Providence, because of this, is not presented in the complete or systematic form that one would expect had the theory been published. However, his manuscripts allow us to see the manner in which he sought to counter the problem of the reconciliation between divine omniscience and human freedom.[17] Most interestingly Cudworth clearly thought that Moveable Providence was an essential component of his account of the freedom of the individual actor. However, before the detail of Cudworth's principles of Plastic Nature and Moveable Providence are explained, it is important to begin with Cudworth's overarching account of the providential harmony of God's intellect.

At the heart of Cudworth's account of providence is a removal of what he perceives to be the stifling and limiting nature of 'divine determinism'. Cudworth's starting point is, therefore, his continued rejection of all forms of voluntarism, exemplified by the theology of Calvinists such as Perkins. Cudworth's discussion of providence continually seeks to reject any suggestion that the actions of man are predetermined. In particular, as we shall come on to see, Cudworth, when discussing the providential actions of God, rejects the voluntarist language of 'will' and 'power'.

---

[17] *FM* 4981: 24-26.

To achieve this Cudworth turns to Plotinus and the Neoplatonic principle of the 'scale of being'. The idea of a scale of being was present in Cudworth's writings as early as the 1630s, as evidenced by his references to 'Jacob's ladder' in letters to his step-father at that time. Central to Cudworth's use of the scale of being was his assertion, following Plotinus, that although creation is unified by the intellect of God, it is not the direct presence, but the reflected, emanated power of God's reason which gives unity and harmony to all creation.[18] This model reflects the Trinitarianism which, as we saw in the previous chapter, Cudworth reads into Plotinus' distinction of the unreflected 'intellect' and reflective 'understanding' of the divine. With relation to the created world Plotinus describes the reflective, understanding power of the divine in terms of the divine artist. On one occasion Plotinus uses this metaphor to describe the world as a stage with humans acting the drama written by the heavenly poet. In another metaphor Plotinus describes God as the musician who:

> brings the conflicting elements into a kind of harmonious concordance, by composing the complete story of the persons in conflict; but in the universe the battle of conflicting elements springs from a single rational principle; so that it would be better for one to compare it to the melody which results from conflicting sounds, and one will then enquire why there are the conflicting sounds in the rational proportions [of musical scales]. If, then, the laws of rational proportions make high and low notes and come together into a unity — being the proportional laws of melody they come together into the melody itself, which is another greater law of proportion.[19]

Cudworth draws heavily on both Plotinus' theory and language of providence when he describes the omniscience of God. Divine art, as Cudworth sees it again mirroring his account of the intelligent substance of God in his Trinitarianism, is the 'unbodied reason of the divine.' In that way it touches the world becoming '*Fuddled* in it.'[20] In this way Cudworth's Neoplatonic understanding of the engagement of the divine artist with creation is based on his Trinitarian definition of the divine artist in the first instance. As we shall see, the Trinity presents Cudworth with a structure through which he is able to argue that, in contrast to the direct providential action of Calvin's God, reality is touched by the divine art of God, but not controlled directly or materially by it. All actions in creation, from the most mundane to the most profound, can be related to

---

[18] *FM*.4980: 151; *TISU*: 464.
[19] *Enneads*: 3.2.16. The metaphor of the 'divine artist' originates in Plato's *Laws*, see: Plato, *Laws*, trans. A.E. Taylor, in *The Collected Dialogues of Plato*, ed. Edith Hamilton and Huntington Cairns. Princeton, NJ: Princeton University Press, 1961: 892.b
[20] *TISU*: 155(2).

the reasoned and loving creation of God. However, for Cudworth each individual action does not need to be caused intimately by God or the expressions of God as Trinity. Plotinus understood the role of the omniscient God to his creation as that of the 'generalship of providence'; judging and guiding all actions in the world, but not determining them absolutely.[21]

In general terms, Cudworth understands providence in Plotinian terms not as a chain of necessarily causal relationships, but as the constant process through which all parts of creation naturally seek after the divine: 'Everything in me seeks after the Good, but each attains it in proportion to its own power.[22] Following this Plotinian approach, Cudworth argues that creation is best understood, not as a unified whole or necessarily determined causal necessity, but as a scale of being with the divine at its head and mundane matter at the base. As Cudworth argues in *FM*.4980:

> Creation is a scale or ladder in wch are all degrees of being possible one below another, ye lowest of all wch is matter & Body So y^t there is a negative defect in all things but God but no positive defect pravity or vitiosity in any thing as it comes out of Gods hands in any nature y^t is no absurdity or Contradiction.[23]

Cudworth argues that there is strength presented by the Neoplatonic account of divine harmony that allows it to move beyond what he perceives to be the weaknesses of divine determinism. Like divine determinism, the scale of being describes creation formed and inspired by the power of God. However, the scale of being broadens, some might say loosens, the account of God's providential action enough to allow space for human action. The Neoplatonic scale of being, which lies at the heart of Cudworth theory of the harmony of providence, overcomes what he argues are the two inherent problems with divine determinism. Firstly, it frees God from being present in all the mundane actions of the created world. Secondly, it liberates man from being solely defined either by the explicit will of God, or the material forces of creation. In Cudworth's account of the harmony of providence this first strength, explaining the relationship of God to the minutiae of creation, is explained by his 'Plastic Nature of Reality' and the second by his theory of 'Moveable Providence.'

---

[21] *Enneads*: 3.3.2.

[22] *Enneads*: 3.2.3.

[23] *FM*.4980:151; *FM*.4970: 5, 14, 88. See also Sarah Hutton, 'Cudworth, Boethius and the Scale of Nature,' in *The Cambridge Platonists in Philosophical Context: Politics, Metaphysics & Religion,* ed. G.A.J. Rogers, et al. Dordrecht: Kluwer: 1997.

'The Plastic Nature of Reality'

At the base of this scale of being are the regulatory principles of the world. This is the realm controlled by Cudworth's 'Plastic Nature.' In the 'Digression on the Plastic Nature of Reality' — which forms the final section of Chapter Three of *TISU* — Cudworth puts forward the theory of Plastic Nature to explain the divine origins of the recurring forms and structures of the natural world. In the face of the dangers of Hobbist materialism it is important for Cudworth to be able to explain the divine hand in mundane actions like the grass growing, the sun shining, or apples falling to the ground. However, it is also important for Cudworth not to make God intimately involved in every aspect of these mundane actions. For this reason Plastic Nature should be viewed, as Sarah Hutton has stated, as the 'ignorant instrument of a knowing and wise providence, a regulatory principle governing the operation of the natural world.'[24] Cudworth uses Plastic Nature to show how all parts of creation relate to, and participate in the creative power of the divine. Secondly, Cudworth uses Plastic Nature to explain the existence of mundane and recurring events in the world.[25] These plastic principles provide, for Cudworth, the foundations of the created realm. By utilising the difference between the intellectual power of God and the immediate presence of the divine Cudworth argues that it is possible to explain the recurring events in the created world whilst at the same time allowing a level of creation which is not controlled and defined immediately by the hand of God. Thirdly, and most importantly, Plastic Nature clarifies the parameters of Cudworth's broader argument for human freewill in the providential form of God's creation.

One of the dangers of Cudworth's theory of Plastic Nature is that it could be interpreted as making God absent from his creation. The strength of divine determinism, as we have seen, is that it never diminishes the omniscience of God, continually stressing the constant and immediate control of God over all things. Particularly, in the causal universe which Cudworth describes in his 'Digression', one could argue that God becomes an architect or motor who, after the initial act of creation, retreats to watch the machine work its course. This possible reading of Plastic Nature, which is close to the position of later Deists who Cudworth

---

[24] Sarah Hutton, 'Aristotle and the Cambridge Platonists: the Case of Cudworth,' in *Philosophy in the Sixteenth and Seventeenth Centuries: Conversations with Aristotle*, edited C.T. Blackwell and S. Kusukawa. London: Ashgate, 2000:342-3.
[25] *TISU*: 147, 151-3.

opposed, is very far from the intention of Cudworth's argument. To counter the possibility that God is removed from his creation he describes God in the active, participatory terms of the divine artist or craftsman.[26] By doing this Cudworth is not only contrasting his ideas with what he perceives to be the limits of divine determinism, but is also distancing himself from mechanical atheists who claimed the world was created by the fortuitous and random motion of matter. As Cudworth pithily states:

> the *Material* and *Mechanical* are altogether *Unphilosophical,* the same *Aristotle* ingeniously exposes the Ridiculousness of this Pretence after this manner; telling us, That it is just as if a Carpenter, Joyner or Carver should give this accompt, as the only Satisfactory, of any Artificial Fabrick or Piece of Carved Imagery...*that because the Instruments, Axes and Hatchets, Plains and Chissels, happened to fall so and so upon the Timber, cutting here and there, that therefore it was hollow in one place, and plain in another, and the like, and by that means the whole came to be of such a Form.* For is it not altogether as Absurd and Ridiculous, for men to undertake to give an accompt of the Formation and Organization of the Bodies of Animals by mere Fortuitous Mechanism.[27]

Cudworth states that God is the author of creation, but not the immediate cause of determined principles. Rather God is the source of the reason that infuses all creation evidenced by the observable order and coherence of all creation. Cudworth, therefore, argues that Plastic Nature, correctly understood, shows how God defines and determines the natural form of creation but is not intimately involved with every mundane facet of that creation. He argues that the failure of divine determinists is not that they reject the existence of God as the determining principle in the world, as material atheists do. Rather it is that they believe this active regulative power to be the highest power in the world, where in reality, Cudworth argues, it is the lowest and basest.[28] Plastic Nature provides, what Leslie Armour has described as, the 'law-like background for our actions.' Divine determinists — the bondsman of God from Cudworth's *Second Sermon* — mistake these regulatory laws for the direct intervention of God. In reality, Cudworth argues, the reasoned form of them shows to us

---

[26] Pierre Bayle and Jean Le Clerc engaged in an extended debate on the place of divine action in Cudworth's 'Digression.' In particular the voluntarist Bayle criticised Cudworth removal of God's direct will and power from creation. See Luisa Simmonutti, 'Bayle and Le Clerc as readers of Cudworth: aspects of the debate on Plastic Nature in the Dutch learned journals' in *Geschiedenis van de Wijsbegeerte in Nederland* 4 (1993): 147-165.

[27] *TISU*: 148-9.

[28] *TISU*: 172-3.

the source of these laws in the intellect of God, but they are not caused immediately and constantly by God.[29]

J.E. Saveson has argued that the plastic principle in Cudworth's philosophy is synonymous with the third hypostasis of the Neoplatonic Trinity. Saveson states that the plastic principle 'is taken persistently from the third hypostasis of the Neo-Platonists; it is the vital and organizing force in Nature.'[30] This assertion would seem to be only partially correct. Cudworth is clear that the plastic principle is not itself divine, stating at one point that:

> though it be a thing that acts for *Ends Artificially*, and which may be also called the *Divine Art*, and the *Fate* of the *Corporeal World*; yet for all that it is neither *God*, nor *Goddess*, but a Low and Imperfect Creature.[31]

Cudworth argues that the error within divine determinism is not the failure to recognise the plastic principle in nature, but to mistake Plastic Nature for the immediate presence of the divine. To do such a thing would be to confuse the individual workman with the intellect behind the entire building project, or the instrument as the source of the harmonies which are in fact brought about by the skill of the musician.[32] Plastic Nature must remain a lower principle, always reliant for its existence on the higher principles of the divine:

> For the *Plastic Life of Nature* is but the mere *Umbrage* of *Intellectuality*, a faint and shadowy *Imitation* of *Mind* and *Understanding*; upon which it doth Essentially depend, as the Shadow upon the Body, the image in the Glass upon the Face, or the Eccho upon the Original Voice. So that if there had been no *Perfect Mind* or *Intellect* in the World, there could no more have been any *Plastick Nature* in it, that could be an *Image in the Glass* without a face, or an *Eccho* without the *Original Voice*.[33]

As the mindless vassal of the divine intellect, Plastic Nature in reality contains no self-consciousness of itself.[34] Contrary to Saveson's claim, Cudworth goes to great lengths to show that Plastic Nature is not synonymous with God. However, Saveson's account of the Trinitarian origins of Plastic Nature does point to the underlying theological explanation for Plastic Nature in Cudworth's philosophy. Plastic Nature presents, for

---

[29] Armour, 'Trinity, Community, and Love': 119.
[30] J.E. Saveson, 'Differing Reactions to Descartes among the Cambridge Platonists,' in *The Journal of the History of Ideas*, 21 (1960): 560-67: 561.
[31] *TISU*: 162.
[32] *TISU*: 155.
[33] *TISU*: 172.
[34] *TISU*: 173.

Cudworth, the clearest evidential proof for the work of the third person of the Trinity, not in the immediacy of plastic principles, but in the evidence of God's reason apparent in all parts of creation. The second and third persons of the Trinity express the reasoned form of God's intellect in the historical fact of the Incarnation and the continual unfolding of this divine principle in history. Although Plastic Nature is only a distant echo of the expression of God's intellect in creation, it presents evidence that God's providential plan finds its way into every nook and cranny of creation.

Along with explaining the relationship of God to the mundane ordering of creation, Cudworth's Plastic Nature plays a second vital role in his theory of providence; defining how and why human action is not determined solely by Plastic Nature. Cudworth does this through one of the earliest developments of the philosophical term consciousness.[35] Cudworth argues that Plastic Nature, because it is mundane, has no consciousness of itself. Man, Cudworth argues, is able to distinguish himself from the mundane, regulatory plastic principles of creation precisely because he is conscious of the existence of these principles. Consequently because man is conscious of the plastic element in reality he cannot, by implication, be solely driven and determined by this slavish Plastic Nature. It is from this assertion that Cudworth begins to develop his account of human agency. Plastic powers, by definition, have no consciousness of themselves, therefore man's ability to consciously recognise the plastic principles in the world acts as an implicit confirmation of the conscious power of man. By this confirmation man is placed above the slavish realm of the mundane and consequently above the teleological, determined world of Plastic Nature. Interestingly, in this context, Cudworth does not contrast the 'conscious' powers of man with the 'unconscious' form of Plastic Nature, but with 'Lower Inconscious Power lodged in them.'[36] Cudworth makes this specific distinction to stress that the vital nature of Plastic Nature which, although not known to the thing being controlled by them, is implanted in the thing from without by the reasoned mind of God, rather than simply acting as a mechanism formed by, but not controlled by God's intellect. Cudworth, therefore, uses his theory of Plastic Nature as a means to an end. It allows him to account for the regulatory principles

---

[35] Benjamin Carter, 'Ralph Cudworth and the Theological Origins of Consciousness' in *The History of Human Sciences*, (forthcoming); Udo Thiel, 'Cudworth and Seventeenth-Century Theories of Consciousness' in *The Uses of Antiquity: The Scientific Revolution and the Classical Tradition*, edited by Stephen Gaukroger. Dordrecht: Kluwer, 1991.
[36] *TISU*: 167

in the world, but it leaves enough latitude for him to argue that above this mundane level exists the powers of human agency which are an essential part of Cudworth's moral theory. Human agency is, therefore, defined by Cudworth as man's recognition of his own consciousness. However, before Cudworth's account of human agency is developed in detail it is necessary to complete Cudworth's theory of providence, with his principle of 'Moveable Providence' which, Cudworth argues, provides an account of God's omniscience which can allow human freedom to exist.

'Moveable Providence'

Cudworth's theory of Moveable Providence is only found in any great detail in Cudworth's manuscripts. Cudworth's discussion of Moveable Providence begins with a criticism of the logical problems of necessity and causation which he argues have clouded and confused previous discussions of the relationship between causality and necessity. For Cudworth the central problem of deterministic systems is that they rely on too strict a reading of the logical principle *post hoc ergo propter hoc* (after therefore because of): that because an action can be understood to have been necessarily caused by a previous act, that that necessary cause was predetermined to be that cause. Cudworth argues that the proofs used by this form of determinism rely entirely on the infallible power of retrospective judgment which have been interpreted too strictly and narrowly by deterministic systems like Calvinism. If the use of hindsight is removed all that can be known is that that every action must necessarily be caused by a sufficient act. However, what cannot be said is that the retrospectively recognised cause was *necessarily* the predetermined cause. As Cudworth puts it in *FM*.4980:

> The necessity of a disjunctive contradictory proposition is so absolute y^t ye same thing should either be or not be, no more y^n it could make it possible y^t it should both be or not be together. Infinite power could no more make it possible y^t Adam should neither eat nor not eat of ye forbidden fruit y^n y^t he should both eat & not eat of it [or that it] is necessary y^t Cato shall kill himself in Africa or not kill himself, But it is not, therefore necessary y^t he should necessarily kill himself, or necessarily not kill himself, & therefore it is a childish illogical argumentation. If it be not necessary it shall rain tomorrow y^t then it must be necessary it shall not rain for neither of y^m might come to passe necessarily but contingently, onely ye whole is necessary y^t one or other of y^m should come to passe necessarily or contingently, it matters not w^{ch}; Here therefore The Author did not observe ye difference between these two affirmations Tis necessary y^t one or other of ye two

should come to passe & this That one or other of y^m must needs come to passe necessarily.[37]

Cudworth terms his understanding of possible future actions which were logical, but not predetermined as necessary causal relationships, the 'disjunctive logical necessity.' This idea Cudworth describes in *FM*.4979 in the following manner:

> So y^t ye meaning of Disjunctive Logicall Necessity is this, not y^t if one of ye Contradictory terms doo not come to pass ye other will necessarily come to passe but if one of them doo not come to passe anyway (though it be contingently unnecessarily) yet it will be necessary y^t ye other shall come to passe some way or other though it may come to passe contigently for all y^t.[38]

By splitting his discussion of providence between the two theories of Plastic Nature and Moveable Providence Cudworth is attempting to refine his account of causality and necessity. All actions have a cause, and it is necessarily true that that cause is sufficient. However, where in Plastic Nature this cause is necessarily determined, in Moveable Providence it is not. The problem, therefore, is not that acts controlled by Moveable Providence — essentially moral acts — do not have a cause, but that man confuses the sufficient cause of a moral act as being the necessarily determined cause.

The problem, however, remains for Cudworth to explain how a system of Moveable Providence, in which 'Infinite power could no more make it possible y^t Adam should neither eat nor not eat of ye forbidden fruit' can be explained in a manner which does not somehow diminish the omniscience of God. Cudworth's response to this recurring problem is to criticise the underlying philosophical assumptions of the theological systems he is rejecting. Cudworth argues that a determinist system like Calvinism understands divine foreknowledge in terms of a direct, predetermined, chain of actions. As we have seen the position of orthodox Calvinism in the seventeenth century on this question was a deal more subtle that Cudworth allows for. However, his criticism is essentially that principles of divine foreknowledge which focus solely on God's will are, too limiting and narrow. Cudworth argues that such a position reduces the intellect of God to the human principles of will and power. Instead,

---

[37] *FM*.4980: 266. It is interesting to note also that the examples used in this quote, of Adam's 'Fall' and Cato's suicide, are suggestive of the possible link that Cudworth believes there to be between Calvinism and Stoicism, both systems ethical arguments being recognisable in these examples, Calvinism through the doctrine of original sin and Stoicism through the justification of suicide.

[38] *FM*.4979: 228-9.

Cudworth asserts, such is the awesome intellect of God, that he can not only foresee all necessary acts, but also all the contingent possibilities that occur from that act. The divine intellect is, therefore, not limited to the strictures of an Adamantine chain of predetermined certainty. Rather the mind of God, as Cudworth puts it:

> doth infallably know all contingent & free actions though not antecedently by necessary causes wch would destroy the freedom & contingency, but yet Consequentially and by ways of Anticipation of Futurity. Soo y^t the object of this prescience is not caused antecedently producing such effects but it is ye consequent truth & futurity y^t must needs fall within ye Comprehensiveness of ye Divine Understanding y^t Grasps & presents all futurity in it.[39]

Cudworth, therefore, in his discussion God's foreknowledge eschews the language of 'will' in favour of 'mind', 'intellect' and 'understanding'. Cudworth argues that the intellect of God, not simply his will, is so vast that all possible 'futurity' is held in it. Actions are, for Cudworth, not defined in terms of necessity but 'ambiguous possibility.'[40] The infinite web of possibility created by this assertion is too vast for the human mind to conceive, but not too great for the limitless power of the wisdom of God. Man can act freely in the vast intellect of the divine because all possible actions and contingencies of actions have been foreseen by God. Providence, in this sense, is not a limited chain of cause and effect but the limitless realm of possibility. Providence is not fixed but 'Moveable' within the harmony of God's intellect and understanding.

As stated above, Cudworth's theory of Moveable Providence is only sketched in his manuscripts and, therefore, does not benefit from as clear and systematic discussion as Plastic Nature. That being said, some interesting conceptual problems are thrown up by Cudworth's account of Moveable Providence. In particular Cudworth remains unclear on exactly what God knows about future events. Is it that God knows all possible future events, or that God's mind can allow for all possible contingent future events, but leaves it to the freewilled actions of man to determine them? Certainly the latter position would seem to be closer to the Molinist account of middle knowledge and the Arminian adoption

---

[39] *FM*.4981: 50.

[40] *FM*.4979: 210. We can identify this principle of the breadth of God's providential plan in the Platonic thought of Cudworth's predecessor Thomas Jackson. As Jackson argues: 'So far is freedom of choice or contingency from being incompatible with the immutability of God's will, that without this infinite variety of choice or freedom of thought in man and angels, we cannot rightly conceive him to be as infinitely wise as his decree is immutable.' Jackson, *Works*: V.90.

of the Molinist theory of providence. It is certainly tempting, given Cudworth's links to Arminian theology, and his own anti-Calvinism, to suggest that this is the position he takes. However, on examination, it would
appear that Cudworth's position is more subtle than this. Where the
Molinist position is a refinement of the traditional scholastic distinction
between God's natural and free knowledge, Cudworth undermines this
distinction by expanding God's free knowledge of all possible things to
account fully for the providential knowledge of God. This reading would
seem to be given credence when we remember that Cudworth distances
himself from the language of 'will' and 'volition' when describing God.
Instead, Cudworth always defines God as a constant, perfect, and
unchanging mind who is only diminished by the language of 'will',
'choice', and 'freedom' which are characteristics of human, and not divine
action. In his manuscripts he constantly talks around the distinction
between divine and human action:

> God is ye most determinate Being in this sense because he is one way; but
> not as if he were under necessity for there is no necessity as yet, but neces-
> sity ariseth from those things yt follow God & are below him. And though
> God cannot be sd to have yt imperfect Free-will yt is in Creatures wch
> plainly implies defectability, yet he is most of all ... a Prince & Lord of
> himself, he is most of all autexiousious in a simple refined sense, under ye
> Power of nothing but himself & his own Perfection, Free-willed Beings are
> not essentially their own perfection & therefore yt self-power of Freewill
> is but an imperfect power over ones self, a staggering & uncertain
> thing.[41]

Cudworth's account of God is, therefore, that above all things he is perfect mind and intellect and any qualification on this in terms of will and
volition is to anthropomorphise God with the language of fallen, human,
freewill. In these terms, Cudworth's account of providence allows space
in the infinite web of known possibilities held in the mind of God for
human freewill to exist in a reasonable and equitable manner. In terms
of the broader context of the seventeenth century debate on providence
Cudworth's theory would appear to differ from the Molinist refinement
of the traditional discussion of providence. Where Molinism (and Arminianism) sought to refine accounts of providence by the addition of
'middle knowledge', Cudworth, by contrast, does the opposite. If we use
the traditional terminology of theological accounts of God's knowledge
Cudworth's theory of Moveable Providence expands the scope of God's

---

[41] *FM*.4980: 43

natural knowledge and, by the rejection of the language of voluntarism, removes the need to assert the existence of God's free knowledge. All things are known and controlled by the harmony created by the mind of God. The harmony of God's creation is held together by the full expression of the reasoned form of God's creation in the actions of the different persons of the Trinity. For Cudworth all of creation comes together in one unified, reasoned system. Although it may not seem so from the human perspective of man all actions, no matter how seemingly small or mundane, fit into the reason and harmony of God's providential mind. On mundane matters Plastic Nature shows that God knows with certainty the form and development of natural things. However, this is merely the background principle to the more important work of Moveable Providence in which man's actions are free to be judged and brought into harmony by the perfect mind of God. Cudworth explains this using the artistic metaphors that run through all his writings on providence:

> The Dramaticall Poem of ye world is wonderfull & extraordinary for it is such as if we should suppose ye Histrionick Actors to pronounce something of their own besides w^t ye Poet hath written down ye Poem itself being incompleat & having certain void Spaces left in it here and there purposly by ye Poet for ye Actors ymselves to Supply & fill up to wch ye Poet forknowing what every one will utter or accomodating w^t he adds thereunto afterwards makes up one coherent & intire Plot of all, so y^t ye Actors are not meer actors of Parts & Speakers of words given them but partiall Poets ymselves, ye grand Poet or Dramatist allways fore knowing w^t every Actor will here and there interpose of himself & still accomodating y^t y^t follows wch is his own so y^t it shall aptly agree wth w^t was interpreted by y^m thereby connecting all into one inntire Plot one coherent dramatical Poem.[42]

As this idea is only present in unpublished sources it would be wrong to extrapolate too broadly from this into the wider seventeenth-century debates on providence. Certainly Cudworth's Moveable Providence presents many problems and ambiguities which are not worked out in the systematic manner that one would hope for. However, what is clear is that even as an incomplete and imperfect account of providence, Cudworth argues that Moveable Providence allows for the maintenance of the omniscience of God whilst still allowing for human freewill which is, for Cudworth, the most important factor within this broader philosophical discussion.

---

[42] *FM*.4980: 206

Cudworth's theory freewill

Cudworth's discussion of providence is used to prepare the ground for his account of freewill. As a consequence it is not a surprise to find that Cudworth's account of human action follows the same bifurcated structure that Cudworth uses to discuss and define his understanding of providence. In particular Cudworth argues that human agency exists in the constant struggle in man between lower animal desires and higher intellectual principles. For Cudworth, freewill is not a sign of perfection in man but 'a staggering and uncertain thing', a sign of man's conflicted and fallen character. This point comes out most clearly when Cudworth briefly discusses man's sinful nature:

> This is ye true attempt of ye original of Sin y^t it is neither caused by God nor by any positive substantiall principle, but ye possibility thereof preceeds only from y^t imperfection & defectibility of Creatures, but actual cause of it is never any other y^n ye rationall Creature itself, not putting forth y^t executive power wch it hath towards ye higher principle in its nature but by sluggish remission & relaxation, sinking down into ye lower.[43]

It is precisely because man is able to move upwards toward God that he is also able to descend downwards into sinfulness. Interestingly the dualism implicit in Cudworth's account of human agency is not a crude duality between the body and soul, or the corporeal and incorporeal. Rather Cudworth's dualism follows Plotinus' duality of higher and lower selves.[44] Man, therefore, resides not in a conflicting world of material and immaterial forces, but in a realm where he is free to choose between the higher principles of the divine or the lower principles of the mundane. Man is a fallible creature who is able to improve himself within this scale of being. The providence of God is, therefore, for Cudworth, found in the infinite possibilities which are suggested, or as Cudworth put it, 'woven into' this divinely ordained scale of being.[45] As we have already seen Cudworth is reluctant to describe the acts of God's intellect in terms of freewill: 'God cannot be sd to have yt imperfect Free-will yt is in Creatures wch plainly implies defectability.'[46] To do so would be describe God with the voluntarist language of will and volition. Cudworth's uses

---

[43] *FM*.4980: 147.

[44] 'In fact the substrate to the free principle is the rational form, and that which has come into existence from the rational form and exists according to it, so that the matter will not be dominant and the formation come second,' *Enneads*: 3.3.4.

[45] *FM*.4981: 24; *FM*.4982: III.66.

[46] *FM*. 4980: 43.

the language of 'will' only with regards to man as this language denotes
the specific place and form of man's particular position. For Cudworth
freewill is a characteristic peculiar to man because it speaks not only of
man's fallibility but also his salvation.

Cudworth begins his account of freewill with a definition of human
will. Human will is, for Cudworth, a faculty that resides between two
extremes; it is 'an amphibious thing, between perfection and nature.'[47]
The implication of this is two-fold. Firstly, Cudworth argues that there
are elements of human action which are necessarily governed by the
mundane, plastic, forces of nature (i.e. hunger, thirst, sleep, etc.). Secondly, above these mundane factors there exist malleable powers which
man can use to improve himself by moving towards the divine principles
of goodness and justice. The defining principle of this moral improve-
ment is reason. Through the correct use of reason man has the potential
to rise above the mundane and to move into participation with the divine.
Man can therefore, Cudworth argues use his reason to participate with God
through the eternal divine principles of justice and wisdom. Cudworth's
use of reason as a means of moving towards the divine returns us to the
link made by Cudworth, and also Whichcote, between reason and God's
grace. As we have already seen Cudworth, in his *First Sermon*, argues
that '*God was therefore incarnated and made man, that he might Deifie
us*, that is… make us *partakers of the Divine nature*.'[48] As was shown in
the previous chapter Cudworth, in *TISU*, develops this idea to make the
incarnation of the *Logos* the immediate and perfect incarnation of the
reasoned form of God's intellect in creation. Therefore the use and utilisation of reason by man becomes the means by which man accepts freely
the grace of God and also participates in God's reasoned, divine nature.
Cudworth's Trinitarian theology underpins his account of man's freewill and the positive and constructive uses he argues man can put that
freewill to.[49]

In his manuscripts Cudworth develops a detailed account of the different faculties that make up human agency. The chief amongst these is the
power of self-determination. Cudworth does not, however, think that all
human actions are self-determined moral actions. Instead he describes
first two non-moral faculties which control mundane actions of man.
These faculties, which Cudworth terms 'hetero-kinetic' and 'epoloustic',

[47] *FM*.4980: 45; *TFW*: 184.
[48] *First Sermon*: 101.
[49] *FM*.4980: 37.

have a two-fold function. Firstly they allow Cudworth to remove certain automatic human actions, such as hunger or tiredness, from the realm of ethical discussion. Secondly, as with his discussion of Plastic Nature, these terms allow Cudworth to frame more clearly the extent and remit of the higher and more important self-determining faculty. The starting point for Cudworth's terminology for human agency is the *Phaedrus* where Socrates defines the immortal part of the soul as that part which 'moves itself' — *to auto eauto kinouv*.[50] This self-moving principle, which Cudworth anglicised to 'auto-kinesis' in his manuscripts, is the self-determining moral power of man. Below this faculty man is still liable to the forces of external action at the most mundane level; these are defined by the regulatory principles of the plastic nature. In the manuscripts Cudworth contrasts the self-moving, auto-kinetic powers of man with the externally moved, hetero-kinetic forces which effect man. Cudworth argues that these hetero-kinetic forces — which man has as much ability to resist as a tennis ball which is struck, or a weather-cock blown by the wind — should not be described in terms of ethics or morality as Hobbes and other material fatalists have described them, because no equitable judgement can be made over man's ability to control them.[51] Included in this sub-ethical layer are what Cudworth terms 'epoloustic' forces.[52] Epoloustic forces describe those human choices where there is an equal determination between two competing factors. According to Cudworth there can be no blame or moral judgment attached to such choices as man is drawn to one option rather than another because of habit rather than any specific moral arbitration. Epoloustic determinations differ, therefore, from hetero-kinetic determinations in that man is determined internally, not externally. This distinction, along with Cudworth's use of the idea of habit, would seem to make epoloustic determinations comparable to the regulatory, plastic, principles in man. As we have seen, Cudworth argues that Plastic Nature describes the mundane determining principle present in parts of creation, existing below the level of ethical judgments. In the 'Digression' Cudworth argues that one of the factors that proves the imprint of the divine intellect on nature is the ability of humans to act from habit. The example Cudworth gives is of a musician

[50] Sarah Hutton, 'Liberty and Self-determination: Ethics Power and Action in Ralph Cudworth,' in *Del necessario al possibile. Determinismo e Libertà nel penserio Anglo-Olandese de XVII seculo,* edited by L. Simonutti. Angeli: 2001: 89.

[51] *FM*.4980: 176; *FM*.4979: 91.

[52] The term 'Epoloustic' only occurs within *FM*.4978 and *FM*.4980, suggesting that *FM*.4978 is related to *FM*.4980. See appendix on the Cudworth's Freewill manuscripts.

being able to play whilst half-asleep; acting from habit, not from conscious power. As Cudworth puts it:

> *Habits* do in like manner, *Gradually Evolve* themselves, in a long Train or Series of *Regular* and *Artificial Motions,* readily prompting the doing of them, without comprehending that *Art* and *Reason* by which they are directed.[53]

Cudworth accepts that man is in many areas of life determined by mundane internal and external factors. Externally man can be pushed this way or that, by the hetero-kinetic power of external forces. Internally man can be drawn to apples over oranges simply through the epoloustic determination of habit. Neither of these actions should, Cudworth argues, be judged in ethical terms because the determination of such actions occurs in a sub-ethical level of natural determination.[54] Neither can effectively account for ethical actions of man, this can only come through the self-determined power, which Cudworth terms 'auto-kinesis'.

Cudworth places the moral faculty of auto-kinesis above the two ethically neutral faculties of epoloustic and hetero-kinetic power. For Cudworth auto-kinesis is the characteristic power in human will that raises man above the level of being mere beast. It is, in short, man's recognition and consciousness of these powers that makes him human. Like the previous human faculties outlined by Cudworth, auto-kinesis does not suggest a retreat from the world, but an active engagement with it. For Cudworth the existence of a self-moving power in man is evidence of man's ability to engage with, and respond to the reason of the divine present in all parts of creation. In making this assertion Cudworth rejects the view that free-will can be explained by the indifference of the will to the world around it, a position found in the moral asceticism suggested by some Stoic and Neoplatonic ethical philosophy. For Cudworth the link commonly made between freewill and indifference in ethical philosophy is implicitly wrong because such a link assumes that the starting principle of the world to be blind will working without the use of reason. Cudworth continually stresses this point because of the role of indifference in scholastic and

---

[53] *TISU*: 157.

[54] As stated an epoloustic judgment is the morally neutral judgement of habit. If, however, using the example stated above, one of the fruits chosen by habit, for instance the oranges, were produced in morally reprehensible circumstance (perhaps in apartheid South Africa) then the choice would be an ethical rather than habitual, and therefore one on which man could be judged. This is because the ethical decision which judges the fruits on their origin and production is an intellectual decision which, within Cudworth's schema, resides above the habitual desire for an apple or orange.

Cartesian accounts of freewill.[55] In his manuscripts Cudworth goes to great lengths to refute indifference as a possible means of explaining freewill. Cudworth argues that the central problem with indifference is that any moral actor who claims to be indifferent to the world in which he resides can never judge the moral truths that exist implicitly in that world. Such a theory completely contradicts the central assertion of Cudworth's moral philosophy, that moral judgments can be known because of man's implicit relationship, through reason, with the intellect of the divine. This can never be the case, Cudworth argues, if the starting point is the indifferent mind as such a theory denies that there is an active, self-guiding power in the soul.[56]

In place of indifference Cudworth asserts his active and engaged account of freewill as an auto-kinetic power. As we have seen, Cudworth takes this terminology from Plato, however his understanding and use of it develops from the theological premises and starting point of all his philosophy. Cudworth argues that man's auto-kinetic power is defined in three ways: it is an internal self-moving power; which is conscious of itself; and active in the external world.[57] Cudworth's tri-partite definition of man's freewill follows his account of the Trinity which we have already encountered: its source is in the incorporeal divine principle which created the world; it is driven by the understanding power of the *Logos*; and defined by the constant active principle of the Spirit. Further links can be found between Cudworth's definitions of this auto-kinetic power and his theology. In particular the process by which man comes to recognise his auto-kinetic power mirrors the means by which man comes to know God. As we have seen in *TISU* Cudworth argues that man uses his reason to tell him of the existence and form of God. In the manuscripts Cudworth utilises this same reasoning power to argue that the auto-kinetic power of man is the means by which man can, through his actions, come closer to, and participate in the divine. Man's auto-kinetic power provides the means through which he can draw himself to God. This power is, however, not an end in itself, merely the means through which man can actively seek and participate with the intellect of God. As Cudworth argues in *FM*.4980:

---

[55] For freewill as indifference in scholastic thought, in particular Ockham, see Copleston, *History of Philosophy*: III.101-3. For freewill as indifference in Descartes see, Descartes, *Works*: I:174-9, 234-6; Cottingham, *Descartes Dictionary*: 86-88; Copleston, *History of Philosophy*: IV.139-42.

[56] *FM*.4979: 6, 33.

[57] *FM*.4979: 26; *FM*.4980: 47, 51.

> for Power is not Power without respect to Good freewill or self-power is
> nothing but a self-promoting Power to Good or Self-professing Power in y^e
> Same. A free-willed Being is such a thing as hath a Power to adde some-
> thing to its own Perfection.[58]

For Cudworth this higher reasoning principle in the soul of man is the
gift of the grace of God. Cudworth argues that God's grace, the perfection incarnated in the *Logos* and communicated to the world by the Spirit,
'excites the free principle' in man. True to his anti-Calvinist Puritan roots
Cudworth argues that is it only through this reasoned grace that man
is able to come into full participation with God. However, crucially this
grace is offered freely and unconditionally by God, with the responsibility for whether this gift of grace is accepted remaining solely with man.
The active principle of the divine, which is such a central part of Cudworth's Trinitarianism, is found, as the grace of God, in the self-moving
power which defines Cudworth's conception of human agency.[59] For Cudworth the centrality of reason to his account of freewill provides the
means by which man is able to be judged equitably by the distributive
justice of God. As Cudworth states in *FM*.4980:

> Besides all wch we Xtians believe y^t though God be not passionate & passive
> in himself y^t after some ages of the world past he humanized his nature in
> our Bl. Saviour Xt & So made it passive & passionate & moveable in him
> who was in all things like unto us & hath a Sympathy & fellow feeling w^th
> our humane difficulties & infirmities ... wth us so y^t this moveable Provi-
> dence may well be exercised by him imploying his Angells as Emisaries &
> Ministering Spirits every where & coming at last himself visibly to judge
> the world & render to every man according to his works.[60]

Most importantly, as this final quote shows, the ethical responsibility of
man is not something which is given only to the elect, but a power which
controls and defines 'every man.' Cudworth's theology, therefore, carries
with it a universalism with regards to grace. The defining term of man's
salvation is, therefore, not man's specific election, but the responsibility
of the individual. For Cudworth this responsibility not only defined man's
humanity, but also his individuality. The individual responsibility which
permeates Cudworth's ethical theory is most clearly seen in his use of
the Stoic ruling principle or *hegemonicon*. Cudworth equates this Stoic
terminology with the Platonic language of auto-kinesis as, for him, they

---

[58] *FM*.4980: 30.
[59] *FM*.4981: 79; *FM*.4979: 224.
[60] *FM*.4980: 218.

both define the active, rational and ethical power of man. However, what Cudworth's use of *hegemonicon* gives us, more so than his use of the Platonic auto-kinesis, is a clear sense of the individualistic imperative in Cudworth's ethical theory. This comes out in Cudworth's translation of this Stoic language through the use of 'self' constructs, most notably self-determination. As Ronald Hall has pointed out many of these 'self' constructs appear for the first time in Cudworth's writing and can rightly been seen as one of Cudworth's most important contributions to ethical philosophy.[61] Cudworth argues that his account of human agency provides an intellectual structure through which man was able to draw himself to the divine whilst not diminishing the omniscience of God. For Cudworth these self-determining ethical powers define man as an individual moral actor, freely able to chose or reject the saving grace of God.

Through his broader discussion of providence Cudworth constructs, with varying degrees of success, an ethical system which allows for the ethical responsibility of the individual moral actor, whilst not diminishing the omniscience of God. This overarching system of providence and free-will, however, only provides the theological and philosophical ground-work for Cudworth's understanding of how man engages productively with the external world and with other members of that external world. Interestingly, as we shall see in the following chapter, Cudworth never suggests an introspective or ascetic account of man's engagement with the external world, but one in which all actions — from the understanding of ethical norms through to the mechanics of political obligation — begin with a reflective engagement with God through his creation. At the heart of this remains Cudworth's 'amphibious' understanding of man's freewill. Writing in the aftermath of the English Civil War Cudworth argues, with some strength, that the only solution to ethical and political dilemmas is for man to take responsibility for this own actions. As we shall see Cudworth argues that it is possible to develop from his account of individual ethical responsibility a pluralistic system of ethical realism in which all members of the community learn to work with one another through their common and shared understanding of the 'eternal and immutable' ethical norms woven into the created order. Political authority for

---

[61] *TFW*: 182-5; Roland Hall, 'New Words and Antedatings from Cudworth's "Treatise on Freewill,"' in *Notes and Queries*, 205 (1960): 427-432; Roland Hall, 'Cudworth: More New Words,' in *Notes and Queries*, 208 (1963): 313-14; Roland Hall, 'Cudworth and his contemporaries: New words and antedatings,' in *Notes and Queries*, 220 (1975): 313-14. Also see Sarah Hutton, 'Liberty and Self-determination': 90-2.

its own sake, so much a byword of the Civil War era and philosophical responses to it, should be avoided at all costs according to Cudworth. As Cudworth argues in his manuscripts, God has placed Ministers and Governors to control the lower passions of man, not to coerce men to act in a correct or good manner. God alone is the source and author of good and it is the free choice of individual moral actors whether or not they use their God-given reason to live a life which is more God-like.[62]

---

[62] *FM* 4981: 26-27.

CHAPTER FIVE

"THE LITTLE COMMONWEALTH OF MAN": ETHICAL RESPONSIBILITY AND POLITICAL OBLIGATION

In many ways the search for political ideas in Cudworth's thought would seem to be a wasted exercise. Cudworth does not, like so many of his contemporaries, present in any systematic manner a political treatise to redefine the form and order of the fractured world in which he lived. Nor is it possible to argue that Cudworth's engagement with *political* thinkers such as Thomas Hobbes is enough to show that he was as concerned with politics as 'that atheist politician.' However, as we have already seen, Cudworth's understanding of the created order, and man's place in it does assume an engagement with the external world of politics. Cudworth's ethics, far from teaching a level of moral asceticism or 'escape', actively calls on man to live a life inspired, not only by the love of God, but also by the love of his fellow men. Cudworth's philosophy is, therefore, intimately concerned with public life and affairs involving questions of authority and obligation. These concerns provide the clearest examples of the ethical imperative which, as we have seen, develops directly from Cudworth's Trinitarian theology, and for this reason it seems perfectly reasonable to posit a political aspect in Cudworth's philosophy.[1]

The problem still remains of how to uncover this aspect within his philosophy. As we saw in the previous chapter, it is possible to identify aspects of the arguments that may have made up the remaining volumes of Cudworth's incomplete *Intellectual System* in his unpublished works. The same is true with these ethical and political ideas, in particular through an examination of his posthumously published *EIM*. To build a comprehensive picture of Cudworth's world view, however, the net needs

---

[1] This text is not the first to recognise the 'political' in Cudworth's philosophy. Also see Cragg, *From Puritans to the Age of Reason*: 60; G.R. Cragg, *The Cambridge Platonists*. Oxford: OUP, 1968, especially 'On Political Sovereignty': 347-365; Hutton, 'Liberty and Self-determination': 81-97; G.A.J. Rogers, 'The Other-worldly philosophers and the real world: The Cambridge Platonists, Theology and Politics,' in *The Cambridge Platonists in Philosophical Context: Politics, Metaphysics & Religion*, edited by G.A.J. Rogers, et al. Dordrecht: Kluwer, 1997; and G.A.J. Rogers, 'More, Locke, and the Issue of Liberty,' in *Henry More (1614-1687) Tercentenary Studies*, edited by Sarah Hutton. Dordrecht: Kluwer, 1991.

to be cast wider to include all of his writings and life. As with all Cudworth's philosophy these political arguments can only be fully unlocked if they are placed in the theological and philosophical context of his *Intellectual System*. This context provides the building blocks for his account of man's place in the political arena. In particular his strong argument for the place and responsibility of individual actors remains a factor in Cudworth's political ideas. This is brought out most vividly in Cudworth's reference to the 'the little-commonwealth of man.' This interesting turn of phrase very neatly describes the bridge between Cudworth's theory of the freely willed moral actor and the development of these actions in the ethical and political arena. The 'little-commonwealth of man' is used by him to describe the form of ethical adjudication which exists in all men. Key to this political man is the reflective, auto-kinetic power which all possess as a mark of their humanity. Cudworth describes this self-reflective faculty as the 'soul-endoubled upon itself.' The auto-kinetic faculty in man is naturally fallible and open to error. But, as he argues in *FM*.4980, 'in ye little common-wealth of man's soul ye naturall Understanding & certain Knowledge is ye Law of Justice & Rule by wch it should be governed.'[2] Cudworth argues that, despite the possibility of failure, it is only through the inner reformation of man that it is possible to create a society governed by self-determined moral actors able to achieve the happiness and liberty of God.[3] Political society is, therefore, formed, Cudworth argues, firstly by man taking responsibility for his actions, and secondly by the mutual agreement and collective responsibilities of all members of that society. The key theme here is that of community. With these principles in mind it is possible to show how Cudworth not only provides powerful and persuasive arguments for how man gains knowledge of ethical and political norms, but also the form and mechanisms required to construct and maintain the political community. By a closer examination of certain key events in Cudworth's biography it is possible to gain a fuller understanding of the practical manifestation of these ideas. In particular his political ideas are given more credence when we understand how they informed his own engagement with the political upheavals and problems of the seventeenth century. More importantly, a reassessment of the political aspects in Cudworth's philosophy allow us to gain a much richer sense of him as a thinker in the intellectual context of seventeenth-century England. It is it not, as we shall see, that political

[2] *FM*.4980: 58.
[3] *FM*.4979: 10, 20.

arguments do not exist in Cudworth's writings, rather that these political arguments can only be reconstructed in the context of the seventeenth-century theological language and world view that Cudworth used. Consequently we can identify in his philosophy a form of political pluralism based on individual responsibility and political obligation, however we can only identify these arguments if we first accept the theological arguments which engendered them.

Ethical knowledge

As we saw in the last chapter, at the heart of Cudworth's ethical theory lies the responsibility of the individual ethical actor. Before we can explore the manner in which Cudworth argued that the individual engaged with in political matters it is necessary to show how he argued that the individual moral actor developed an understanding of the ethical norms which underpin political action. This argument is most fully developed by Cudworth in his *EIM*. *EIM* was first published in 1731 in an edition prepared by Edward Chandler, Bishop of Lichfield and later Durham at the request of Cudworth's grandson, Francis Cudworth Masham.[4] This publication was prompted by the growth in debates on ethical rationalism in the eighteenth century, and it is in this context which it is often read and understood.[5] Although the original version of *EIM* was almost certainly circulated in manuscript it is not known whether Cudworth ever intended to publish the work in its present form.[6] From what we know of Cudworth's stated intentions we can, however, tentatively place the work in the broader context of his published and unpublished works. In terms of

---

[4] Jacqueline Broad, 'A Woman's Influence? John Locke and Damaris Masham on Moral Accountability,' in *The Journal of the History of Ideas* 67 (2006): 489-510: 501.

[5] *EIM*: xiv; L.A. Selby-Bigge, ed., *The British Moralists, being selections from Writers principally of the eighteenth century.* Oxford: The Clarendon Press, 1897: 813-43. One of the consequences of *EIM*'s place in eighteenth-century debates on ethical rationalism has been the development of a Neo-Kantian reading of Cudworth's ethical thought, particularly ones, like that of Stephen Darwall, which argues that '[f]or Cudworth as for Kant, ethics is possible only if pure reason can be practical.' See: Darwall, *British Moralists*: 109, 325. This Neo-Kantian reading of Cudworth can be traced back to Coleridge's reading of the Cambridge Platonists. See Samuel Taylor Coleridge, *Coleridge on the Seventeenth century*, edited by Roberta Florence. Durham, NC: Duke University Press, 1955: 109. Also see Arthur J. Lovejoy, 'Kant and the English Platonists,' in *Essays Philosophical and Psychological: In honour of William James by his colleagues at Columbia University.* New York: Longmans, Green & Co., 1908: 263-302 and Beiser, *Sovereignty of Reason*: 174.

[6] *EIM*: xiv.

subject area *EIM* can be related to Cudworth's planned second volume
of his *Intellectual System*, arguing, as it does, against the view of God as
not 'meer Arbitrary Will Omnipotent, Decreeing, Doing, and Necessitating
all Actions, Evil as well as Good, but Essentially Moral, Good and Just.'[7]
It may even have been based on the initial ideas which Cudworth described
as his 'Metaphysical Ethics' in letters to John Worthington in the 1660s.[8]
The title, *A Treatise Concerning Eternal and Immutable Morality*, even
relates the work back to Cudworth's B.D. disputations in 1644.[9] It is,
however, impossible to verify exactly when, and for what purpose, *EIM*
was written as the original manuscript is now lost. What can be said for
certain is that *EIM* is not a work on ethics as one might naturally understand it. Rather it is a prolegomenon to an ethical work which Cudworth
failed to complete. That being said, certain arguments are discussed in
EIM and, as we shall see later, certain ethical and political arguments in
Cudworth's manuscripts, particularly his discussion of political oaths,
rely upon assumptions and arguments put forward in *EIM*.

In the seventeenth-century context in which Cudworth wrote *EIM*
the text presents a fascinating bridge between the traditional 'innatist'
arguments of Neoplatonic epistemology and the strengthening arguments
of empirical philosophy which culminated in the publication of John
Locke's *Essay* in 1689. What is most interesting about *EIM* is not only
that it presents, unsurprisingly for a critic of Hobbes, a general criticism
of empiricism, but also that Cudworth goes to great lengths to distance
himself from 'anamnesis', the traditional Platonic theory of knowledge.
In Platonic philosophy this argument is found most clearly in the *Meno*
where Socrates argues that knowledge is not taught so much as drawn
out from knowledge which pre-exists in the mind. The task of the teacher
is not to give knowledge but to coax from the pupil the knowledge locked
in his mind: 'knowledge will not come from teaching but from questions,
he will recover it for himself.'[10] The assumption of Plato's theory is that
the soul of man possesses this knowledge because of its pre-existence
from its present, embodied form. In the *Meno* Socrates argues that the
ability of the slave boy to grasp the basics of geometry merely through
the questioning of the teacher is proof that this knowledge is held in the
soul from eternity. As we have already seen, Cudworth cites the argument of the *Meno* approvingly in his discussion of the existence of God.

---

[7] *EIM*: v.
[8] Worthington, *Diary*: I.157.
[9] 'Memoirs of Ralph Cudworth': 27.
[10] Plato, *Meno*, 85d.

In *EIM* Cudworth agrees with the starting position anamnesis, that the soul of man is immortal. However, Cudworth rejects the belief that because the soul is immortal all knowledge resides in it from eternity as this would mean accepting the pre-existence of the soul.[11] Cudworth argues that if souls pre-existed before they were joined with the body God would become merely a spectator observing the world from afar after his initial work of creation is done. As Cudworth argues in *TISU*:

> The effect of such a Hypothesis as this [the pre-existence of souls], to make men think, that there is no other God in the World but Blind and Dark Nature. God might also for other good and wise Ends, unknown to us, reserve to himself the continual exercise of this his creative power, in the successive Production of new Souls.[12]

For this reason Cudworth develops an account of the development of knowledge which comes from the internal reasoning power of the mind participating in the intellect of the divine, rather than through the recollection of locked away, pre-existing knowledge.[13] The internal power of the mind for Cudworth is not a means of accepting the pre-existence of the soul, but rather a means of confirming the relationship between man's reason and the intellectual principle of the divine. Cudworth argues, the mind has a 'diaphanous power' which can recognise the intellectual forms in the created world and recognises the source of these intellectual forms, in their purest and most perfect form, as coming from the founding intellectual principle in the divine.[14]

Cudworth argues that this participatory process does not occur in a process of mental retreat and introspection from the external world. Rather

---

[11] By contrast Henry More accepted the pre-existence of the soul. See Henry More, 'The Præexistency of the soul,' in Henry More, *The Complete Poems of Henry More (1614-1687)* edited by Alexander B. Grosart. Hildeshiem: Georg Olms, 1969: 119-128. See in particular 119:

For I would sing the Præexistency
Of humane souls, and live once more again
By recollection and quick memory
All what is past since we first all began.
But all to shallow be wits to scan
So deep a point and mind to dull to clear
So dark a matter; but Though, O more then man!
Aread though sacred Soul or *Plotin* deare
Tell what we mortals are, tell what of old we were.

[12] *TISU*: 44.

[13] Dominic Scott, 'Reason, Recollection and the Cambridge Platonists,' in *Platonism and the English Imagination*, edited by Anna Baldwin and Sarah Hutton. Cambridge: CUP, 1994: 145.

[14] *EIM*: 77; Scott, 'Reason': 147.

man uses his reason to recognise the mark God on all parts of creation.
In *EIM* Cudworth defines this through a tri-partite structure which coheres
with the Trinitarian theology of *TISU*. In this structure man, through
his experience of the external world, is drawn into a participatory relationship with God, contemplating and understanding God through his
growing understanding of God's creation. In this account Cudworth
argues that the intellect and goodness of God is the central point of an
infinitely expanding circle. The radii extending from this central point
are the understanding and wisdom of God. The outer edge of this ever
extending circle is the action of God. Therefore, the external workings of
God in the world are related directly to the infinite intellect and goodness
of God by means of the wisdom and understanding of God.[15] Man, by
the use of his reason is, therefore, able to comprehend this evidence of
God's action in the world, and from this come to understand these actions
and the embodiments of the wisdom and intellect of God which lies at
the heart of this structure. The initial data for this comes from man's
sense perception. However, these sensations do not create knowledge
in themselves, but provide the means by which man comes to recognise
the imprint of God's intellect on all things. Sensations are, therefore, only
comprehensible when, by use of his reason, man links these sensations
to, what Cudworth terms, 'inward characters written within itself.'[16]
Although the impetus for the creation of knowledge can come from external factors, the appreciation of knowledge is always an internal action,
'[f]or knowledge is not a knock or thrust from without, but consisteth in
the awakening and exciting of the inward active powers of the mind.'[17]

Cudworth's concentration on the internal power of the intellect over
sensory perception in man means that in *EIM* we encounter much the
same reflexive language that we found in Cudworth's freewill manuscripts. At one point Cudworth describes knowledge as not '"the perception of things abroad without the mind", but the mind comprehending
itself.'[18] Cudworth also cites Boethius in this connection, commenting
that:

> knowledge is not a passion from anything without the mind, but an active
> exertion of the inward strength, vigour, and power of the mind displaying
> itself from within, and the intelligible forms by which things are understood
> or known are not stamps or impressions passively printed upon the soul

---

[15] *EIM*: 27.
[16] *EIM*: 60.
[17] *EIM*: 60.
[18] *EIM*: 135.

from without, but ideas vitally protended or actively exerted from within itself.[19]

This account of how man comes to develop knowledge of the external world, and so the ethical norms that govern that world is predicated on the dualism that runs throughout Cudworth's philosophy. The internal, discerning principle of the mind is, by definition for him, incorporeal. In that way it is not only distinct from the corporeal reality of sensory perception, it is also directly related to the infinite and incorporeal principle of the intellect of the divine. The 'innate cognoscitive power' of the soul of man is drawn directly from, and judged by intellectual principles in the divine.[20] The knowledge of the nature of an external object, for instance, does not come from the implicit nature of that object: whether it is itself hard or soft, square or triangular, etc. Rather knowledge of its form comes from the mind's ability to recognise and compare the various combinations of local motion that make up that object to intellectual principles perceived by the mind. Only by this comparison to innate principles in the mind is man able to come to effective knowledge of the object. The argument of *EIM* is interesting because it presupposes the individual moral actor's direct engagement with the external world. Cudworth argues that for true knowledge to be formed, both of external objects and ethical norms, the individual must partake in an active engagement with the external world and not simply a passive acceptance of, or passive retreat from it. Cudworth's fully developed account of the moral actor, therefore, demands the direct engagement of that actor with the objects of the external world and the community of ethical actors living in the external world for him to come into a closer participatory relationship with God.

The ethical community

The theme of community occurs through all of Cudworth's theology and philosophy. His definition of the Trinity, as we have seen in Chapter Three, draws on an understanding of the equal coexistence of the three persons of the Trinity, a relationship which Thomas Wise, one of Cudworth's earliest followers, described as 'a community of nature.'[21] As we

---

[19] *EIM*: 73-4.
[20] *EIM*: 75.
[21] Thomas Wise, *A Confutation of the Reason and Philosophy of Atheism being an abridgement of Dr Cudworth's True Intellectual System of the Universe: In which the arguments for and against atheism are clearly stated and examined.* London: 1706: 28.

shall see, there are some parallels that can be drawn between Cudworth's account of the Trinity as a model of a community of equals, and his political ideas.[22] However, it only remains a model and so it would be incorrect to draw a direct parallel between Cudworth's immanent definition of the Trinity and his understanding of the political community. Rather Cudworth argues that the political community is the realm in which the ethical characteristics of man, which are predicated on the principles of Cudworth's Trinitarian theology, are most fully developed. The idea of the community is present in Cudworth's earliest writings, most interestingly in his 1642 text *The Union of Christ and the Church in a Shadow*. In this text Cudworth argues that the Church or, using my terminology, the ethical community was both the structure through which man came to know God, as well as the earthly fulfilment of man's participatory relationship with the divine. In *The Union* Cudworth, through a discussion of marriage, defines marriage as a metaphor of the relationship between Christ and the Church. In marriage Cudworth argues that as women are wedded to men by marriage so the Church is wedded to Christ. As the woman submits herself totally to man in marriage, so the Church submits itself totally to Christ. Crucially, however, Cudworth argues that this is not a one-way relationship, for in marriage as man promised to honour his wife, so Christ honours his Church with his body, through his Passion.[23] A Church created out of the membership of, using the language of the *Second Sermon*, God's freemen is unified through its shared experience of the principle of Christ, understood fully as an active principle, at play in the hearts of all men. So as marriage can be broken by the licentious desire of adultery, so the Church — the human community — can be broken by the sinful lusts of men. The unity of the ethical community is, therefore, controlled not by external laws and threats, but, in the first instance, by the inner reformation and self-determined power of man. The desire to live in the light of Christ, by the means of inner reformation, and the fulfilment of this through the creation of an ethical community, are inseparable in Cudworth's mind.

In *The Union* Cudworth, through a detailed discussion of Chapter Five of St Paul's letter to the Ephesians, argues that the Christ and the Church are bound together through the principle of reason; reason which emanates down to man through Christ, and reason which brings man into a participatory relationship with the divine. Although not fully developed

---

[22] Armour, 'Trinity, Community and Love': 128.
[23] Ralph Cudworth, *The Union of Christ and the Church in a Shadow*. London: 1642: 4-6.

in *The Union* by linking of the life and work of Christ with the workings of reason we can relate this early work to the more fully developed Trinitarianism of *TISU*. For Cudworth this active participatory process is only developed in direct engagement with the external world. Therefore all ethical actions should be judged as part of man's participation with God through the correct application of his reason. As a consequence political actions are essentially a development of a deeper theological relationship. In this fully participatory nature Cudworth argues, man emancipates himself from the dangers of self-love that typified the stale, legalistic relationship found in systems of arbitrary authority. As we have seen such legalistic constraints are only required, Cudworth argues, if man turns away from the higher intellectual principles. At the heart of the ethical community are not a set of proscriptive legal, doctrinal or liturgical principles, but a collective acceptance by the members of that community that they have a responsibility to participate individually with the divine and through this come to a collective understanding of the truth of God's wisdom. Cudworth's conception of the ethical community as a participatory structure of equal moral actors underpins Cudworth's liberal theology. However, to say that Cudworth's theology is 'liberal' is not to say that it lacks a firm basis. As Sarah Hutton has noted, 'Cudworth's liberal theology entails a conception of God, the fixity of which might appear to belie the latitude of his religious views.'[24] This latitude relies on the active divine principle that we have seen Cudworth develop systematically and consistently through all his theology and philosophy. In political terms Cudworth allows all to be members of the community. Consequently membership of the ethical community has a breadth that it is available to all, but also has definition in that all members of that community must recognise the eternal and immutable principles of the divine that define the created order. Cudworth argues that the emancipation of man, the life of 'God's freeman', can only come when man is loosed from the strictures of legalism; only if man completely accepts that all creation is defined by the overflowing love of the divine can he be truly at liberty.

Cudworth defines this in the language of 'love' in *The Union*, however, it would be wrong to assume that this is an amorphous principle. Love is, in these early writings, synonymous with Cudworth's later understanding of the reason of God's intellect. As Cudworth stated in his *First Sermon*, five years after the publication of *The Union*, 'God who is

---

[24] Sarah Hutton, 'Ralph Cudworth: God, Mind, and Nature': 62.

absolute goodness, cannot love any of his Creatures & take pleasure in
them, without bestowing a communication of his goodness and Likeness
upon them.'[25] This principle of 'love' can be equated with the link that
Cudworth, following Whichcote, made between reason and the grace of
God. Love, in this context, exists as the animating and verifiable presence
of God in creation which Cudworth, in *TISU*, links more explicitly to the
reasoned mind of God expressed to creation in the incarnation of the
Logos.

In *The Union* Cudworth also equates the love of God with the principle
of natural law. Citing the scholarship of the English legal theorist and
scholar of Jewish prophesy John Selden, Cudworth argues that the example of the marriage of Christ and the human Church is not only confirmed
by the evidence of the Epistle to the Ephesians, but also supported by the
principles of natural law.[26] Cudworth's use of Selden in this context is
interesting with regards to the political implications of these texts. Cudworth was, at this time, well acquainted with Selden. It appears that the
young Cudworth's reputation as a scholar of Jewish prophesy had caught
the attention of the older Selden. It is not clear who made the first
approach, but through the early years of the 1640s Selden and Cudworth
corresponded. These letters, which are now held with Selden's papers
in the Bodleian Library, largely discuss the minutiae of Jewish texts.
However they also show the high regard in which Cudworth was held in
the eyes of the older and more illustrious Selden. They also reveal something of Cudworth's understanding and interest in Selden's more well
known ideas on natural law. In a letter dated 28 November 1643 Cudworth states that 'under yᵉ Christian State, there is scarcily any thing of
Jus Divinum [the 'Divine Right' claimed by Charles I] besides the Universal and Catholick Law of Nature.'[27] This statement, which could have

---

[25] *First Sermon*: 102.
[26] *The Union*: 33.
[27] Letter of Ralph Cudworth to John Selden, Bod MS Selden Supra, 108-9: 270.
Cudworth's comment here draws on Selden's reputation as a Natural Law Theorist.
Explicit arguments for Natural Law are not necessarily apparent in Cudworth. However
Nathaniel Culverwell, often included as one of the Cambridge Platonists despite his more
orthodox Calvinism, was clearly influence by Selden. For Culverwell's relationship to
Selden see Nathaniel Culverwell, *An Elegant and Learned Discourse on the Light of
Nature*, edited by Robert A. Greene and Hugh MacMullum. Toronto: University of
Toronto Press, 1971: xiv, xxiv, xxxiii; also Jason P. Rosenblatt, *Renaissance England's
Chief Rabbi: John Selden*. Oxford: OUP, 2006. For Culverwell's tempered Cambridge
Platononism, particularly with relation to his theory of Natural Law, see Knud Haakonssen,
Natural Law and moral philosophy: From Grotius to the Scottish Enlightenment. Cam-
bridge: CUP, 1996: 50.

been meant to flatter Selden, does hint at a potential, if guarded, political radicalism in the young Cudworth. If we can take this statement at face value then it does seem to suggest that Cudworth was intellectually opposed to the 'Jus Divinum' claims of the Stuart monarchy. It also seems to allow for a fuller explanation of why Cudworth was, like Selden, so willing a supporter of those who opposed the King during the Civil War.[28] Above all Cudworth's defence of the supremacy of natural law gives us a sense of his interpretation and definition of the political realm. As we have seen in earlier chapters, Cudworth argues at all times that the world is created and defined by the grace of God and revealed to man through the love and reason of the divine. The ascription of the principles of natural law to the creative principle of the divine means that for Cudworth the freedom which man's ethical nature aspires to can only be found through man's strict adherence to the divinely ordained principles of natural law. The seeming paradoxical nature of this relationship is not lost on Cudworth. At one point in the *First Sermon* he comments that 'Love is at once a Freedome from all Law, a State of purest Liberty, and yet a Law too, of the most constraining and indispensable Necessity.'[29] However, this paradox in Cudworth's political utterances is again clarified with reference to his intellectualism. Man can reject the love of God, but true freedom can only come with the free acceptance of God's love. This action of free choice is only possible because God's love is, for Cudworth, universal and unchanging.

The external 'political' acts of man are, therefore, always dependent on the existence of unchanging internal 'intellectual' principles of God. The seeming paradox that an internal action can confirm an external community in Cudworth's philosophy in part explains how this political aspect is so difficult to account for. On one level one could reason that such is Cudworth's concentration on the internal working of the intellect that the external and political becomes secondary and of lesser importance. However, as Cudworth argues in his manuscripts — particularly *FM*.4983 which is misleadingly titled 'On the eternity of the torments' — the relationship of internal to the external is not one of hierarchy but one of equality. The dangers of human sin and self-will are so great that man's personal, internal, love of God is not enough in itself to overcome

---

[28] For Selden's place in the Civil War see, Richard Tuck, '"The Ancient Law of Freedom": John Selden and the Civil War' in *Reactions to the English Civil War: 1642-1649*, edited by John Morrill. London: Macmillan, 1982.

[29] *First Sermon*: 124. The importance of this paradox in Cudworth has been noted by C.A. Patrides, ed., *The Cambridge Platonists*: 124, n. 88.

it. Instead, he argues, that sin can only defeated if both parts of the 'New Covenant' are fulfilled, to love God and to love one's neighbour. In this manuscript Cudworth states that the political realm (as with his attitude to the Church in *The Union*) takes on something of the form of the body of Christ on earth reflecting both the divinity and humanity of Christ. Consequently man's individual appreciation of this divinity through his participation in the divine image, leads to a collective, even democratic, recognition of this participation in the humanity of other men. The unity of men through Christ by reason, therefore, is not only confirmed but necessarily completed by the ethical actions of men in the world. As Cudworth states in *FM*.4983, 'yᵉ Love of God is too weak a principle to conquer sin yᵉ great duty of Xian law is to love God and love men'[30] The creation of the ethical community is the central purpose and responsibility of life, as it is only through this political mechanism, Cudworth states, that men create the means through which their participatory relationship with God is fulfilled.

Individual moral certainty

For Cudworth the ethical community is formed by the collective action of individual moral actors. This would seem to present the recipe for chaos. After all, Cudworth was writing at a time when England had been arguably torn apart by the continual claims of different, individual beliefs. However, Cudworth's philosophy, although advocating pluralism, is not saying that this would be groundless. Rather it would be given firm foundations, made 'real', by the eternal and immutable principles of God's wisdom. Such is the solidity provided by the eternal and immutable principles of God that Cudworth argues that these ethical truths can be known with the same certainty as man can come to know the laws of mathematics.[31] Such a claim naturally places Cudworth in agreement with Benjamin Whichcote's aphorism that '[i]n *Morality*, we are sure as in *Mathematics*.'[32] Cudworth's use of the *Meno* shows that ethical principles can be known through the same process by which mathematical principles are known, by the intellect judging and understanding the form and nature of the created realm. Or, as Cudworth put it, 'they are all as

---

[30] *FM*.4978: 100.
[31] *EIM*: 88.
[32] Benjamin Whichcote, *Moral and Religious Aphorisms*, edited by W.R. Inge. London: Elkin Matthews and Marrot: 298.

it were ectypal prints…and derivative signatures…from one archetypal intellect, that is essentially the *rationes* of all things and all verities.'[33]

On the most practical level Cudworth argues that this can be shown by refuting the nominalist belief that ethical norms can be determined by the naming of things. Such a position, which Cudworth identifies in the philosophy of Hobbes, fatally confuses the means for the ends.[34] Words are an important means to transport and transfer knowledge. They are, however, only the means of transport. Just as a physical, external stimulus could remind the mind of some innate principle, so words on the page will bring out of the mind of man the 'inward anticipations of learning.'[35] Without the intellect of man to interpret or understand these words they might as well be little more than 'several scrawls of lines of ink drawn upon white paper.'[36] This idea of the active nature of divine law, as opposed to the stale language of legalism, is present throughout the arguments of Cudworth's *First Sermon*. In an argument directed against what he perceives to be the limitations of ethical legalism he argues:

> The Gospel, that new Law which Christ delivered to the world, it is not merely a *Letter* without us, but a *quickening Spirit* within us. Cold Theorems and Maximes, dry and jejune Disputes, lean syllogistical reasonings, could never yet of themselves beget the least glympse of true heavenly light, the least sap of saving knowledge in any heart.[37]

Ethical principles, therefore, cannot be summed up merely in a form of words or a set legalistic code. Rather these written codes act as a means by which each moral actor comes to know the truth and profundity of these moral laws in the actions of their every day lives.

That is not to say that Cudworth argues that this active process of knowing and understanding ethical principles is infallible. The failings that occur comes not from the imperfection of divine principles, but in the fallibility of the mind of man.[38] If the mind is working correctly it is, Cudworth argues, 'clearly and mathematically demonstrable from what we have already proved that there is some eternal mind.'[39] Man, therefore, needs to 'listen to one and the same original voice of the eternal voice which is never silent.'[40] The source of this voice is the intellect of God

---

[33] *EIM*: 131.
[34] *EIM*: 116.
[35] *EIM*: 99.
[36] *EIM*: 99.
[37] *First Sermon*: 92.
[38] *EIM*: 136; Passmore, *Ralph Cudworth*: 22.
[39] *EIM*: 130.
[40] *EIM*: 132.

expressed to the world in the persons of the Trinity. More accurately in the expression of the *Logos* which Cudworth describes in the *EIM* as 'the eternal and first-begotten offspring of the first original goodness.'[41] This perceptive power which Cudworth outlines in *EIM* mirrors the divine power of understanding which Cudworth argues for in *TISU*. The *Logos* acts as the divinely ordained means by which man can come to know of the existence, form, and nature of the divine in the world. This in turn leads man to the Spirit, where, through a consistent and reasoned engagement with the created world, man is able to find the consistent and reasoned expression of God's love and intellect in all parts of creation.

As the principle of the divine intellect permeates every aspect of reality it necessarily becomes the means by which, according to Cudworth, an ethical community can be created. All ethical principles have their source in the intellect of the divine. Any man, as long as he attempts to understand these truths in the correct way, can come to the same conclusion as other members of the community. Cudworth argues that by asserting the unifying power of the divine intellect, his theory allows him to overcome the arbitrariness and uncertainty created by Hobbist nominalism. So just as Cudworth argues that the written word can be understood because it stimulates intellectual principles in the reader, so it is possible for men to exist harmoniously in an ethical community because the members of that community 'partake of one and the same intellect.'[42]

Beyond these comments on the creation and maintenance of the ethical community there is very little in *EIM* to suggest in detail how this ethical community would be constituted. However, in Cudworth's manuscripts there are some suggestions of the form that he conceived the ethical community taking. It is clear from *EIM* and from the desire to allow for 'Distributive *or* Retributive Justice' that Cudworth makes in *TISU*, that this ethical community would be made up from independent, self-determining and, eventually, independently judged moral actors.[43] Cudworth's argument here is a extension of his rejection of the ethical legalism of contemporary Calvinism and arbitrary legalism of Hobbism. For Cudworth, ethical legalism, like other forms of arbitrary authority, suggests that man could not be held personally responsible, or be individually judged, for his actions.

Cudworth's attack on legalism can also be shown by his concentration on goodness over duty in his ethical writings. Although duty and

---

41 *EIM*: 132.
42 *EIM*: 131.
43 *TISU*: v.

obedience are important, it is essential for Cudworth that obedience is given freely for the action to carry any form of ethical validity.[44] From this position we can begin to place many of Cudworth's early attacks from his *First Sermon* on the dangers of 'self-love' in a broader ethical and political framework. As with his use of 'self' constructs in his freewill manuscripts, Cudworth concentrates on *self*-love because he is concerned with the status and role of the individual in his moral theory. As we have seen Cudworth argues that man's freewill is an 'amphibious' thing; as capable of going in one direction as the other. Therefore, the threat of self-love is so great precisely because the individual is the defining principle in ethical discussion. Just as he stresses the virtuous possibilities of the individual in his ethical philosophy, particularly his definition of the *self*-determining power of the individual; so his concern with *self*-love stresses the dangers presented when ethical responsibility is placed in the hands of the individual. Arguably in a system such as Hobbes' the dangers of selfish egoism are removed by the imposition of a strict, legalistic ethical code on all in civil society. However, Cudworth rejects this because such a system denies the importance of the individual in the ethical community. Cudworth, in this sense, makes a rod for his own back, asserting on the one hand the dangers implicit in the excesses of individualism, whilst trying to create an ethical system entirely based on the virtuous actions of individuals. There is, therefore, in Cudworth's ethical and political ideas, a constant structural danger of a descent into anarchy driven by the hedonism of self-love. He appears to be aware of, and willing to risk, this danger. He is confident that the dangers of self-love can be defeated if the virtues and liberty which he asserts can be found in the divine are asserted as the central aim of humanity. As he argues in his *First Sermon*:

> Happinesse is nothing but that inward sweet delight, that will arise from the Harmonious agreement between our wills and Gods will. There is nothing contrary to God in the whole world, nothing that fights against him but *Self will.*[45]

This release from selfishness allows man to discover the liberty which he can only find in the love of God. Following the dictates of Christ, as the principle of the divine intellect, means that man 'will not be put in a State of Bondage, but of Perfect Liberty.'[46]

---

[44] Passmore, *Ralph Cudworth*: 51, 68.
[45] *First Sermon*: 98.
[46] *First Sermon*: 126.

Cudworth's terminology here is interesting. Hobbes, for instance, makes no qualitative distinction between actions that are done by 'freedom' or those carried out through 'liberty.' Sometimes Cudworth, like Hobbes, uses these terms interchangeably, discussing, for instance, both the 'freedom of the will' and the 'liberty of the will.' However, Cudworth at times, particularly within his manuscripts, makes a qualitative distinction between the actions of 'freedom,' and the state of 'liberty.' In this sense, for him, all men possess freewill. This allows men to aspire to become, in the terms of the *Second Sermon,* 'God's freeman.' Man's freewill is also a fallible faculty leading, as it can, to life as 'Sin's freeman.' The bondage which comes from the sinful life is a direct consequence of man's freedom, and consequently men are responsible for these sinful actions. 'Liberty', by contrast, is used by Cudworth to describe both a faculty and a state. A state of 'liberty' in Cudworth's philosophy only occurs when man's virtuous action leads to pure communion with the divine. Cudworth, therefore, makes a particular linguistic distinction between the 'freedom' and 'free powers' which man possesses and the 'liberty' which he is attempting to achieve with those powers. The supremacy of 'liberty' over mere freedom is confirmed by Cudworth in *FM*.4979 where Cudworth argues that 'liberty is only in good.'[47] For Cudworth all men are free, but only those who follow the higher principles of the mind can achieve liberty. As Cudworth argues in his *Treatise on Freewill*, 'he who has liberty has conquered himself.'[48]

The political oath

Cudworth's vision of politics develops out of his Trinitarian theology. For Cudworth the political realm is not divorced from the theological basis of reality, rather, the political is simply another manifestation of the divinely informed nature of creation. This created realm is expressed, as we have seen Cudworth argue throughout his writings, in its fullest and truest form by the Trinity. Political actions, therefore, follow the same participatory form that ethical actions do; using reason to draw man to the inherent reasonableness of God. Reason is given to man by God so that he can freely choose whether or not he participates in this relationship.

---

[47] *FM*.4979: 40.
[48] *TFW*: 167.

Underlying this is the creative intellect of God. As Cudworth states in the *TISU*:

> there are yet other *Phaenomena*, no less *Real*, though not *Physiological*, which *Atheists* can no way *Salve*; as that of *Natural Justice*, and *Honesty*, Duty, and Obligation; the true Foundation both of *Ethicks* and *Politicks*; and the...*Liberty of Will*, properly so called.[49]

Freewill, when used correctly, lifts man from his baser emotions to the higher virtues of justice and equity, principles only found in the liberty of the divine. Although this is a common theme throughout all Cudworth's writings, there is a political necessity derived from this principle. He argues that man can, as a self-determined moral actor, learn and know the correct, ethically virtuous path to take in life. However this life is, he argues, futile if it remains a private concern. The ethical life implies for Cudworth the discarding of private interest for the greater good of the wider community. In the preface to his *First Sermon* Cudworth, perhaps a little sycophantically, suggests that the members of the House of Commons, if they considered the public good, would 'reflect so much lustre and honour back upon yourselves.'[50] We find the same argument in *TISU*. In the concluding section of the whole work Cudworth calls for a society in which the good of the public always rises above the wants of the private individual.[51] It is in this political aspect in the mature writings of Cudworth, of civil society defined and controlled by the dictates of divine justice, that we find the fullest expression of Cudworth's belief in living the Christian life through the creation of an ethical community.[52]

Cudworth's intentions in this endeavour are clear, but in his published works there is very little to make one believe that these claims are little more than the idle wishes of a cloistered academic. To find the true implications of Cudworth's political utterances we have to delve below the surface of not only these sections of his published works, but also sections of his manuscripts, to find exactly how he envisaged such an ethical community taking shape. Cudworth's political arguments are most clearly seen in his discussion of political oaths. It is not a surprise to see Cudworth drawing on these examples in his writings. The codification of

---

[49] *TISU*: 690.
[50] Ralph Cudworth, 'Preface' to 'A Sermon Preached before the Honourable The House of Commons, On March 31st, 1647,' in *Cambridge Platonists Spirituality* edited by Charles Taliferro and Alison J. Teply. Mahwah NJ: Paulist Press, 2004: 58.
[51] *TISU*: 898.
[52] *TISU*: 697, 896.

matters of conscience in oaths was a recurring political tool throughout the seventeenth century. As David Martin Jones argues, 'the oath... constituted a singular mechanism for attempting to secure an English *universitas*, a unified and incorporated English body politic.'[53] Oaths acted as political punctuation marks through the political upheavals of the century, with nine different oaths being put forward in Cudworth's lifetime, seven of them during the twenty years between the outbreak of the Civil War and the Restoration.[54] Cudworth, as a prominent member of the University, would have been required to take many of these oaths. At a minimum he would have been required to take the 'Solemn League and Covenant' to keep his fellowship during the Earl of Manchester's purge in 1644, 'The Engagement' in 1650 confirming the legitimacy of the Republic, and the oath of allegiance at the Restoration to keep his place as Master of Christ's. Cudworth later took the oaths attached to the Clarendon Code which explicitly denied oaths previously taken, particularly the 'Solemn League and Covenant.'[55] The use of these oaths as political instruments opens up two readings of Cudworth's attitude to political matters. On one hand, Cudworth's apparent willingness in acquiescing to the changing political climate would seem to confirm the common view of Cudworth, and the other Cambridge Platonists, as politically quietist. However, viewed in conjunction with his writings on these issues, a much more subtle and politically astute image of Cudworth emerges. Cudworth's use of the political oath, when understood in the context of his arguments for freewill and moral responsibility, show how he argues that it is possible to rise above the contemporary political wrangling that accompanied these oaths. Cudworth, instead, asserts the oath as a practical means by which the individual could show his ethical responsibility and moral goodness in political society, whatever the political colour of the current regime.

The clearest means of examining Cudworth's writings in this area is by a comparison with Hobbes' writings on the same issue. Quentin Skinner argues that Hobbes' arguments for oaths and allegiance to political authority should be understood in the context of the 'Engagement Crisis'

---

[53] David Martin Jones, *Conscience and Allegiance in Seventeenth century England: The Political significance of Oaths and Engagements*. Rochester, NY: University of Rochester Press, 1999: 15.

[54] Jones, *Conscience and Allegiance*: 115, 272-81.

[55] Twigg, *University of Cambridge*: 293-7 & 302-3. Cudworth subscription to the Act of Uniformity is recorded in Bod. MS Rawlinson, B375: 5b. Also see Jones, *Conscience and Allegiance*: 280.

which immediately followed the execution of the King in 1649. Following the regicide, there was a pressing need to legitimise the new political regime in a form that would make it more than simply the usurper of the authority of the King. One of the clearest defences for the new regime came in John Milton's *The Tenure of Kings and Magistrates*, published in 1650. In this Milton, as chief propagandist to the Commonwealth, defends the regicide in terms of natural law. The King had been lawfully executed, Milton argues, because Charles I was acting as a tyrant. The regicide was, therefore, the re-assertion of the natural right of men to limit the powers of government.[56] However, Milton's argument could never create obligation to the new regime from those who believed that the King ruled by divine right, and so was not bound by the dictates of natural law. From this impasse developed a new form of argument for allegiance, which based political obligation solely on the *de facto* power of the regime. Allegiance was drawn not from philosophical or theological principles, but from the physical power of the regime to maintain and control the political order. The chief defenders of this *de facto* argument in England at the time were Anthony Ascham and Marchamont Nedham. Skinner argues that Hobbes, although at the time living in exile in France, was writing in the context of this debate. Although J.G.A. Pocock has argued that many of these *de facto* arguments drew on the Old Testament covenants of the power of the elected Kings of Israel, Skinner argues that the strength of the *de facto* argument was its 'secular' nature.[57] Hobbes argues, primarily in *Leviathan*, that political obligation is defined entirely by the human emotion of fear which initially created political society. Obligation is defined by man's overriding human emotion of the fear of not being dragged back into the chaos of the state of nature. Oaths are therefore, Hobbes argues, not of central importance because the form of words in an oath cannot bind a man more surely to civil society than the bond already created by fear.[58] Although Skinner does not conclusively prove Hobbes' relationship to the Engagement Crisis, we can recognise the way in which Hobbes' arguments

[56] Quentin Skinner, *Visions of Politics*, 3 vols. Cambridge: CUP, 2002: III.288; John Milton, *Political Writings*, edited by Martin Dzelzainis. Cambridge: CUP, 1991: 9-10. The clearest account of the political arguments of the Engagement Crisis is the introduction to John M. Wallace, *Destiny his Choice: the loyalism of Andrew Marvell*. Cambridge: CUP: 1968.
[57] J.G.A. Pocock, *The Political Works of James Harrington*. Cambridge: CUP, 1977: 36; Skinner, *Visions*: III.303.
[58] *Leviathan*: 198, 201.

would have been popular to those politicians wishing to legitimise a civil society created by the fall of an axe.[59]

From Cudworth's perspective there are two major failings of Hobbes' theory. Firstly, it diminishes the political power of the individual. Hobbes' theory does demand the twin obligations of the subject's obedience to the magistrate and the obligation of the magistrate to protect the individual. However, the individual's obligation is not created in the ethical realm of intellectual activity, but rather by the base human reaction of fear. Secondly, a system that bases obligation solely on the *de facto* power of political authority undermines the ability to create a stable political community. This is because, Cudworth argues, that such a society would not be based on rationally verifiable principles of justice, but on who possess the largest sword. As Hobbes argues famously, 'covenants without the Sword, are but Words, and of no strength to secure a man at all.'[60] At the heart of Cudworth's criticisms is his strong assertion that justice is eternal and immutable and so cannot be 'created' by arbitrary power.[61] Political society can never be asserted simply by the will of the sovereign but, as with all parts of creation, it must be understood as a manifestation of the intellect of the divine. Consequently Cudworth's political argument is always reliant on what he sees as the correct understanding of the principles that underpin political society. This argument comes out most clearly in Cudworth's manuscript FM.4980:

> they might have agreem[ts] & Lawes & a leviathan Commonwealth, but yn there could be no other obligation upon any to keep those lawes but only from their own private Utility of wch ymsleves were Judges, no obligation truly morall in y[t] wch would be called Injustice, ye breach of Lawes & Covenants.[62]

Cudworth, as in his ethical arguments, states that the community is only bound together by a collective understanding of the absolute moral norms found in God. This is only achieved if all in that community learn to place aside their lower desires and move, through their freewill, to the higher principles of the divine. As we have seen previously, Cudworth argues that political and religious leaders are only needed if man chooses not to follow the higher intellectual path of personal responsibility. As a consequence it is worth noting that Cudworth does not doubt

[59] Skinner, *Visions*: III.304.
[60] *Leviathan*: 223; Jones, *Conscience and Allegiance*: 153, 164.
[61] *TISU*: 103, 890.
[62] *FM*.4980: 9.

that a Hobbist Civil Sovereign could create effective laws. Rather he argues that the principle of justice would have been arrived at through force and not choice making it implicitly weaker. For instance, Cudworth argues, it is possible to imagine a polity governed by a Civil Sovereign who would proscribe that murder was unjust. Such a conclusion is in keeping with eternal and immutable ethical norms. However, Cudworth argues that because the Leviathan's legitimacy comes from his *de facto* power, he can only prohibit a man from killing another man through an equally destructive threat of force. The laws of the Leviathan, therefore, cannot bind men to them as effectively as Cudworth's model where, through the individual verification, the members of that community bind themselves to the collectively and intellectually understood principles of justice. The vicious circle created by this Hobbesian logic, Cudworth argues, simply leads to the splintering of the society, not because the original law is wrong, but because the legitimacy of the law is based on a political justification that cannot morally bind man to it. He points out the implicit paradox he sees in Hobbes' use of private utility in the *TISU*:

> *Civil Obedience*, cannot be derived...from men's *Private Utility* onely, because every man being Judge of this for himself, it would then be Lawful for any subject, to Rebel against his Sovereign Prince and to Poyson or Stab him, whensoever he could reasonably perswade himself, that it would tend to his own Advantage.[63]

Cudworth contends that Hobbes' argument, in one move, both diminishes the dignity of man and undermines the foundation of the ethical community.

For Cudworth the foundation of any society must always be the wisdom and justice of God. Man, through his freewill, is presented by God with the means by which this community can both be created and exist as a reflection of the intellect of the divine. Interestingly Cudworth does not argue that the Hobbist state is illegitimate as such, but that it qualitatively poorer than the ethical community. For Cudworth the cohesion of the ethical community does not come from dictates or rules of a leader, but from the collective will of the members of that community.

Central to this community is, Cudworth argues, the correct understanding of the oath within the political society. In using this argument Cudworth follows the central seventeenth century belief, undermined by Hobbes' argument, that oaths form the basis of the political organisation of the state. So Cudworth argues in FM.4980:

[63] *TISU*: 698.

> Promises, Pacts, Covenants, & Promisiory Oaths wch men take as a security to ymselves & firmly acquiesce in y^m wn they are made by vertuous persons wch are ye foundations of politicall societies.[64]

What lies behind the use of the oath, Cudworth argues, is the principle of freewill. As he goes on to say in FM.4980, 'Promises, Covenants & promisory Oaths would be Errant Nonsense if a man had no-more power over his future Actions y^n a weather-cock hath of standing North or South tomorrow.'[65] An oath can only ever carry any moral weight if man has freely entered into the oath and accepts that all oaths have been entered into willingly by the other members of that community. The binding quality of an oath carries with it not only an obligation to keep a promise to God, but also a recognition that this promise also requires man to keep and maintain his obligations to the other members of the community. The central building block of Cudworth's political principles, the oath, consequently carries with it dual obligations to God and man. In doing so, it maintains Cudworth's central theological and political principle, already stated, that 'ye great duty of ye X^{ian} laws is to love God & to love men.'[66]

Political obligation

Cudworth's argument for political obligation is a logical development of his ethical theory. For this reason, obligation is not created, as in the Hobbist state, through the force and power of the civil sovereign, but through the participation of the morally responsible individual in a divinely ordained reality. Cudworth's theory of political obligation is, therefore, another facet of his overall theological and philosophical project. The founding principle of political obligation is, Cudworth argues, the eternal and immutable justice expressed by the intellect of God. Man's obligation is, therefore, first and foremost, to the justice of God as the founding principle of reality. As he argues in the *TISU*:

> The *Right* and *Authority* of God himself is Founded in *Justice*; and of this is the Civil Sovereignty also a certain *Participation*. It is not the meer *Creature* of the people, and of men's *Will*, and therefore *Annihilable* again by their *Wills* at pleasure; but hath a *Stamp* of *Divinity* upon it.[67]

---

[64] *FM*.4980: 177.
[65] *FM*.4980: 177.
[66] *FM*.4983: 100.
[67] *TISU*: 896.

Cudworth argues that political society grows naturally out of the reasonable divine principles woven into the fabric of the created realm. Political society is not founded on fear or necessity, but the natural and fullest working out of the ethically virtuous life. As the above quote shows, for Cudworth political society develops naturally out of the eternal principles of justice in the world. Cudworth completely rejects Hobbes' assertion that political society is formed by the creation of an artificial body politic. In contrast, he argues that a just political society cannot be created through the artificial and violent commands of a absolute ruler. Rather, just political society is based upon the ability of the individual political actor to understand the commands given as the natural and lawful commands of a just ruler. This confirmation is brought about by man recognising in political commands not the command but the implicit justice that lies behind those commands. As Cudworth comments in FM.4983, 'y^e: Lawgiver has power to inforce his laws with reasonable penalty, but no Lawgiver has just right to inforce his laws beyond equality and justice.'[68] The means of ensuring this obligation is created, he argues, from each individual's ability to use his reason to recognise the implicit justice, or otherwise, of a command.

There is an implicit weakness created by Cudworth's system. By making obligation dependent on the individual judgment of the justness or otherwise of a specific command, Cudworth opens himself up to accusations of political antinomianism. Cudworth counters this dilemma in two ways. Firstly he argues that, although natural justice is the founding principle of political society, society cannot be so reflexive as to meet and judge every situation with an appeal to natural justice. Consequently he argues that principles of natural justice over time become codified into principles of 'positive justice.' These principles of positive justice are freely commanded by the political leader. The obligation to them is, however, not invested in the power of the commander, but in the assumed natural justice of the command.[69] Secondly, Cudworth further maintains the stability of political society by arguing that obligation to the commands of positive justice should be followed not simply because they follow natural justice, but because to follow legitimate political authority is itself a command of natural justice. This argument for political obedience as a natural good comes out most clearly in his final remarks in *TISU*:

[68] *FM.4983*: 22.
[69] *EIM*: 21.

> Conscience and religion oblige subjects actively to obey all the lawful com-
> mands of the civil sovereigns or legislative powers though contrary to their
> own private appetites, interest and utility; but when these same sovereign
> legislative powers command unlawful things conscience, though it here
> obliges to 'obey God rather than man,' yet does it, not withstanding, oblige
> not to resist.[70]

Cudworth, in this published work, argues that even if the positive commands of the civil sovereign are deemed by the individual to be contrary
to natural justice, the desire to resist is negated by the overriding obligation to the dictates of natural justice not to resist. Cudworth's arguments
for political obligation do, however, vary from this strict line if we examine those occasions where he deals with the same issue in his unpublished
writings. One could go so far as to say that this final clause in *TISU* is
an attempt by Cudworth to allay any fears that the moderate theological
and philosophical position advocated in *TISU* would necessarily undermine the political *status quo*. This would certainly be the case if the
reports of the objections to Cudworth's publishing *TISU*, as discussed in
Chapter Two, were correct. The assertion that Cudworth's unpublished
political views were more radical than those he presented in print would
seem to be backed up when we compare this argument from *TISU* with his
use of the same arguments in *EIM*. Cudworth presents, in *EIM*, a far more
subtle argument for political obligation, in which he asserts that in certain
cases, natural justice can, and should, lead to the resistance of the positive
commands of an arbitrary ruler.

When dealing with the same issue of political obedience, in the those
works which remain unpublished in his lifetime, Cudworth does not make
non-resistance a dictate of natural justice, as he does in *TISU*. Instead he
stresses that the overarching obligation in political society is that all political commands correspond to the dictates of natural justice. In *FM*.4983
Cudworth wrestles with this dilemma arguing:

> ye Laws of ye Land may make a thing unlawful wch is unjust, & yet y^e
> penalty if justifiable & obedience required but ye Supreme power must be
> necessarily lodged & fixt in some hands, for ye preservation of government,
> y^t power must be obeyed, but ye thing therefore does not become just or
> reasonable, it [does] not [make] obligations to ye minds & consciences of
> men any further y^n it is just and equitable, for we are obliged by better &
> more equitable laws within ourselves. To suffer any inconvenience y^n to
> give obedience to laws y^t: are themselves unjust, those who make unjust
> laws, who have ye supreme power in their hands, do not thereby alter y^e

---

[70] *TISU*: 899.

nature of things, & make things unjust, just & just, unjust. They are themselves accountable to a greater power y^n themselves for ye laws they make.[71]

Cudworth does not invest the necessity of political authority with absolute power, it always remains 'accountable to a greater power'. The limits of divinely ordained natural law remain to control and constrain the excessive powers of political authority. For this reason Cudworth argues in these unpublished works that positive commands remain, but only as pragmatic and, consequently, malleable principles. Man is, therefore, only obliged to follow positive commands if they still follow the dictates of natural justice. In Cudworth's terms, the covenant made by man to the political community is not binding in itself. The covenant does not in itself create a new moral entity, rather new covenants are only modifications of man's existing obligation to the eternal and immutable dictates of natural justice. Cudworth does recognise that part of this obligation is to the person of the commander however, unlike in *TISU*, this is not a blind obedience, but an obligation that could be refused if the dictates of natural justice were circumvented by the commander. Cudworth puts this argument like this in *EIM*:

> And it is not the mere will of the commander that makes these positive things to oblige or become due but the nature of things appears evidently from hence because it is not the volition of every one that obligeth, but of a person rightly qualified and invested with lawful authority. And the liberty of commanding is circumscribed within certain bounds and limits, so that if any commander go beyond the sphere and bounds that nature sets him, which are indifferent things, his commands will not at all oblige.[72]

An obvious example of this would be that of the duty of the soldier to his superior officers. In war time, assuming the war is itself has a *just* cause, a soldier is obliged to follow the orders of his superior officer. The soldier is following a positive command, such as attacking a village, which, because of the specific context of that positive command, follows the natural justice implicit in that struggle. However, if the same positive command to attack the same village is given in peacetime the soldier would be obliged to refuse to follow the positive command because at that point in time the positive command was running contrary to the dictates of natural justice. Thus, he argues, that when the positive commands of the commander move beyond the bounds of natural justice they no longer oblige man to follow them. In this way he offers, in *EIM*, a sophisticated defence for a limited right to resistance.

[71] *FM*.4983: 37b.
[72] *EIM*: 21.

Cudworth argues that this occurrence would be impossible in a correctly formed political society. His ideal society is united by the collective realisation of the higher, ethical truths that emanate from the mind of God. The unifying principle being, as in all his moral writings, the assertion that the eternal and immutable principles of justice are available to all men through the use of their reason. Cudworth describes this collective political will when he says that:

> Wherefore *Conscience* also, is in itself not of a *Private* and *Partial*, but of a *Publick* and *Common Nature*; it representing *Divine Laws, Impartial Justice*, and *Equity*, and the *Good of the Whole*, when clashing with our own *Selfish Good*; and *Private Utility*. This is the only thing, that can *Naturally Consociate Mankind* together, lay a Foundation for *Bodies Politick*.[73]

Cudworth's theory relies on the existence of a society made up of autonomous moral actors to exist. Only in a society made up of morally autonomous, self-determined individuals can the collective principles of natural justice be known with certainty by all men. Cudworth's political principles when examined in detail present us with a powerful, almost democratic defence of a society based on equality and justice for all.

For Cudworth the only constant factors in political society are the principles of natural justice that underpin it. The organisation of that society could change as the political institutions of a society are, in Cudworth's mind, simply the pragmatic structures which ensure that the dictates of natural justice are fulfilled within a specific context. For instance, an aristocracy is to be respected, Cudworth argues, because it may, at a certain point in time present the most effective form of government, not because it personally holds any natural virtues in itself. As Cudworth argues pithily in *FM*.4983:

> Nothing does so crave ye esteem of a Nobleman to himself as ye sense of his honour or greatnesse; this he estemes naturall: but if he do go back, but to of 7 ages: he w^d see from how low a degree they are risen to ye condition they are in y^t they will see it is rather owing to ye industry or fortunes or to ye injustice of their ancestry they find they are the possesser of ye advantages.[74]

Cudworth's desire to concentrate on the underlying principles of political society would seem, therefore, to present a means of understanding his own ambiguous political actions. If his actions were true to his philosophy Cudworth would have felt justified in moving his allegiance from the Crown, to Parliament, to the Protectorate, and back to the Crown,

---

[73] *TISU*: 898.
[74] *FM*.4983: 21.

because each presented imperfect manifestations of a positive justice which could open the way to full manifestation of the natural justice discoverable through the perfect political community.

Toleration and the ethical community

In all of Cudworth's writings the nearest we come to a practical account of what this ethical community might look like is through an examination of Cudworth's progressive and influential advocacy for religious toleration. As we have already seen, Cudworth was an active supporter of the Republic and the Protectorate, and it would not be too bold an assertion to state that Cudworth was an active supporter of the religious policy of both these regimes. Certainly at the Restoration Cudworth came under attack for his advocacy of religious tolerance. This can been seen most clearly in the attacks made on him by Ralph Widdrington, a disaffected fellow of Cudworth's College. Through a bitter legal wrangle which dominated Cudworth's professional life in the 1660s Widdrington criticised Cudworth on three grounds. Firstly he attacks Cudworth's role in the readmission of the Jews, complaining that Cudworth had 'been ye protectors... advocate to break the laws and bring in the Jews.'[75] Certainly Cudworth was consulted by Cromwell over the readmission of the Jews and in 1655, before their formal readmission on 14 December, Cudworth met with the Menasseh ben Israel.[76] Secondly Widdrington accuses Cudworth of lax religious observance and discipline in the College. At one point Widdrington complains of the irregular practice in the Chapel and the lack of surplices. Cudworth's failings included, for Widdrington, a certain vanity in dress and his closeness to the previous protectorate regime. As Widdrington claims:

> when the King and government are restored it no salve in Dr Cudworth to wear a velvet coat in the exchange among Merchants and Presbyterians and a cassock when he visits a bishop and both upon the same day. Well had the complainant been ye protectors chaplain or favorite or pensionary or advocate to break the laws and bring in the Jews had he preached to humour the rebels in a short cloak open sleeves and 36 dozen ribband at his knees.[77]

[75] CUL MS Mm.5.48: 15.
[76] David S. Katz, *Philo-Semitism and the Readmission of the Jews to England: 1603-1655*. Oxford: The Clarendon Press, 1982: 234. Also see David S. Katz, *The Jews in the History of England, 1485-1850*. Oxford: The Clarendon Press, 1994.
[77] CUL MS Mm.5.45: 15.

Thirdly, and most importantly, Widdrington criticises Cudworth's continued advocacy for comprehension in religious belief. Widdrington, in his letters of complaint to the King, writes that Cudworth continually states:

> the old dear plea for liberty of conscience and for allowing every conceited fellow to follow the light within and to do everything upon a principle of acceptance as this is to men who desire a greater latitude to walk in than our statute will permit.[78]

The seeming bitterness and pettiness of Widdrington's attacks belie the perceived political danger and radicalism of Cudworth's advocacy for religious tolerance. Importantly Widdrington attacks Cudworth's assertion that the individual, 'every conceited fellow,' is the best judge and arbiter of his own moral actions. Widdrington also alludes to the 'latitude' or breadth of approach in which, as we have seen, Cudworth argues these ethical principles could exist. The ethical life for Cudworth does not, as Widdrington argues, need to be limited and defined by structures or 'statute.' Instead Cudworth, as we have seen, argues that the form of the ethical life can be changeable and moveable as long as the central principles of God's justice and natural law are maintained.

This argument comes through in Cudworth's writing most clearly in his *First Sermon*. Given in the Palace of Westminster against the backdrop of the First Civil War and on the eve of the Second, Cudworth argues passionately for a respect for religious latitude and tolerance in political society. In open criticism of the reactionary religious practices of the Long Parliament and the Westminster Assembly, Cudworth warns that:

> many of us, that pull down idols in churches, may set them up in our hearts; and whilst we quarrel with painted glass, make no scruple at all of entertaining many foul lusts in our souls, and committing continual idolatry with them.[79]

The dogged determination to replace one form of religious exclusivism with another (Laudianism with the Calvinism of the Westminster Assembly) would, Cudworth argues, simply shift and not solve the political turmoil which was, in his view, based on these different forms of religious intolerance. Later in the *First Sermon* Cudworth makes explicit reference to political and military dangers of the self-willed nature of this religious exclusivism when he states that 'carnal and fleshy zeal is like gunpowder set on fire, that tears and blows up all that stands before it.'[80]

---

[78] CUL MS Mm.5.24: 14b-15.
[79] Cudworth, 'Preface': 56.
[80] *First Sermon*: 119.

Cudworth argues that the only practical means of creating 'a good peace, well settled in a commonwealth' is if, quoting from *Isaiah*:

> the wolf shall dwell with the lamb, and the leopard shall lie down with the kid, and calf, and the young lion, and the fatling together, and a little child lead them...for the earth shall be full of the knowledge of the Lord, as the waters cover the sea.[81]

Even after the failed experiment of the Republic and the Protectorate Cudworth continued publicly and privately to advocate religious toleration as the basis for a sound political settlement. In his *Second Sermon*, preached in early 1664 when the level and extent of comprehension and toleration within the Church was a particularly live issue, Cudworth calls for the Church to be the union of all reformed beliefs, as otherwise the reformed Church would be 'pulled into complete confusion and ruin by infinite sects and divisions.'[82] This view of the broad nature of the Church is backed up by a letter to the Dutch Remonstrant Peter van Limborch, in 1674, in which he calls for the Church of England to be 'a Noah's ark' of comprehension, in which all reformed religious groups, Calvinists, Remonstrants and even Socinians could live together.[83] For Cudworth the exact structure of the Church was of secondary importance to the role it played in the political realm, as he argues in *FM*.4983, 'I would understand ye temple to be a type of the universal society of Christians, ye true temple of God.'[84] Religious pluralism, therefore, provides the basis for a society in which freely willed individuals are able to live and to interact peaceably with one another.

Beyond these writings on religious toleration there is no evidence that Cudworth supported the wholesale reform of the political community. However, what Cudworth did advocate is a reformation in the method by which the legitimacy and sovereignty of a political society was defined. Political liberty is created, he argues, by the collective appreciation of the divinely inspired principles of justice in the world. For Cudworth the motor for this collective understanding of justice is the reasoning faculties man posses through the expression of the reason of God's intellect to all parts creation by the persons of the Trinity. However, the central argument to be taken forward from Cudworth's idea of religious toleration is that man is only able to achieve the liberty found in the divine in

---

[81] Cudworth, 'Preface': 56-7.

[82] *Second Sermon*: 255.

[83] Letter from Cudworth to Limborch, 16 March, 1674, quoted in Hutton, 'Liberty and Self-determination': 82-3.

[84] *FM*.4978: 20.

a world defined and controlled by morally determined individuals. The political community, he argues, has to be liberated from the legalism of statute and from fixed organisation as an end in itself. These forms and institutions must be understood as the pragmatic constructs around which the fundamental, divinely inspired, principles of justice and equity can be maintained. What we find in Cudworth is a shift in the justification of political legitimacy away from the traditional principle of self-preservation or divine fiat, to a legitimacy which is entirely defined and maintained by the individual. Cudworth's argument for political legitimacy and obligation relies on the self-conscious movement of man away from the bounds of ethical legalism, to the position of individual moral responsibility. To borrow the terminology from Cudworth's *Second Sermon,* political legitimacy is created when man develops from 'God's bondsman' to 'God's freeman.'

Cudworth's political utterances, however sparse they may be, play a vital role on the definition of Cudworth's philosophy. Firstly, they continue his movement away from the limitations of arbitrary authority in whatever form it took. Secondly they show the way in which the political individual, 'the little commonwealth of man' was defined by Cudworth as a divinely ordained means to recognise the justice of God. For Cudworth political legitimacy is identified by the collective acceptance of the justice of a political institution. The source and confirmation of this legitimacy relies on the existence of human agency which, as we have seen, Cudworth argues is created and defined by the differing expressions of the reasoned form of God by the persons of the Trinity. Consequently in Cudworth's philosophy we can identify a symbiotic relationship between his theology, particularly his Trinitarianism, and his ethical and political thought. The identification of this theological principle is found not only in Cudworth's writings but in the practical working out of the Puritan anti-Calvinist position he always espoused. So for Cudworth the salvation of man still comes by the explicit action of God's grace alone. However, man has to choose to accept and use the grace given freely and lovingly by God in all areas of life, including the political, if he is to achieve reconciliation with God and salvation. The political working out of Cudworth's theological arguments present an important bridge between the political cultures that blighted his own lifetime, and the more progressive political ideas, based on the political responsibility of the individual, which marked the political ideas of the final decades of the seventeenth century.

CHAPTER SIX

'THE REAL TRINITY':
CUDWORTH IN LATE SEVENTEENTH-CENTURY
ENGLISH THEOLOGY

Cudworth died on June 26, 1688 at the age of 71. An account of his death given in the 'Memoirs' describes how he was taken ill during a journey to London and carried back to Cambridge through the night so that he could die at his home of the previous thirty-four years, Christ's College.[1] It is there that Cudworth is buried next to Henry More who predeceased him by three years. Their grave stones now lie under the altar in the college chapel with a commemorative plaque, to both men, on the wall of an anteroom of the chapel. The account of Cudworth's death given in the 'Memoir' states that Cudworth was, even on his deathbed, railing against heresy in theology. In particular Cudworth is said to have '*believed not anything at all of Deism.*' The source of this information is said to have thought that Cudworth's comments might have shown a rejection of theism by the ailing man, so much so that he died 'a very Infidel.' However, the author of the 'Memoirs' suggests that these comments against Deism were in reality a confirmation of Cudworth's 'steadfast Attachment to Xianty.'[2] There is no source given for these comments and so it is impossible to know whether this account has any truth in it all. It is a surprise to find such a detailed account of the death of a man whose life has left so little in terms of definite biographical detail. However, it is possible to surmise that this account of Cudworth's death shows that he held, until the end of his life, a critical view of contemporary developments in theology, particular the growing rational, anti-Trinitarian theology of Deism. Certainly Cudworth seems to have been aware of the growing trends of Deism, commenting on them in his commonplace book in the mid 1680s, seeming to show that Cudworth was both intellectually active and curious

---

[1] Cudworth continued in his post as Master and Bursar of Christ's until his death. College records show his active involvement in College business until a few days before his death. However the marked deterioration of his handwriting in the last few entries, particularly one on June 23rd, seems to suggest a swift decline his health in the final weeks of his life: Christ's College MS C.6.13.1: 53.

[2] 'Memoirs of Ralph Cudworth': 29-30.

until his death.[3] This is evidenced not only by his commonplace book but by his continued and active role as Master and Bursar of Christ's until his death. With relation to this study we can see that Cudworth retained an active interest in and defence of what he understood as Christian orthodoxy right to the end of his life. Certainly it was this aspect of his theology, particularly with reference to his understanding of the Trinity, which dominated the reception and use of his work in the immediate years following his death.

As has been argued throughout this book, the Trinity is the *leitmotif* of Cudworth's philosophy. The particular character of his Trinitarian theology, particularly his use of an immanent account of the Trinity, placed him at odds not only with anti-Trinitarians, but also with more orthodox Trinitarians. However, Cudworth's account of the Trinity was championed by some theologians, who like Cudworth, wished to defend the doctrines of Christianity against the attacks of theological heterodoxy and philosophical innovation. It would be incorrect to say that Cudworth caused the increase in debates on the Trinity in the later decades of the seventeenth century. However, his strong defence of the Trinity inevitably made him a central, if unwitting, actor in these debates. Orthodox thinkers like John Turner attacked Cudworth's introduction of Cartesian thought into questions of Christian orthodoxy. As a consequence Cudworth's Trinitarian theology not only provided a means by which his thought was transmitted in the years after his death, but also acted as one of the central means by which the categories of Cartesianism was first debated in English theology and philosophy. William Sherlock adopted and stretched Cudworth's immanent account of the Trinity bringing, unwittingly on Cudworth, the castigations of the orthodox Robert South, and the ridicule of the Unitarian Stephen Nye. Most importantly Cudworth's account of the Trinity provides us with an intellectual model through which we can trace the use of his theology and philosophy by Latitudinarian divines such as John Tillotson and Edward Fowler. This intellectual link helps confirm the already clear biographical relationship that existed between the Cambridge Platonists and the Latitudinarians. More importantly the importance of the Trinity to both Cudworth and the Latitudinarians shows the manner in which these liberal thinkers sought to maintain the efficacy of Christian doctrine against the structures of high-churchmen, and the radicalism of heterodox thinkers such as Socinians, Unitarians, and Deists. This middle position, which as we

---

[3] *FM*: 4984: 17-9. Also Passmore, *Ralph Cudworth*: 108.

have seen Cudworth sought to take in all things, is arguably his most important contribution to English theological discussion. The moderation and temperance which typifies Cudworth's Puritan anti-Calvinism, can be traced through to the Latitudinarians many of whom developed, like Cudworth, as Puritan critics of Calvinist orthodoxy. In particular, through a concentration on the Trinity, it is possible to trace in the Latitudinarians the same direct link that we have traced in Cudworth from the tri-unity of God through the reasoned inner reformation of man to an advocacy for the Christian life as the practical and tolerant engagement with all members of society. Although not providing a intellectual manifesto to these men, Cudworth's work acted as an intellectual pattern through which the individual could engage with the world within the models and doctrines of orthodox Christianity.

Early criticisms of Cudworth's Trinitarianism

In 1706 Thomas Wise presented an edited and abridged version of the *TISU* published as *A Confutation of the Reason and Philosophy of Atheism*. Even in the abridged form this volume ran to over five hundred pages. What is of more interest than this project of abridgement, is the introduction to the volume which gives us a clear insight into Cudworth's intellectual reputation in the decades following his death in 1688. The overriding theme of this introduction is the use and abuse of Cudworth's theology in the debates on the Trinity. As Wise states:

> there has hardly been a Pamphlet or Book writ for some years about the *Blessed Trinity* especially in *England* ... which does not bring in Dr. *Cudworth* upon the Stage, and vouch his Name and Quotations for the Purpose.[4]

The most vehement early attack on Cudworth's Trinitarianism came from John Turner, a fellow Christ's College, where Cudworth was Master. In his *Discourse concerning the Messias* published in 1685, Turner sees clearly that Cudworth's concentration on the Trinity *ad intra* was designed to counter the dangers presented by contemporary Trinitarian heresies, particularly the supposed 'Sabellianism' of Hobbism.[5] However, Turner

---

[4] Wise, *Confutation*: 25-6.
[5] Turner, *Discourse*: xvi. The earliest published attack on Cudworth's *TISU* was the Jesuit John Warner who added a letter to Cudworth to his *Anti-Haman* published in 1679. See John Warner, *Anti-Haman, or an Answer to M.G. Burnet's "Mistery of Iniquiti unvailed"... To which is annexed a letter to R. Cudworth, By W.E. Student of Divinity.* Amsterdam, 1679.

argues that Cudworth in stressing the individual substances of the persons of the Trinity, had in fact reduced the Trinity to Tritheism.[6] The heart of Turner's criticism of Cudworth is a rejection of Cudworth's ascription to the Trinity the qualities of *res cogitans*. In making this criticism of Cudworth's Trinitarianism Turner is calling into question the efficacy of Cudworth's use of Cartesian categories. In particular Turner turns on Cudworth's interpretation of *homoousious*. As we have seen, Cudworth defines this term as meaning a unity of essence, and not of number. This unity of essence is, Cudworth argues, provided by the indivisible form of immaterial and thinking substance. Turner argues that this distinction is illogical, for to claim that God shares the same indivisible and eternal substance is merely to create *one* God, and that further persons of the Trinity are merely lesser, subordinate Gods sharing a similar, *not* the same entity. In this manner Turner argues that Cudworth's Trinitarianism is merely a reversion to Arianism.[7]

In answer to Cudworth's Trinitarianism Turner presents two arguments which are of historical and philosophical interest. Firstly he reverts to an economic interpretation of the Trinity, defining the Trinity in terms of the operations and qualities of the persons of the Trinity, rather than Cudworth's language of essence and substance. Secondly, Turner develops this traditional economic account of the Trinity in such a way as to undermine the assumptions of Cartesian *res cogitans* used by Cudworth. Turner argues, as previous economic accounts of the Trinity had, that the qualities of the persons of the Trinity revealed something of their own shared eternal unity. However, developing from his criticism of Cudworth, Turner asserts that this substance, whilst being eternal and immaterial, is at the same time extendable, and this extension explains the different workings of the three persons of the one Trinitarian God:

> The *Father* is the *simple divine substance* by *himself*, the *Son* is the *vital Union* of an *human Soul* to the *Substance* and *Person* of *God* the *Father*, and the *Holy Ghost* is nothing else but an *Æternal* and *Emanitive matter*, *vitally united* to both the former. That which make them all to be *God*, is the same *Numerical Divine Substance* belonging to them all, and that which makes the distinction of the *Persons* is the addition of a *Created immaterial nature*, in the *Second Person* of the *Blessed Trinity*, of a *Created material one* in the *third* and the substration or precision of *both* of these in the *first*.[8]

[6] Turner, *Discourse*: xxix.
[7] Turner, *Discourse*: xxiii-xxix.
[8] Turner, *Discourse*: cliv.

The principle that runs through Turner's definition of the Trinity is that the divine substance that vitally unites the persons of the Trinity is extendible. Turner's interpretation of immaterial substance, therefore, openly rejects Cudworth's use of the Cartesian model of immaterial substance.[9]

Wise, despite being a self-confessed disciple of Cudworth's attacks on atheism, also expressed opposition to Cudworth's account of the Trinity. It is possible to see aspects of Turner's rejection of Cudworth in Wise's more reserved commentary on Cudworth's Trinitarianism. In the introduction to his *Confutation* Wise, like Turner, criticises Cudworth's definition of *homoousious*. However Wise's criticisms, as one might expect, are much more charitable that those of Turner. Where Turner criticised the philosophical underpinnings of Cudworth's Trinitarianism, Wise merely saw the attacks on Cudworth as a misunderstanding of terms.[10] Wise argues that Cudworth was misunderstood because of the 'manner of his expression.'[11] Although Wise presents an over simplified account of the use of Cudworth's account of the Trinity, the mere existence of these criticisms is instructive for two reasons. Firstly, Wise's introduction confirms the central role that the Trinity played in Cudworth's thought. Secondly, Wise's introduction shows how the reception of Cudworth's work concentrated on his Trinitarianism, rather than his attacks on atheism. In fact it is possible to argue that it was Wise's abridgement of *TISU*, rather than *TISU* itself, which did most to define Cudworth as the opponent of atheism. Consequently for the majority of those who used Cudworth's work in the years after his death it was his Trinitarianism which stood out. This is no more clearly seen than in Cudworth's place and importance in the Trinitarian debates of the 1690s. It is true to say that these debates, which occurred after Cudworth's death, were not caused by Cudworth's definition of the Trinity. However, the overt use of not only Cudworth's immanent Trinity, but also the vocabulary and principles of his wider philosophical project by William Sherlock, inflamed and exacerbated the debates. Therefore, although Wise's attempt to rehabilitate Cudworth may have been a little too simplistic, it is certainly possible to argue that Cudworth was ever present in the 'Great Trinitarian Debate' of the 1690s.

---

[9] Turner, *Discourse*: clxii
[10] Wise, *Confutation*: 45-6.
[11] Wise, *Confutation*: 80.

The 'Great Trinitarian Debate' of the 1690s

Philip Dixon has recently shown that debates on the Trinity were a constant theme in English seventeenth-century theology.[12] Despite their continued importance there is little doubt that these grew in intensity and ferocity in the 1690s. The key factor in this development was the publication, in 1687, of Stephen Nye's *Brief History of the Unitarians, called also Socinians, in Four Letters to a friend*. Nye was educated at Magdalene College, Cambridge, and was, from 1679 the rector of Little Hormead in Hertfordshire. Nye's text was written as part of the wider debate on religious toleration which had again become a live issue in English thought following the accession of the Catholic James II to the throne in 1685. James' desire to reintroduce Catholicism into English life led him to an active interest in arguments and policies for religious toleration. In an attempt to maintain his own authority, and to destabilise the political power of the Anglican Church, James sought to bring about the alleviation of persecution against Roman Catholics, and then widespread religious freedom for all religious dissenters. James' prime instrument in this was his *Declaration of Indulgence* of 1687.[13] This not only suspended the legal prohibitions on all dissenters, including Catholics, but also allowed for their freedom of worship. James hoped that this would win him the support of those Protestant dissenters who, like Roman Catholics, had been persecuted under the Clarendon Code of the 1660s. The political aims of James' move failed, particularly because of his open advocacy for Catholicism, with his policy of unchecked religious toleration helping hasten his fall in the Revolution of 1688/9. In theological terms James' actions had an unforeseen consequence. His policies provided the most complete religious toleration England had known to that date. As a consequence, religious groups which had never been considered for toleration — both Catholics and, in particular, anti-Trinitarian dissenters — began to engage in vigorous defences of their own right to religious pluralism. The possibility of the freedom of worship for Protestant dissenters offered by James' *Declaration* also opened up the possibility that anti-Trinitarians, who viewed themselves as Protestant dissenters, might also be afforded religious toleration. In many ways this might be viewed as a vain hope as anti-Trinitarians were consistently denied religious freedom

---

[12] Dixon, *Nice and Hot Disputes*.
[13] J.P. Kenyon, ed., *The Stuart Constitution: 1603-1688*. Cambridge, CUP, 1986: 389-391.

under previous schemes of toleration both during the interregnum and after the restoration of the monarchy.[14]

Despite these obstacles Nye's text, which was paid for by the English Socinian (and friend of John Locke) Thomas Firmin, argued that Socinians, or Unitarians, as Nye terms them, had the right to religious freedom.[15] Theologically Nye's text does not differ greatly from the Socinian declaration of belief, the *Racovian Catechism*. Nye argues that Christ, although begotten of the Virgin Mary, was not himself God, merely a messenger of God — *divinitas* not *deitas*.[16] For this reason the doctrine of the Trinity diminishes the character of God as 'the maker of Heaven and Earth.' Accordingly the duty of true believers is to renounce 'all Doctrines and Religions to be vain which proceed not from him alone,' in particular the Trinity.[17] Nye characterises the Trinity as 'Tritheism'; the assertion of three separate Gods which destroys the unity of the one true God-head. Socinianism is, therefore, presented by Nye, in contrast to the Trinitarianism of orthodox Christianity, as a more authentic and truthful understanding of the faith of the New Testament. For Nye the crucial evidence for this claim came in the coherence of Socinianism with what he saw as the biblically sound Apostles Creed. By contrast, Nye argues, the only creedal definition of the Trinity comes in the philosophically complex and theologically dubious Nicene creed.[18] Through this evidence Nye argues that the strength of Socinianism is that it allowed for a clear definition of the

[14] For a comprehensive account of the importance of the Trinity in debates for toleration see Joshua Toulmin, *An Historical View of the State of the Protestant Church in England and the Progress of Free Enquiry and Religious Liberty from the Restoration to the Accession of Queen Anne*. London: 1814. For a general account of James II's policy of religious toleration see: John Miller, 'James II and Toleration' in *By Force or By Default? The Revolution of 1688-1689*, edited by Eveline Cruickshank. Edinburgh: John Donald, 1989; and Barry Coward, *The Stuart Age 1603-1714*, third edition. London: Pearson, 2003: 336-341. For the place of anti-Trinitarians in this debate see; Stephen Trowell, 'Unitarian and/or Anglican: The Relationship of Unitarianism to the Church from 1687-1698' in *The Bulletin of the John Rylands Library*, 78 (1996): 77-102; Redwood, *Reason, Ridicule and Religion*: 157-172; J.A.I. Champion, *The Pillars of Priestcraft Shaken: the Church of England and its Enemies, 1660-1730*. Cambridge: CUP, 1992: 116-120. The persecution and non-tolerance of Socinians was a pattern repeated across Europe. For a study of this trend see Martin Mulsow and Jan Rohls, eds. *Socinianism and Arminianism: Anti-Trinitarisnism, Calvinits, and Cultural Exchange in Seventeenth-Century Europe*. Leiden: Brill, 2005.

[15] Nye's use of the term 'Unitarian' is important in the historical development of English Socinianism. However, as will be argued, the theological similarity between Nye and Socinianism, means that the two terms will be used interchangeably in this text.

[16] Stephen Nye, *A Brief History of the Unitarians, Called also Socinians. In Four Letters, Written to a Friend*. London: 1697: 3.

[17] Nye, *Brief History*: 8, 4.

[18] Nye, *Brief History*: 8.

basic tenets of the Christian faith. The simplification of faith allowed by
Socinianism then gave a theological structure through which all Protestants
could be accommodated to scripture and so insulated against the potential
corruptions of the Roman Church.[19] As already stated, there was nothing
innovative in Nye's advocacy of Socinianism as such. The controversy
caused by his publications came not so much from the fact of publication,
but the debate it engendered. This debate took two distinct forms: firstly
the differing 'Trinitarian' responses to Nye's affirmation of Socinianism,
particularly in the debate between William Sherlock and Robert South;
secondly in Nye's ability to ridicule and satirise the contradictions
between the 'orthodox' responses to his Socinianism.

The debates on whether or not anti-Trinitarians should be tolerated
continued after the Revolution of 1688/9. Accompanying Nye's defence
of Unitarianism came other texts calling for a simplification of the creeds
of the Church, particularly the doctrine of the Trinity, to allow for the comprehension of all Protestant dissenters. Most notably amongst these was
Authur Bury's *The Naked Gospel* published in 1690. Against these perceived attacks on the Trinity came a series of defences of the Trinity.
Two of these responses stand out. In 1690, John Wallis, the Savilian
Professor of Geometry at Oxford University, published *The Doctrine of
the ever-blessed Trinity explained*. This text rejected the calls of Socinians
and reasserted the traditional economic account of the Trinity.[20] However,
in addition to Wallis' text came William Sherlock's response to the threat
of Socinianism. Sherlock was educated at Peterhouse, Cambridge and
was, at the time of the publication of his *Vindication of the Doctrine of
the Holy and Ever Blessed Trinity* in 1690, Dean of St Paul's Cathedral.
Published three years after Nye's pamphlet, Sherlock's text was designed
as a significant contribution to the debates on the Trinity. As we will see
below it is clear that in the lengthy formation of this text, Sherlock drew
heavily on Cudworth's *TISU*, not only for his modes of argument, but also
for his philosophical language. Consequently it is Sherlock's use of Cudworth, as much as his *TISU* which makes Cudworth such a vital character
in this debate.

The basis of Sherlock's definition of the Trinity is essentially a defence
of the Trinity *ad intra* which Cudworth advocated in *TISU*. Like Cudworth,
Sherlock argues that a clear definition of the substance of the Trinity is
necessary because recent 'New Philosophies' had rejected the existence

---

[19] Nye, *Brief History*: 49.
[20] Victor Nuovo, *John Locke and Religion*. Bristol: Thoemmes Press, 1997: 111.

of immaterial substance and matter. Sherlock's criticism in this area is clearly aimed at the materialism of Thomas Hobbes. It is also possible to suggest that Sherlock was also concerned by the possible latent materialism that many read into Locke's recently published *Essay*.[21] To reject the possible dangers of materialism Sherlock, again like Cudworth, uses the Cartesian category of *res cogitans*. Sherlock goes as far as to state that we must 'strip ourselves' of material assumptions of God when talking of the substantial form of the divine.[22] It was only through the categories of immaterial substance, Sherlock argues, that God could be understood coherently. God must be defined in terms of the infinite and indivisible properties of immaterial substance because the attributes belonging to God — infinite wisdom, power, and goodness — are only comprehensible through the properties of immaterial substance.[23]

Where Sherlock's Trinitarianism diverges from Cudworth is in his attribution of these immaterial qualities directly to the persons of the Trinity. Although Cudworth uses immaterial substance as a means of understanding the unified substance of the Trinity, and the numerical uniqueness of the Trinity, he remains largely agnostic on the specific nature of the interaction between the different persons of the Trinity. Sherlock, by contrast, hangs his definition of the Trinity on his ability to make strong claims about how the different persons of the Trinity know themselves as persons, and recognise their unity as God.[24] What is interesting here is that, even when Sherlock moves beyond Cudworth's arguments he does so by using and developing the arguments of Cudworth's philosophical system. In this area his specific means is the attribution of the qualities of Cudworth's theory of consciousness to the persons of the Trinity. As we saw in Chapter Four, Cudworth's *TISU* provided one of the first philosophical definitions of the idea of consciousness.[25] There Cudworth uses consciousness

---

[21] William Sherlock, *A Vindication of the Doctrine of the Holy and Ever Blessed TRINITY, and the Incarnation of the Son of God*. London: 1690: 3

[22] Sherlock, *Vindication*: 49, 77. Compare with Turner, *Discourse*: 67.

[23] Sherlock, *Vindication*: 69.

[24] Sherlock's approach here marks him out as a 'Social' Trinitarian — beginning with the persons and to explain the unity of the Trinity — against Cudworth's 'Latin' explanation which begins with the unity of the Trinity and then explains the persons. For the distinction between the 'Latin' and 'Social' Trinities see: Cornelius Plantinga, Jr. 'Social Trinity and Tritheism', in *Trinity, Incarnation, and Atonement: Philosophical and Theological Essays*, edited by Ronald J. Feenstra and Cornelius Plantinga Jr. Notre Dame IN: University of Notre Dame Press, 1989, and Brian Leftow, 'Anti Social Trinitarianism,' in *The Trinity*, edited by Steven Davis and Daniel Kendall. New York: Oxford University Press, 1999.

[25] Udo Thiel has done much to stress the importance of discussions of Cudworth and Sherlock's Trinitarianism on the development of early modern theories of consciousness.

to define the intellectual character of human agency. The term is defined, in the first instance in contrast to the mundane actions of the material world. Cudworth argues that the intellect of man, unlike dull matter, is able to perceive his own actions, therefore man is *conscious* of those actions. Cudworth describes this reflexive action of self-perception as, 'as reduplicated upon itself comprehending it selfe and Conscious of all its own capacities & congruities.'[26] Sherlock takes Cudworth's reflexive understanding of consciousness and relates this to the interrelationship of the different persons of the Trinity. He argues that consciousness, defined in Cudworthian terms as self-perception, allows him to explain the relationship of the persons of the Trinity to one another. Building on his definition of the shared substantial form of the Trinity, Sherlock argues that each of the persons of the Trinity shares the same unified divine consciousness. However, in addition to this shared consciousness, Sherlock asserts that each of the person of the Trinity also possess a self-consciousness of its own personhood. So Sherlock defines the Trinity as, 'the Three Divine Persons, as Three Infinite Minds, distinguished from each other by a self-consciousness of their own, and essentially united by a mutual consciousness to each other.'[27] For Sherlock the strength of this definition of the Trinity was that it allows for a structure and language in which the specific persons of the Trinity are comprehended in their individuality without diminishing the equal knowledge, wisdom, goodness, justice, and power of the mutual consciousness of the Trinity.[28] The problem was that Sherlock's definition of the interrelated consciousness and self-consciousness of the Trinity gave rise to a version of the Trinity which has been described pithily by Philip Dixon as a 'cosmic *ménage a trios*.'[29] The use of Cudworth in Sherlock's fully developed immanent definition of the Trinity is clear. Whether this is a faithful completion of Cudworth's doctrine of the Trinity is a matter of conjecture.[30] What is clear is that Sherlock's Cudworthian Trinity, far from silencing the threat

---

See 'Cudworth and Seventeenth-Century Theories of Consciousness', in *The Uses of Antiquity: The Scientific Revolution and the Classical Tradition* edited by Stephen Gaukroger. Dordrecht: Kluwer, 1991; 'The Trinity and Human Personal Identity', in *English Philosophy in the Age of Locke*, edited by M.A. Stewart. Oxford: OUP, 2000; 'Self-Consciousness, and Personal Identity' in *The Cambridge History of Eighteenth-Century Philosophy* edited by Knud Haakonssen. Cambridge. CUP, 2007.

[26] *FM*.4979: 40.

[27] Sherlock, *Vindication*: 73.

[28] Sherlock, *Vinidication*: 81.

[29] Dixon, *Nice and Hot Disputes*: 113.

[30] For a reading of Sherlock which places him as the heir of Cudworth's Trinity see Armour, 'Trinity, Community, and Love'.

of Socinianism resurrected by Nye, provided the spark for more than ten years of fierce debate on the form and structure of the Trinity.

Sherlock's text proved particularly controversial because it not only brought inevitable opposition from Socinians, but also fierce rebukes from orthodox Trinitarians. As has been argued previously, orthodoxy on matters of the Trinity in the seventeenth century involved an adherence to the economic Trinity. Therefore, the immanent Trinity of Cudworth and Sherlock, brought criticism from both sides. For this reason we find the most vociferous early criticism of Sherlock coming not from a Socinian, but from the high-church cleric Robert South. South's *Animadversions upon Dr. Sherlock's Book* published in 1693, presented a blistering attack on the philosophical basis of Sherlock's definition of the Trinity. In particular, South criticised Sherlock's inability to understand the Trinity in 'its proper *Mode* of *Substance*.'[31] Mirroring John Turner's earlier criticisms of Cudworth, South argues that the discussions of the immaterial substance of the divine was both incorrect and damaging to the efficacy of the doctrine of the Trinity. Instead South argues that the only constructive way to discuss the Trinity was through the 'operations of the Trinity'. In short, South rejects Sherlock's immanent argument by returning to the economic Trinity. South argues that men are able to comprehend the '*common general nature*'[32] and the operations of the persons of the Trinity as revealed to man in the economy of salvation. However, it was impossible to know anything of the internal form and interrelationships of the Trinity which would remain 'Internal, Incommunicable, and distinguishing.'[33]

The real damage to the status of the Trinity in this debate was, however, made by Stephen Nye. As well as being a passionate defender of the rights of Socinians, Nye was able to exploit and highlight the fissures created within the Trinitarian camp to his own advantage. Nye recognised the deep debt that Sherlock's definition of the Trinity owed to Cudworth. In doing so Nye was able to criticise both Cudworth and Sherlock for bringing into these debates a detailed discussion of the substance of the Trinity. In particular Nye ridiculed what he saw as the presumption of Cudworth and Sherlock that it was possible, through a linguistic slight-of-hand, to overturn what was logically plain to him: that one substance equalled one person.

---

[31] Robert South, *Animadversions upon Dr Sherlock's Book entitled a vindication of the Holy and Ever-Blessed Trinity.* London: 1693: 242.
[32] South, *Animadversions*: 241.
[33] South, *Animadversions*: 243.

> Words are *Arbitrary* Signs, applied to things according as Men please, and
> therefore are capable of Alteration in their Use; but the Nature of things is
> absolutely unchangeable *three* Persons can *never* be *one* Substance, Essence
> or *individual* Nature.[34]

Nye argued that however effective the sophistry of philosophers like
Cudworth and Sherlock was, it could never overturn the overwhelming
biblical evidence that supported Socinianism. These criticisms mirrored
Nye's original claims from the *Brief History*, for the biblical orthodoxy of,
and coherence of Socinianism with, the Apostle's Creed, and for the philosophical contortions of the Trinitarian Nicene Creed. Nye's criticism of the
philosophical imperative of Trinitarian theology led him to dub Cudworth's
Trinity a 'Platonic Trinity' and Sherlock's a 'Cartesian Trinity.'[35]

More importantly, Nye's criticisms of the interlocutor's in these
debates reveals the more fundamental divergence between the different
defences of the Trinity. In his 1695 *Discourse concerning the Nominal
and Real Trinities* Nye, borrowing from the language of Locke's *Essay*,
defines the two camps within the Trinitarian debate as either 'Nominal'
or 'Real'. The Nominal Trinitarians, amongst whose number Nye
includes South, present the Trinity of the historical church. The Nominal
Trinity, with its concentration only on the revealed operations of God,
was in reality a form of hidden Socinianism because the characteristics
of God were mistakenly interpreted as Persons by Nominal Trinitarians
when, in fact, these were merely aspects of *One* God.[36] In contrast to
this is the Real Trinity advocated by Cudworth and Sherlock. Their
theology, Nye argues, derived from their disquiet over the place and
discussion of substance by the Nominal Trinitarians.[37] The 'Real Trinity', with its concentration on the substance of the different persons of
the Trinity presents, Nye argues, a philosophically valid, but theologically bogus Tritheism.[38] Nye's purpose in making this distinction was
to show how, in reality, the doctrines of the established Church, through
the form of the Nominal Trinity, were in reality the same as those of
Socinianism. Therefore, Nye argued that — returning to the argument
of his *Brief History* — toleration and comprehension should be extended

[34] Stephen Nye, *Consideration of the Explications of the Doctrine of the Trinity By
Dr Wallis, Dr Sherlock, Dr South, Dr Cudworth, and Mr Hooker*. London: 1693: 15.

[35] Nye, *Consideration of the Explications of the Doctrine of the Trinity By Dr Wallis,
Dr Sherlock, Dr South, Dr Cudworth, and Mr Hooker*: 16, 10-11.

[36] Stephen Nye, *Discourse concerning the Nominal and Real Trinities*. London: 1695:
4-12.

[37] Nye, *Discourse*: 13.

[38] Nye, *Discourse*: 20-27.

to Socinians as they were in reality, more orthodox that Real Trinitarians. Nye's assertions — 'Buffoonery' according to Thomas Wise[39] — did not win him favour on either side of the debate. However, Nye's caustic observations, on the debates on the Trinity, do highlight the theological and philosophical significance of these debates. Perhaps most importantly, Nye shows the central, if unwitting role that Cudworth played in their definition.[40]

Cudworth and the Latitudinarians

It is clear that Cudworth's theology played an important role in the definition of the 'Great Trinitarian Debate'. What is of historical interest is that Cudworth's Trinitarianism also provides a strong intellectual link between Cudworth and the Latitudinarians, the leading churchmen of the following generation. When dealing with the relationship between Cudworth and the Latitudinarians there is a modicum of confusion over who we are talking about when we use the term Latitudinarian. Like the Cambridge Platonists the, so-called, Latitudinarians were not a self-conscious school of thought. Instead the term Latitudinarian is best and most commonly used to describe a collection of London based, liberal, Anglican divines who found preferment following the Glorious Revolution.[41] Chief amongst their number were John Tillotson, Edward Stillingfleet, Simon Patrick, Edward Fowler and Gilbert Burnet. However, it should be noted that the Cambridge Platonists were also known by the sobriquet Latitudinarian. In fact the term Latitudinarian was first coined

---

[39] Wise, *Confutation*: 83.

[40] Nye, *Discourse*: 27.

[41] The classic account of the life and work of many of the Latitudinarians comes in Gilbert Burnet's *History of My own Time*. This was expanded in 1902 by H.C. Foxcroft's edition of many of Burnet's diaries and notebooks as *A supplement to Burnet's History of My own Time*. In recent years there has been growth in studies specifically on the Latitudinarians. Chief amongst these has been Louis G. Locke's 1954 study, *Tillotson: A Study in Seventeenth century Literature*. Copenhagen: Rosenkilde and Bagger, 1954. More general surveys have included: Barbara Shapiro, *Probability and Certainty in Seventeenth century England: A Study of the Relationship between Natural Science, Religion, History, Law and Literature*. Princeton NJ: Princeton University Press, 1983; W.M. Spellman, *The Latitudinarians and the Church of England, 1660-1770*. Athens GA: University of Georgia Press, 1993. Isabel River's excellent two volume *Reason, Grace and Sentiment*; and various essays by John Spurr, chiefly, '"Rational Religion" in Restoration England' in *Journal of the History of Ideas*, 49 (1988): 563-85, and, '"Latitudinarianism" and the Restoration Church' in *The Historical Journal*, 31 (1988): 61-82.

in the 1660s in Cambridge as a term of abuse against the Cambridge Platonists.[42] It has, however, been common in recent scholarship to ignore or down play the relationship between the Cambridge Platonists and the Latitudinarians, painting the Cambridge Platonists as ivory-towered academics in contrast to the metropolitan worldliness of the Latitudinarians. Barbara Shapiro's definition is indicative of this view. 'Their lives were spent rather differently,' Shapiro points out:

> the Platonists preferring the retired scholarly life to the hurly burly of an active city pulpit, or efforts to gain the high ecclesiastical posts which could enable them to pursue actively their moderate policies. It was Wilkins, William Lloyd, Sprat, Stillingfleet, Tillotson, and Gilbert Burnet, not the Platonists, who became deans, bishops, and arch-bishops.[43]

Next to the practical Churchmanship of the Latitudinarians, the Cambridge Platonists' philosophical theology has been read as a luxury. As W.M. Spellman argues, 'the speculation of the cloister and the college were ill-suited to the demands of the busy urban parish.' The obverse of this view is that the Latitudinarians are seen as intellectually thin; popular in their time but lacking the rigour and power of the Cambridge Platonists. Spellman again argues that the Latitudinarians, compared to the Cambridge Platonists, 'seem to be without ...spiritual commitment or otherworldly direction, often emerging as little more than complacent heralds of religious rationalism and tepid moralism.'[44]

---

[42] Although I will argue in this chapter that the Cambridge Platonists and the Latitudinarians should only be considered as different generations of the same liberal theological and philosophical movement, for the sake of clarity I will use the traditional descriptions of the two groups to avoid confusion. It is, however, interesting to note at this point that the term 'Latitudinarian' was first coined in Cambridge in the 1660s. In a letter to Anne Conway, Henry More complains that in Cambridge during the 1660s those who opposed the Cambridge Platonists would 'Push hard at the Latitude men as they call them, some in their pulipitts call them sons of Belial, others make the Devill a Latitudinarian,' Conway, *Letters*: 243.

[43] Shapiro, *Probability and Certainty*: 107. It is more likely that the sort of ecclesiastical preferment the Cambridge Platonists received was as much to do with the theological-political make-up of Restoration England as with any conscious desire on the part of the Cambridge Platonists to distance themselves from the realities of the seventeenth century. All the main Cambridge Platonists accepted the act of Uniformity. This allowed Whichcote to take up his various livings in London after 1660, also both Cudworth and More were also Prebendaries of Gloucester Cathedral. However, preferment beyond this was most likely limited because of the perception, by the hierarchy of the Restoration Church, of the Cambridge Platonists as willing accomplices with the Protectorate.

[44] Spellman, *Latitudinarians*: 2, 116. Also see John Gascoigne, *Cambridge in the Age of the Enlightenment: Science, religion, and politics from the Restoration to the French Revolution*. Cambridge: CUP, 1989: 42.

This sort of clear separation assumed by some recent commentators is at odds with the contemporary assessment of the relationship between the two groups. Although there are obvious differences in style between the Cambridge Platonists and the Latitudinarians, the closeness of the relationship between them is difficult to deny. Many of the latter school were educated by the Cambridge Platonists, the obvious examples being Simon Patrick, who was taught by John Smith whilst a student at Queens', and John Tillotson who was a student and later fellow of Clare Hall under Cudworth. The Latitudinarians also largely shared the same Puritan anti-Calvinism which, as we saw in Chapter One, characterised Cudworth's intellectual development. In fact this link is made explicit, particularly between Cudworth and Tillotson, in a pamphlet published in 1706 entitled *An Historical Account of Comprehension and Toleration. From the Old PURITAN to the New LATITUDINARIAN.*[45] In fact Isabel Rivers attributes the general antipathy of the Latitudinarians towards Calvinism to the influence of the Cambridge Platonists on their education and intellectual development.[46] This pedagogical debt is shown by the fact that Simon Patrick preached the sermon at the funeral of John Smith and Tillotson fulfilled the same task at the funeral of Benjamin Whichcote. Perhaps most tellingly, the earliest defences of the Cambridge Platonists, as 'men of latitude', were published by members of the later group. Chief amongst these are Edward Fowler's *The Principles and Practices of Certain Moderate Divines of the Church of England (greatly mis-understood) Truly Represented and Defended*, and Simon Patrick's *A brief account of the New Sect of Latitude-men together with some reflections upon the New Philosophy.*[47] This link is made more explicit by Joseph Glanvill, a student of Henry More, in his account of the fictional 'University of Cupri,' a thinly veiled allusion to the Cambridge of the time. In this he describes a gallery of portraits of the luminaries or 'Cupri-Cosmits' of 'Cupri Univeristy' by

[45] Anon, *An Historical Account of Comprehension and Toleration. From the Old PURITAN to the New LATITUDINARIAN; with their continues projects and Designs, in opposition to our more Orthodox Establishment.* London: 1706: 42-61.

[46] Rivers, *Reason, Grace, and Sentiment*: I.30. Also see, Locke, *Tillotson*: 18; Mark Goldie and John Spurr, 'Politics and the Restoration Parish: Edward Fowler and the Struggle for St Giles Cripplegate' in *English Historical Review* 109 (1994): 572-96: 582.

[47] Fowler, *Principles and Practices*; P.[atrick], *Brief account*. This latter text was only published under the initials S.P. although it is widely accepted to be from the hand of Simon Patrick. John Gascoigne has argued that Patrick published this defence of the Latitudinarianism of the liberal Cambridge Divines, of which he was one at the time, after he was denied the Presidency of Queens', see Gascoigne, *Cambridge*: 35, 41. John Spurr has cast doubt on the accepted belief that Patrick was the author of this tract, see Spurr, '"Latitudinarianism"': 70.

the use of anagrams. These 'Cupri-Cosmits' included both members of
the Cambridge Platonists and the Latitudinarians. Making no distinction
between the two groups, Glanvill includes in his roll-call Cudworth,
Whichcote, Patrick, George Rust, Smith, More, and Stillingfleet.[48] Other
recent commentators have been more willing to follow the accepted line
of members of the group by noting the obvious links between the Cambridge Platonists and the Latitudinarians. Moving beyond the obvious
distinctions of style and geography G.R. Cragg argues that, 'Stillingfleet,
Tillotson, Patrick, Fowler and Burnet...might modify the teachings of the
Platonists, but the imprint of the older men was upon them to the end.'[49]
Theologically this imprint is found explicitly in their shared understanding of the Trinity.

This is most clearly visible in works on the Trinity written by two of
the leading Latitudinarians: Edward Fowler's *Certain Propositions By
which the Doctrine of the Trinity is so Explained*, first published in 1694,
and John Tillotson's *Sermons Concerning the Divinity and Incarnation
of our Blessed Saviour* which were delivered at St Lawrence Jewry,
where Benjamin Whichcote was incumbent, in the very early 1680s but
not published in 1693. Importantly, within the context of the Trinitarian
debates outlined above, Stephen Nye described both Fowler and Tillotson
as 'Real Trinitarians' and explicitly as disciples of Cudworth.[50] This link
is significant because it shows not only the intellectual link between Cudworth and these central figures of the Williamite church, but also the theological sophistication of the both Tillotson and Fowler. Most importantly,
by establishing this relationship we are able to see the way in which the
ethical imperative which is apparent in Cudworth's Trinitarianism also
develops in the writing of both Tillotson and Fowler.

[48] Jackson I. Cope, '"The Cupri-Cosmits": Glanvill on Latitudinarian anti-Enthusiasm'
in *The Huntington Library Quarterly*, 17 (1954): 269-86: 273-85.

[49] Cragg, *From Puritanism to the Age of Reason*: 60. The quote continues, 'In ethics,
the Cambridge Platonists established a tradition which determined the character of English
moral philosophy for a century and a half. In political theory they interpreted the idea of
sovereignty in a way which Locke expanded, popularized, and established as the ruling
principle in English political thought. But the Cambridge Platonists are not important
simply because of the nature and extent of their influence. They represent as profound a
restatement of Christianity as English theology has produced, and their unswerving conviction of the grandeur and scope of the divine activity gives to their writing a dignity and a
persuasive power which neither the changes of fashion nor the passage of time have
obscured.'

[50] Stephen Nye, *Considerations on the explications of the Doctrine of the Trinity occai-
sioned by Four Sermons preached by his Grace, the Lord Bishop of Canterbury*. London:
1697: 37, 67.

The Trinity in the theology of the Latitudinarians

As we have already seen, the biographical links between the Cambridge Platonists and the Latitudinarians are undeniable. What is of interest with both Fowler and Tillotson is, however, not that they developed in the light of the thought of the Cambridge Platonists, but that both men owed a great deal, both personally and intellectually to Cudworth. Edward Fowler, it is important to note, was in the minority of the Latitudinarians in not being educated at Cambridge. Instead he received his education at Corpus Christi College Oxford, the former college of Thomas Jackson. Despite this geographical separation, Fowler appears to have quickly fallen into the intellectual world of the Cambridge Platonists. As we have already seen, his 1670 work, *The Principles and Practices of Certain Moderate Divines of the Church of England*, was one of the first public defences of the Cambridge Platonists. He also benefited from the patronage of Henry More, becoming a Prebendary of Gloucester Cathedral in 1676 when More resigned his position in Fowler's favour. Fowler was also close to the Cudworth family. He was, with John Locke and Edward Clark, one of the executor's of the will of Cudworth's wife Damaris. He was also a beneficiary of that will, receiving from Mrs Cudworth a 'broad mirror' which had belonged to Henry More and a share with the other executors of the remainder of her estate once her eldest son, John Cudworth, had received £350.[51]

Fowler's *Propositions* take the form of 28 arguments which he argues can account for the Trinity in the reasonable terms used by the Nicene Fathers. In this endeavour Fowler explicitly recognises his debt to Cudworth.[52] This work should not be viewed as an original work, but as a pamphlet which simply outlined the reasonable defence of the Trinity defined by works like Cudworth's *TISU*. Fowler's *Propositions* are primarily aimed at defending this definition of the Trinity against accusations, similar to those made by Turner in his *Discourse Concerning the Messias*, that such a Platonic and reasoned defence of the Trinity inevitably leads to the heresies of Arianism or Socinianism. For this reason, Fowler concentrates his attack on what he perceives to be the misplaced belief that the second person is subordinate to the first person of the Trinity and so that, necessarily, the second person is created. This, Fowler argues, is

---

[51] Christ's College MS. Box.77, The Will of Damaris Cudworth.

[52] Edward Fowler, *Certain Propositions By which the Doctrine of the Holy Trinity Is so Explained, According to the Ancient Fathers as to speak it not Contradictory to Natural Reason*. London: 1719: no.28.

a deliberate misinterpretation of the Trinity by Arians and Socinians. Fowler argues that both heresies fail to recognise the relationship of the second person to the first of a 'necessary emanation'. This Neoplatonic definition, which we have already encountered in Cudworth, is enough, Fowler argues, to dispute the belief that 'there was at least a Moment of Time when the Son was not; and that He is a Creature.'[53] Fowler again alludes directly to an argument Cudworth uses in *TISU* when he defines this emanation using the metaphor of the relationship of the light to the sun. Fowler argues:

> *Light* doth exist by necessary *Emanation* from the *Sun*, and therefore the *Sun* was not before the light which proceeds from thence in Order of *Time*, though it be in Order of *Nature* before it.[54]

Fowler uses this metaphor to define the Trinity as a substantive unity, which still maintains a distinction in the persons of the Trinity.[55]

In the same year that Fowler's *Propositions* appeared, Tillotson, at the time Archbishop of Canterbury, published his *Sermons Concerning The Divinity and Incarnation of our Blessed Saviour*. Tillotson published these sermons to refute anti-Trinitarian accusations made against him.[56] The *Sermons* were originally preached during two successive Christmas-tides in 1679 and 1680 at St Lawrence Jewry where Whichcote was minister. Tillotson's defence of the Trinity, like Fowler's, betrays an intellectual debt to the Cudworth and *TISU* in particular. Tillotson's intellectual debt to Cudworth is matched by the high personal regard with which each held the other. As previously mentioned, Tillotson was a student and later fellow of Clare Hall whilst Cudworth was Master there in the 1640s and 1650s. In 1664 Cudworth preached, and later published, a sermon given at Lincoln's Inn whilst Tillotson was chaplain there. In the same year Cudworth, during his dispute with Henry More as described in Chapter Two, asked John Worthington to seek Tillotson's advice on how Cudworth could best publicly acknowledge his debt to Archbishop Sheldon.[57] Also Cudworth was, late in life, complementary about Tillotson's work on devotion.[58] This respect was reciprocated by Tillotson, in

---

[53] Fowler, *Certain Propositions*: no.21.
[54] Fowler, *Certain Propositions*: no.18, compare with *TISU*: 595: '*Both the Father and the Son is God: But he as it were an Exuberant Fountain, this as a Stream derived from him: He like to the Sun, This like a Ray extended from the Sun.*'
[55] Fowler, *Certain Propositions*: no.22.
[56] Locke, *Tillotson*: 93.
[57] Worthington, *Diary*: II.142.
[58] *FM*.4983: 104.

his sermon at Benjamin Whichcote's funeral in 1684, where he described his former master as the 'ancient and learned...Dr Cudworth.'[59]

Tillotson was apparently urged to publish his *Sermons* by Princess, later Queen, Anne to convert the leading Socinian Thomas Firmin to orthodoxy.[60] The *Sermons* take the form of an exegesis of the clauses of the prologue to John's Gospel. To overcome accusations of anti-Trinitarianism Tillotson continually stresses the existence of the second person of the Trinity, the *Logos*, from eternity. The eternal nature of the *Logos* places it, he argues, in the unified understanding of the triune Godhead. To explain the complicated relationship of the *Logos* to the first person of the Trinity, the *Father*, Tillotson relies on the Neoplatonic metaphor of the first person as an emanating fountain. He defines the relationship of the *Logos* to the *Father* in the following terms:

> The *Evangelist*, adds ... *the same was in the beginning with God*, that is though the *Word* was truly and really God, yet was not *God the Father*, who is the Fountain of the Deity, but an Emanation from him, the only begotten Son of God from all eternity *with him*.[61]

This Neoplatonic emanation is further reinforced by Tillotson's interpretation of the *Logos* not merely in the form of the person of Christ but as the incarnation of the perfect reason of the divine intellect.[62] The *Logos*, Tillotson argues, is not simply a guiding principle, but also the creative principle in the world. The creative nature implicit in the *Logos* allows Tillotson to distance himself from criticisms of Socinianism by arguing that the *Logos*, as a creative principle, cannot itself be a creature.[63] Tillotson's interpretation of the eternal nature of the *Logos* follows almost exactly that which we find in Cudworth. The *Logos* fulfils the role of the active and creative principle in the divine, the perfect incarnation of the intellect of God. Tillotson's separation of the intellectual source of the divine from the perceptive and creative nature of the *Logos* follows Cudworth's Plotinian distinction between intellect and understanding in the divine.

Tillotson, like Cudworth, finds historical credence for the *Logos* as the creative principle in the world, from the ancient theology of the Jewish

---

[59] John Tillotson, T*he Works of the Most Reverend Dr John Tillotson, Late Archbishop of Canterbury: Containing Fifty Four Sermons and Discourses, on several Occasions. Together with the Rule of Faith*. London: 1696: 268.

[60] Dixon, *Nice and Hot Disputes*: 107.

[61] John Tillotson, *Sermons Concerning the Divinity and Incarnation of our Blessed Saviour*. London: 1693: 23.

[62] Tillotson, *Sermons*: 24.

[63] Tillotson, *Sermons*: 38.

Cabala and from the Platonic tradition. Tillotson argues that, in both traditions, the *Logos* is used to describe the efficient cause in the world. So Tillotson argues:

> And so likewise *Philo* the *Jew* calls him *by whom God made the World, the Word of God,* and *the son of God.* And *Plato* probably had the same notion from the *Jews* which made *Amelius,* the *Platonist,* when he read the beginnings of *St Johns* Gospel to say, *this* Babarian *agrees with Plato, making the* Word *in the order of the Principles*; meaning that he made the *Word* the *Principle* or efficient Cause of the World, as *Plato* has done.[64]

Tillotson, therefore, follows the *prisca theologia* which is so prevalent in *TISU,* by arguing that ancient wisdom was ultimately fulfilled in the Gospel revelation of Christ as *Logos.* [65]

Tillotson, although recognising these Cabalistic and Pagan sources, does not rely on them as heavily as Cudworth. Tillotson prefers instead to base his interpretation primarily on the revealed truth of Christianity. Tillotson argues that without this revealed truth the ancient knowledge of the *Logos* as a creative principle can only descend into 'fancies and conceits.' The central failure of the '*Jewish Cabalists* and the *Schools* of *Pythogoras* and *Plato*' was that they lacked the correct structure through which to interpret the *Logos* as both God and creator.[66] Without the revealed truth of Christ as *Logos* they simply revert to a 'confused *Genealogy* of *Deities.*'[67] The purpose of John's prologue is, for Tillotson, to refute and deny pagan interpretations of *Logos,* replacing them with the full revealed truth of Christ as *Logos.* As Tillotson puts it in his first sermon:

> the *Evangelist* shows that all this fanciful *Genealogy* of *Divine Emanation* ...was a mere conceit and imagination: and that all those glorious Titles did really meet in the *Messias* which is the *Word,* and who before his Incarnation was from all eternity *with God,* partaker of his Divine Nature and Glory.[68]

The vehemence of Tillotson's criticism of pagan theology would, as already stated, appear to distance him from Cudworth. Tillotson in this sense relies much more on biblical proofs in his sermons than Cudworth who, as we have seen, bases much of his defence of the Trinity on the specific claims of Plato and Plotinus.[69]

---

[64] Tillotson, *Sermons*: 9.
[65] *TISU*: 557.
[66] Tillotson, *Sermons*: 12.
[67] Tillotson, *Sermons*: 12.
[68] Tillotson, *Sermons*: 16.
[69] *TISU*: 550, compare with Tillotson, *Sermons*: 125.

Despite his attacks on the short comings of pagan and ancient theology, Tillotson maintains a Neoplatonic structure for not only the eternal creation of the *Logos* but also the internal structure of the Trinity. Tillotson, like Cudworth and Fowler, uses the metaphor of the sun to explain the relationship of the *Logos* to the *Father*. He argues that the *Logos* is 'God by participation of the Divine Nature and Happiness together with the *Father*, and by way of derivation from this as the light from the Sun.' This quote, is, he argues, the 'best and fittest that can be given' for the mystery of the Trinity.[70] Tillotson, again like Fowler, uses this metaphor to distinguish between the unified substance of the Trinity and the distinct persons of the Trinity. Here he follows Cudworth's contentious interpretation of the *homoousian* form of the triune God. This interpretation for the relationship of the *Logos* to the *Father* allows Tillotson to, as he says, 'describe to us that which is commonly called the *Divine* and so any thing I could ever see properly enough, *the distinction of person* in the Deity.[71]

Tillotson's concentration on the biblical proofs of the Trinity in a Neoplatonic framework allows him to counter the threats and accusation of Socinianism made against him. He argues that, by concentrating on the words alone, the characteristic rational biblical exegesis of Socinianism fails to appreciate the full meaning and truth of scripture. For this reason he derides Socinian opponents of the Trinity for claiming they have reason on their side. As with Cudworth's defence of the Trinity, Tillotson argues that Socinians cannot claim to have reason on their side if they propagate a theory which undermines the Trinitarian God as the source of that reason.[72] Because the Trinity is incomprehensible to limited human reason, that in itself should not undermine the implicit and infinite reasonableness of the Trinity.[73]

Tillotson's defence of the Trinity did not silence the accusations of Socinianism made against him. As we have seen Socinianism had long been used as a shorthand for those who brought too much of the principle of reason into theological debate. Tillotson was all too aware of this when he complained:

[70] Tillotson, *Sermons*: 36, also see *TISU*: 595.
[71] Tillotson, *Sermons*: 23.
[72] Tillotson, *Sermons*: 115-8.
[73] Tillotson, *Sermons*: 162. Tillotson's argument here mirrors Cudworth's assertions in the *TISU* that the Christian Trinity, 'though a mystery,' is still more reasonable in form than any other explanation of the Trinitarian form of the divine, *TISU*: 560.

> I know not how it comes to pass, but so it is, that every one that offers to give a reasonable account of his faith, and to establish religion upon rational principles, is presently branded for a Socinian.[74]

Despite the publication of his sermons many of Tillotson's opponents continued to accuse him of being a Socinian. This accusation was made most forcefully by the non-juror Charles Leslie who continued to accuse him of Socinianism after Tillotson's death in 1695. Perhaps alluding to the Platonism of Tillotson's defence, Leslie argues, 'he does not really believe it; tho' he endeavours with all his Art, to cast a Mist before the Reader's Eyes, in other Expressions, which to some might seem Testament, as *Arius* and his followers did.'[75] For Tillotson the end of the Trinity always resides in the practical and moral code that it teaches man. The Trinity, he argues, is the fulfilment of the redemption of man and the reconciliation of God to man.[76] The *Logos* is the principle of inward reformation which leads to outward change. He states in his fourth sermon, '[a]ll that He hath done for us *without us* will avail us nothing, unless we be *inwardly* transformed and *renewed in the spirit of our minds*: unless we become *new creatures*'[77] Far from being a 'complacent herald of...tepid moralism,'[78] both Fowler and Tillotson present sophisticated defences of the Trinity which have their basis in Cudworth's Trinitarianism.

The Trinity and the ethical and political ideas of the Latitudinarians

What is of particular interest in Tillotson and Fowler's use of Cudworth is not simply the fact of his being used in the Trintarian debates — Cudworth's influence here is clear from a reading of Sherlock — rather it is the way in which their Trinitarianism informed their ethical and political ideas. Tillotson's teachings are redolent with calls for man to turn to and serve God not only in his words, but also in his deeds. These are the teachings which have elsewhere been viewed as 'tepid moralism'. However, Tillotson's use of the Trinity shows that this human action was informed and animated by the inward power of the *Logos*. This inner

---

[74] John Tillotoson, *The works of the Most Reverend Dr. John Tillotson*, 3. vols. London: 1752: III.443.

[75] [Charles Leslie], *The Charge of Socinianism Against Dr Tillotson considered. In Examination of Some Sermons He has lately Published on purpose to clear Himself from that Imputation... By a True Son of the Church.* Edinburgh: 1695: 1.

[76] Tillotson, *Sermons*: 47, 181.

[77] Tillotson, *Sermons*: 217.

[78] Spellman, *Latitudinarians*: 2.

reformation, which mirrors the same theory that we have encountered in Cudworth's ethical philosophy, stresses that the transforming power of the Trinity brings with it the demands of service towards God. This is, however, as with Cudworth, not to take the form of an inward looking asceticism, but as the basis of an active, outward looking, tolerant, and humble life. Tillotson argues that man cannot mirror God in the form of divinity or miracles, but can resemble the life of 'Innocencey, Humility, Meekness and Patience.'[79] The Trinity brings man to an inward moral reformation, a theory that mirrors Cudworth's own belief in the moral responsibility of man. As with Cudworth, Tillotson argues that the ethical life of man is driven by this inward reformation where man chooses to accept and live in the light of God's grace. As Tillotson states:

> All that He hath done for us *without us* will avail is nothing, unless we be *inwardly* transformed and *renewed in the spirit of our minds*: unless we become *new creatures*, unless we make it in the continual and sincere endeavour of our lives to *keep the commandments of God*.[80]

The Latitudinarians' continual instance on the moral nature of Christianity has led many, as already stated, to down play the intellectual and theological core of their thought. However, if we place the Latitudinarians together with the Cambridge Platonists we can identify a theological core to their moral and ethical rationalism. This moral rationalism is explicable in the Latitudinarians if we understand that, for them, all activity is implicitly ethical. The actions of grace are therefore synonymous with virtue.[81] This elision between grace and activity is explicable when all life is understood, in Platonic terms, as the participatory activity of man in all parts of a divinely ordained creation. This focus on the centrality of grace comprehended by man by his reason also provides a link to Cudworth's understanding of grace as the reason of the divine woven into creation. Tillotson shares something of Cudworth's Puritan anti-Calvinism when he argues that man's salvation can only come through the active acceptance of God's grace by the individual moral actor. What is clear, however, is that this shared ethical position is grounded in deeply held and coherently argued shared theological position.

We can find a similar link between the theological and ethical in the writings of Edward Fowler. Because of the brevity of the *Propositions* we need to look deeper into Fowler's work to establish this link. The

---

[79] Tillotson, *Sermons*: 233.
[80] Tillotson, *Sermons*: 217.
[81] Rivers, *Reason, Grace and Sentiment*: I.74-5.

explicit political implications of Fowler's Trinitarianism can be identified in his *Principles*, where he argues that the priesthood of Christ is not given privately to his apostles but publicly to all men. Fowler, therefore, rejects one of the central tenets of the sacerdotal justification for the authority of the established Church, which is that the authority of the Church was created by the apostolic succession of the ordained Priesthood. Fowler argues that the priesthood of man was given to all collectively. This is, of course, a teaching central to Reformed Christianity and therefore cannot be viewed as peculiar to the Latitudinarians or the Cambridge Platonists.[82] However, if Fowler's claim is viewed in the light of his use of Cudworth, we can interpret Fowler's use of this central argument of the Reformed tradition as a continuation of Cudworth's assertion of the active and divinely inspired faculty of reason in all men. This link to Cudworth is made even more explicitly when Fowler, in his *Principles*, identifies the divine nature of the faculty of reason through an allusion to Cudworth's argument for the eternal and immutable nature of morality. As Fowler's interlocutor Theophillus states: '*[t]here is an eternal Reason, why that which is good should be* so *and required, and why that which is evil should be* so *and forbidden*; *which depends not so much on the divine* will *as the divine* nature.'[83] Through the recognition of these principles by reason, Fowler argues that man is able to make his outward moral actions an expression of his inward reformation. Again in a very Cudworthian manner, Fowler argues that, '[m]oral righteousness …consisteth in the Regulation of both the *outward* and *inward* man, according to the unchangeable Laws of righteousness.'[84] Fowler argues, as in Cudworth, that the necessarily ethical nature of this inner reformation leads man inevitably to an outward political position. Fowler acknowledges that the moderation that he is suggesting would be interpreted by many as undermining the authority of the Church and the King.[85] Despite these accusations, Fowler argues, like Cudworth, that a political community should be legitimised by the collective will of the members of that body politic. He follows Cudworth in developing an account of the legitimisation of the political community, one that holds the priesthood of all believers as its founding principle. Fowler in his *Principles* suggests a political structure in which the ethical implications of man's individualism can be realised. Both Tillotson and Fowler take from Cudworth not

---

[82] Fowler, *Principles and Practices*: 326.
[83] Fowler, *Principles and Practices*: 12-13.
[84] Fowler, *Principles and Practices*: 119.
[85] Fowler, *Principles and Practices*: 332.

only an ethical imperative for the inner reformation of man, but that that reformation is possible because of the ability of man to know something of the divine through the exercise of his reason. The link between Cudworth and the Latitudinarians shows not only that they shared the same principles of liberal theology, but that the terms of their liberal theology, particularly their definition of the Trinity, helped define their liberal and latitudinarian approach to ethics and politics.

Conclusion

The closeness of the Latitudinarians to the Cambridge Platonists is undeniable in both biography and theology. This closeness came not only through the role of the Cambridge Platonists in the education of the Latitudinarians but also in the formation of the theology of the Latitudinarians. However, as we have seen, what binds Cudworth and the Latitudinarians together is not simply congruence in matters of theology, but the manner in which the rejection of the theology of Calvinism brought with it the rejection and replacement of the strictures of Calvinist ethics. In particular the Cambridge Platonists and the Latitudinarians both argued that the correct actions of man in the created world must be defined in the first instance by a correct understanding of man's relationship to God in and through creation. Most importantly, especially in the context of late seventeenth-century thought, this relationship was one defined through the structures and forms of orthodox Christianity. This link is, I would argue, not one that can be defined simply in terms of influence, but more deeply through the shared theological and religious temper which both the Cambridge Platonists and the Latitudinarians possessed. The intention to show how a Christian God could be understood by use of reason in the changing structures of early-modern thought lies at the basis of this shared religious culture which informed Cudworth, the Latitudinarians, and to a lesser extent thinkers like Sherlock. This intellectual culture did not assume an agreement in all things, however it did promote, in differing forms and to different extents, human reason as the central term through which men fulfil their obligation to God and, through him, to other men.

The broader intellectual significance of the Puritan anti-Calvinism — Gibbon's 'secret reformation' — which Cudworth developed and advocated is too great to be outlined in this brief conclusion. However, it is possible to argue that the rejection of dogmatism and respect for individual action which both Cudworth and the Latitudinarians advocated was a product of their rejection of the authoritarianism of the interregnum, mixed with a natural distrust of the 'priestcraft' of the Laudian and Restoration churches. The intellectual culture of Puritan anti-Calvinism drew these thinkers to argue, often in very different forms, that the tenets and principles of Christianity should be understood primarily through the structures of human reason, and that these reasonable principles should then provide the definition and structure of human society. In this process the central term is that of the individual, who comes to know himself as an individual through his reason, and then engages with the external world through the power of that God-given reason. The congruence between reasonableness and true religion which Cudworth advocated is perhaps most eloquently summed up in the main theological work of John Locke, a friend of the Latitudinarians and Cudworth's philosopher daughter Damaris Masham.[86] In his work, *The Reasonableness of Christianity*, Locke talks of his conception of God, saying:

> He that made use of this candle of the Lord, so far as to find what was his duty, could not miss to find also the way to reconciliation and forgiveness, when he had failed of his duty, though if he used not this reason this way, if he put out or neglected this light, he might perhaps see neither.[87]

In this context 'the candle of the Lord', although most commonly linked to the Cambridge Platonists, sums up eloquently the shared temperament of the Puritan anti-Calvinism which Cudworth, the Cambridge Platonists, the Latitudinarians, and even Locke shared. Although all these men differed markedly on specific issues (one could say dramatically in the case

---

[86] For the social and intellectual links between Locke and the Latitudinarians see: Locke, *Correspondence*: 2112, 2294, 2814, 3501, 3633, 3635, 3647; Maurice Cranston, *John Locke: A Biography*. Oxford: OUP, 1985: 368; John C. Higgins-Biddle, 'Introduction' in John Locke, *The Reasonableness of Christianity as delivered in scriptures*. Oxford: The Clarendon Press, 1999: lvii-lxxiv. For Locke's relationship with Cudworth's daughter, Damaris Masham, see: Locke, *Correspondence*: 677, 684, 687, 688, 690, 693, 695, 699, 704, 710, 710, 720, 726, 730, 731, 734, 740, 744, 751, 752, 760, 763, 779, 784, 787, 805, 815, 823, 827, 830, 837, 839, 847, 870, 882, 896, 930, 942, 950, 967, 975, 1003, 1040, 1322, 2280; Mark Goldie, *John Locke and the Mashams at Oates*, private publication by the Parish of High Laver: 2004; For discussions of Masham's philosophy see: Jacqueline Broad, *Women Philosophers in the Seventeenth Century*. Cambridge: CUP, 2002; Lois Frankel, 'Damaris Masham' in *A History of Women Philosophers, vol.3: Modern Women Philosophers, 1660-1900*, edited by Mary Ellen Waithe. Dordrecht: Kluwer, 1991. For a detailed discussion of the influences at play on Masham's philosophy see Sarah Hutton, 'Damaris Cudworth, Lady Masham: Between Platonism and Enlightenment' in *The British Journal for the History of Philosophy* 1 (1993): 29-54.

[87] Locke, *The Reasonableness of Christianity*: 140.

of say Cudworth and Locke)[88] all can be placed together in attacking atheism, dismissing enthusiasm, championing reason, and promoting toleration as the defining principles of individual Christian life. Many would argue that this Christian advocacy of reason merely presented the last stand of orthodox Christians before the eventual and inevitable rationalism of Deism and the eighteenth-century Enlightenment.[89] However, it is not enough to say that because Cudworth defined human reason as, in some qualified sense, God-like that it was inevitable that others would make rationality divine. As we have seen throughout this study, Cudworth, and latterly the Latitudinarians, only promoted the advocacy of reason within the bounds of orthodox Christianity. It is certainly the case that others, most notably Locke, made similar arguments whilst not openly committing themselves to orthodox Christian doctrines such as the Trinity. However, what remains with all these member's of Gibbon's 'secret reformation' is a belief that human action cannot be divorced from the explicitly theological principles that define them.

In this context Cudworth's importance as a thinker is only partially revealed to us by identifying who he influenced, or how his work was received. Cudworth needs to be understood as one of many English thinkers who sought to reconcile the dictates and obligations of religious

---

[88] Certainly Locke and Cudworth differed on many issues. Theologically it has long been argued that Locke was a Socinian; for a full debate on this matter see: John Marshall, *John Locke: Resistance, Religion, and Responsibility*. Cambridge: CUP, 1994; John Marshall, 'Locke, Socinianism, "Socinianism", and Unitarianism' in *English Philosophy in the Age of Locke*, edited by M.A. Stweart. Oxford: The Clarendon Press, 2000; Victor Nuovo, 'Locke's Theology, 1694-1704' in *English Philosophy in the Age of Locke*, edited by M.A. Stewart. Oxford: The Clarendon Press, 2000; John Locke, *Writings on Religion*, edited by Victor Nuovo. Oxford: OUP, 2002. Philosophically also Locke's attack on innate ideas would appear to present an explicit rebuttal of Cudworth's Platonism; see: Robert L. Armstrong, 'Cambridge Platonists and Locke on Innate Ideas,' *Journal of the History of Ideas*, 30 (1969): 187-202; Dominic Scott, *Recollection and Experience: Plato's theory of learning and its successors*. Cambridge: CUP, 1995: Chapter 10. However, in certain specific areas it is possible to find agreement between the two men. In theology it is possible to see Cudworth's influence on Locke's 'proof' of the existence of God; see: Locke, *Essay*: 4.10.10. compare with *TISU*: 30-34. Also see: M.R. Ayres, 'Mechanism, Superaddition, and the Proof of the God's Existence in Locke's Essay,' *The Philosophical Review*, 90 (1981): 210-251; Michael Ayers, *Locke: Epistemology and Ontology* 2 vols. London: Routledge, 1991: 2.190-196. In ethics Stephen Darwall has argued strongly for the influence of Cudworth on Locke's definition of 'self-determination'; see: Darwall, *British Moralists*: 172-5. This argument has recently been questioned in Broad, 'A Woman's Influence'. The argument at hand though is not to what extent was Locke agreeing, or disagreeing with Cudworth on specifics, but that both men developed their liberal positions from a shared approach to, if not engagement with, theological and philosophical issues.

[89] See, Beiser, *Sovereignty of Reason*.

belief with the ethical and political problems of his time. Particularly next to more overly practical men like the Latitudinarians many of Cudworth's proscriptions and theories seem archaic to the modern reader. However, the theological arguments helped define not only many of the central arguments of early-modern thought, but also the generally tolerant approach which came to typify English philosophy and theology in the late-seventeenth century. What a focus on Cudworth's theology and philosophy shows is how the explicit theology of Puritan England began to develop into the characteristic philosophy of the early Enlightenment. Cudworth's place is, therefore, not as the high-priest or prophet of this tradition, nor as its greatest and most perceptive advocate. Rather, Cudworth should be best remembered as one of the first thinkers in this tradition to develop the overtly theological intentions of Puritanism, as generally understood, into the more easily recognisable form and language of early-modern liberal philosophy.

CUDWORTH'S FREEWILL MANUSCRIPTS

The purpose of this brief appendix is to describe the form, style, composition and age of Cudworth's freewill manuscripts. Cudworth's freewill manuscripts are recognised to be the British Library Additional Manuscripts 4978-4982. In this text I have also included *FM*.4983, which is normally, and misleadingly, titled 'On the Eternity of the Torments,' and two 'Commonplace books', *FM*.4984 & 4985 as part of this group because they also deals with the philosophical and ethical issues discussed in *FM*.4978-4982.

As discussed in Chapter Six it is not immediately clear what happened to Cudworth's unpublished manuscripts on his death in 1688. It has normally been argued that they were taken by Cudworth's widow to Oates. This is certainly the belief of Thomas Wise, who commented on the supposed whereabouts of Cudworth's manuscripts in 1706, and also in an account of the changing ownership of Cudworth's manuscripts during the middle decades of the eighteenth century published in the *Critical Review* in 1783. Certainly contemporary observers, who were aware of the existence of Cudworth's unpublished manuscripts, assumed that they were housed at Oates.[1] However Jacquline Broad recently uncovered evidence, in the form of a letter from Masham to Jean Le Clerc, that suggests that the manuscript for the *Eternal and Immutable Morality*, and so probably all the manuscripts, were not held at Oates but in the care of her elder brother John Cudworth. John Cudworth, who was a fellow of Christ's between 1678 and 1697, was left in Cudworth's will 'all my books except such English books as my wife shall take for herself or for her daughter Masham.'[2] Broad argues that the evidence of the will and Masham's letter to Le Clerc seem to suggest that the manuscripts were not at Oates until 1726 when they were bequeathed to Francis Cudworth Masham, Damaris Masham's son, by the childless John Cudworth. The date of John Cudworth's death also, Broad argues, helps explain the publication

---

[1] Thomas Wise, for instance, stated in 1706 in the introduction to his abridgement of Cudworth's *System* that the 'Remainder is said to be in MS' and in the possession of '*The Lady* Masham, *Dr*. Cudworth's *Daughter*.' See Wise, *Confutation*: 10.

[2] Christ's College MS, Box 77.

date of the *Eternal and Immutable Morality* in 1731. Through a close examination of the manuscripts is possible to find evidence which would appear to confirm Broad's theory. John Cudworth, who was born in 1656, was educated at Christ's and elected to a fellowship in 1678 in place of Locke's friend Thomas Burnet. In 1697 he resigned his fellowship and retired to the family estate in Southwold, Suffolk.[3] There is evidence from the manuscripts themselves which appear to back up Broad's theory that some of the manuscripts were held in Suffolk, and not at Oates, chiefly in BL.Add.Ms. 4985 described as a 'Moral Commonplace Book'. In this assorted and confused selection of papers appear several pages outlining the management of an estate in 'Suffolk', in particular a survey of the 'Oaks 15 Sept 1715'. It would appear from this that, far from being the 'scholarly son' that Broad describes, Cudworth's manuscripts became included with John Cudworth's papers on estate management![4] What is known is that the manuscripts were, according to an account in the *Critical Review*, sold by the last Lord Masham (described by the author of the *Critical Review* as 'the right honourable Goth') to Robert Davies, a London bookseller 'to make room for books of *polite amusement.*' It appears that Davies bought the manuscripts under the pretence that they were composed by Locke. The manuscripts seem then to have been severely neglected — 'exposed to rats, and the depredations of his maid' — and were only saved in 1777 by 'a gentleman, who had veneration for the name of Mr Locke.' On discovering that the manuscripts were authored by Cudworth and not Locke the anonymous benefactor organised for the manuscripts to be taken into the Additional Manuscript Collection of the British Museum (now Library) where they now remain.[5] The manuscripts held at the British Library are an incomplete reflection of those which Cudworth left on his death. For instance the manuscript of *EIM* is not amongst these manuscripts. Also the anonymous author of 'Memoirs' lists several manuscripts which do not appear to mirror those currently held in the British Library. Amongst these missing manuscripts are listed: 'A Discourse of Moral Good and Evil' and 'An explanation of Hobbes's notion of God and of the extension of spirits.'[6]

[3] Peile, *Biographical Register*: II.46.

[4] The section is found in *FM*.4985: 120b-121b, or 87-89 depending on which numbering is followed.

[5] 'Ayscough's Catalogue of MSS. in the British Museum' in *The Critical Review* 55 (1783): 389-92.

[6] 'Memoirs of Ralph Cudworth': 36-38. This list is also replicated almost exactly in Birch's 'Life': 32-34.

Of the manuscripts on freewill now held at the British Library the one which most obviously stands alone is *FM*.4978. It is the only one of the complete manuscripts to have been published, as *A Treatise of Freewill* in 1838 in an edition by John Allen. Of the remaining manuscripts by far the most substantial and complete manuscripts are *FM*.4979 and *FM*.4980 which both run to well over 250 folios each. *FM*.4981 contains two distinct sections. The majority of this volume is an attack on 'divine fatalism.' Added to the end of this volume is a summary chapter of Cudworth's arguments on freewill of 11 folios in length. This has recently been published as 'On the Nature of Liberum Arbitrium' in an edition by J.L. Breteau which appears as an appendix to the 1997 collection, *The Cambridge Platonists in Philosophical Context*.[7] Finally *FM*.4982 is a collection of three shorter, and unrelated sections of manuscript which have been bound into one volume.

To date the only comprehensive survey of these manuscripts appears as an appendix to John Passmore's *Ralph Cudworth — An Interpretation*. In this, Passmore attempts to place the manuscripts in chronological order, using the differing handwriting styles within the manuscripts as a guide. This ordering is based on what Passmore describes as the 'natural assumption' that there was a steady and identifiable development in Cudworth's writing from a traditional Elizabethan 'secretary' hand, to a more modern 'Italian' or 'Italic' hand. In this analysis Passmore concentrates particularly in Cudworth's inconsistent use of the letters 'c' and 'e.' Using this method, Passmore categorises the freewill manuscripts into four distinct groups:

Group 1: *FM*.4982 Bk.II, *FM*.4980 (old 'c' and 'e').
Group 2: *FM*.4982 Bk.III, *FM*.4979, *FM*.4981 (erratic 'c' and old 'e').
Group 3: *FM*.4978 (new 'c' and old 'e').
Group 4: *FM*.4982 Bk.I (new 'c' and erratic 'e')

Passmore's thesis is based on two assumptions. Firstly that Cudworth's handwriting style changed gradually and consistently over this time. This is possible, Passmore claims, if one compares Cudworth's letters with his manuscripts. Secondly, Passmore assumes that Cudworth used the same writing style in both his letters and his manuscripts.

Although this thesis is persuasive it does begin to fall down upon examination. Passmore struggles to explain why Cudworth's hand will change

---

[7] Ralph Cudworth, 'Additional Manuscript no.4981 (On the Nature of Liberum Arbitrium),' introduced by J.L. Breteau, in *The Cambridge Platonists in Philosophical Context: Politics, Metaphysics & Religion,* ed. G.A.J. Rogers et al. Dordrecht: Kluwer, 1997: 219-31.

[8] Passmore, *Ralph Cudworth*: 108.

between several types in one page. He explains this by suggesting that Cudworth may have begun a passage in an older style halfway down a page and then returned to the same sheet some years to fill in around this initial work in what Passmore judges to be a later hand.[8] Despite the peculiarities of Cudworth's working habits I believe that Passmore's explanation of how Cudworth wrote his manuscripts can be dismissed for four reasons. Firstly, if we are to believe Passmore's assertion that Cudworth began sections half way down a page at some point and then return to the manuscript some years later to complete the process, then Cudworth was very consistent in this practice. There are, by my reckoning, very few sections of the freewill manuscripts which begin half way down a page with no text around it. In the most substantial manuscripts, that is *FM*.4979 and *FM*.4980, Cudworth uses all the pages available to him. Secondly Passmore's theory cannot explain why Cudworth, on occasions, corrects and amends sections written in 'Italic' hand in what he judges to be the earlier 'secretary' hand. Thirdly, Passmore's theory cannot explain satisfactorily how and why Cudworth's hand often changes abruptly mid-sentence. Such changes would, I believe, be better explained by a change of stylus rather than by a baroque working habit.[9] Fourthly, as we shall come on to see, there are philosophical similarities between certain manuscripts, which are not held in others, which would appear to transcend the groupings suggested by Passmore's analysis. This is particularly the case with the obvious similarities which exist between *FM*.4978 and *FM*.4980, which Passmore places in his Groups 1 and 3 respectively.

   Although Passmore's analysis is instructive I think, for the reasons outlined above, it has to be viewed as flawed. I will below lay out the evidence for a more detailed analysis of Cudworth's freewill manuscripts. To do this I will examine not only the handwriting style, but also paper watermarks, Cudworth's references to published works, and the internal arguments of the manuscripts to establish a new chronology for Cudworth's freewill manuscripts.

Handwriting and style

Although I do not hold to Passmore's handwriting thesis as a means of dating the manuscripts it is instructive to examine the differing styles of

---

[9] See *FM*.4979: 194; *FM*.4981: 51 for examples of pages where Secretary hand changes to Italic hand during the page, and *FM*.4981: 79 for an example of a change from Italic to Secretary hand.

handwriting that Cudworth uses within the manuscripts. This allows us
to understand more fully the method he employed whilst composing his
manuscripts. Cudworth's hand falls into three distinct styles: style [1] is
a plain Italic script, style [2] is an angular secretary hand, and style [3]
(which is almost exclusively in *FM*.4979) is a rounder secretary hand.
It has been suggested that [3] is that of an amanuensis. However I would
argue that all three hands are Cudworth's. Evidence for this comes in two
forms. Firstly, there exists in more than one hand a common spelling
inconsistency. Cudworth has a tendency at times to reverse the letters
within a word on certain occasions. Two clear examples of this appear
in *FM*.4979 where both [2] and [3] reverse the letters 'i' and 'n' within
a word. On fol.16 Cudworth uses [3] to spell 'contingent,' 'contnigent,'
then on fol.21 he uses [2] to spell 'in,' 'ni.' Secondly, the evidence linking all three handwriting styles to Cudworth comes in the way that the
styles change abruptly within the text. As already stated, Passmore
explains this as an idiosyncrasy in Cudworth's working method. However the fact that these styles often change mid-sentence would appear to
suggest a change in stylus, rather than a change in the time of composition
or penman. Two examples of this are, firstly, *FM*.4979 fol.194 where [3]
changes to [1], second, again in *FM*.4979, fol.194, where [2] changes to
[1] mid-sentence.

If we accept, as this evidence would seem to show, that all three
hands are Cudworth's this gives us an insight into his working methods.
Generally speaking the manuscripts are written in long sections of con-
tinuous prose on the recto side of each sheet. This is almost always
done in a single style, most commonly style [1]. These sections appear
to have been written in long single sessions with Cudworth making
little in terms of correction of amendment as he wrote. There are also,
in contrast to Cudworth's published works, relatively few direct quotes,
in stark contrast to *TISU*. Following the writing of the manuscripts
Cudworth then appears to have come back to them at a later date to
correct and amend his text. These amendments are generally written in
style [2]. Cudworth marks the existing script with a mark, usually a
capitalised letter of either the Roman or Greek alphabet. He then adds
comments of extra information on the facing, verso page. The fact that
Cudworth often mixes the symbols by which he marks amendments and
alterations on the same page (i.e. in *FM*.4979 fols.47, 47b, 48 where
Cudworth uses both Roman and Greek letters to mark amendments) suggests that Cudworth returned to and revised these manuscripts more than
once.

Paper

Cudworth's manuscripts are written on three different sizes of paper bound into booklets of differing length. Most, that is *FM*.4980-4982 are written on sheets that are approximately 14.5" by 9", *FM*.4979 is on 12" by 8" paper, and *FM*.4978 is on 9" by 7" paper. When the watermarks of these manuscripts are examined it is possible to give rough start dates after which the manuscripts were written. Although this is rather approximate and inexact, it does add to the picture of how and when Cudworth wrote the manuscripts. All the volumes, except *FM*.4982, which is a collection of 3 separate sections collated together by a later librarian, use the same water mark throughout the volume. This would seem to back up my premise that the manuscripts were composed by Cudworth as single projects and not dipped in and out of as Passmore suggests. The approximate dates suggested by the watermarks are as follows. Both *FM*.4980 and the first section of *FM*.4982 use a coat of arms water mark which originates after 1680,[10] *FM*.4981 uses a fleur-de-lis water mark dating from after 1670,[11] and *FM*.4979 uses a 'foolscap' watermark dating from around 1671.[12]

Reference to published works and authors

Throughout the manuscripts Cudworth constantly refers to other authors, most notably and consistently, Thomas Hobbes. Cudworth does refer explicitly to the published debates between Hobbes and Bishop Bramhall, however, as the last of these, Bramhall's *Castigations of Mr Hobbes*, was published in 1658, this does not assist us in the accurate dating of the manuscripts. However it is not simply the publications that Cudworth refers to, but also the manner with which he refers to them, that allows for more definitive conclusions to be drawn over the dating of Cudworth's manuscripts. The only manuscript which this form of evidence is helpful with is *FM*.4979. Firstly in *FM*.4979 Cudworth describes Hobbes as 'the Late author of Necessity.'[13] This could simply refer to Hobbes as the recent author of works on necessity. However if it referred to the 'Late author' as the deceased author, then this would place this manuscript after Hobbes' death in 1679. Secondly Cudworth describes Hobbes' philosophy as making

---

[10] Edward Heawood, *Watermarks of the 17th and 18th Centuries*. Hilvershum: The Paper Publications Society, 1950: no.678.
[11] Heawood, *Watermarks*: no.1785.
[12] Heawood, *Watermarks*: no.2003.
[13] *FM*.4979: 125.

God a 'Leviathan or Behemoth.'[14] This mirrors Cudworth's style in *TISU* where he says that the civil sovereign is 'no *Leviathan*.'[15] As Hobbes' work *Behemoth* was not published until after his own death in 1679 it is possible to argue that this comment is an explicit reference to Hobbes' work. Also, further to Passmore's handwriting thesis this comment is written in handwriting style [1]. If the link of this comment to the publication date of Hobbes' *Behemoth* is correct two conclusions can be made: firstly that this is further evidence of the incomplete nature of Passmore's handwriting thesis; and secondly that Cudworth was working on, or revising this manuscript after the completion and publication of *TISU* in 1678.

Internal comparisons

Although Cudworth's freewill manuscripts are generally seen as a single unit it is possible to differentiate between the different manuscripts. Although it is not possible to use these internal differences to suggest definitively which manuscripts were written first, by examining the manner with which specific arguments develop within the manuscripts it is possible to surmise that some manuscripts develop and expand ideas suggested in a previous manuscript.

It is possible tentatively to link *FM*.4979 with the first section of *FM*.4981. This link is made by Passmore who shows that the reference in *FM*.4981 to a second chapter on divine prerogative is almost certainly to the second chapter of *FM*.4979.[16] This link would also appear to be logical as *FM*.4981 and *FM*.4979 deal broadly with the differing problems of divine and mechanical fatalism respectively. This group, which I shall describe as Group I, can be differentiated from the other manuscripts — in particular *FM*.4980 — by the use of further internal evidence, in particular Cudworth's changing vocabulary of ethical self-determination, his use of the terms 'autokinsey', heterokinsey', and 'epoloustic'. The philosophical nature of these arguments has been discussed in detail in Chapter Four. As evidence for the composition of the manuscripts the occurrence of only 'autokinsey' and 'heterokinsey' in Group I of the manuscripts can be used as further evidence of the link between these manuscripts. The term 'epoloustic', along with 'autokinsey' and 'heterokinsey', appears in *FM*.4978 and *FM*.4980.

---

[14] *FM*.4979: 148b.
[15] *TISU*: 896.
[16] Passmore, *Ralph Cudworth*: 111.

These two pieces of internal evidence would seem to suggest that *FM*.4978 and *FM*.4980 can be placed together as a group — what I will call Group II. This leaves the individual sections bound together in *FM*.4982 unaccounted for by this grouping. Although Passmore suggests that the first section of *FM*.4982 could be linked to Group I (*FM*.4979 &4981), there is nothing to link the other manuscripts bound together in *FM*.4982 to the composition of the other, more substantial manuscripts.

Conclusion

From the evidence outlined it is possible seriously to doubt Passmore's claim that some of these manuscripts 'were probably written before the appearance of the *True Intellectual System*, perhaps a good many years earlier.'[17] Although it would be naïve to think of the freewill manuscripts as being synonymous with the suggested third section of Cudworth's entire *Intellectual System*, it is possible, I believe, to show that the manuscripts were composed after the completion of *TISU* in 1671. This would therefore substantiate my argument that the manuscripts should be read in the light of the philosophical and theological principles which Cudworth outlines in *TISU*. It is, however, I believe not possible from the present evidence to order them other than as two different groups of manuscripts which Cudworth worked on some time after 1671 and, in the case of Group I, after Hobbes' death in 1679.

That being said I would argue that Group II, on the balance of the evidence, would appear to be the fuller and more philosophically sophisticated account of freewill of the two groups of manuscripts outlined above. This is merely conjecture made on the rather flimsy evidence of the more complete forms of the manuscripts as works in their own right (in particular when *FM*.4979 from Group I and *FM*.4980 from Group II are directly compared.) If this theory is correct then that would push the production of Group II into the 1680s, after the composition of Group I. If this holds then it is possible to suggest that *FM*.4978 (which is the manuscript of Cudworth's *Treatise of Freewill*) is an abridgment of the ideas of *FM*.4980. This then could have been used by Cudworth either to create interest for the later publication of *FM*.4980, or as a more manageable version of Cudworth's fullest account of what he entitles, *Libero Arbitrio*, which we find in *FM*.4980.

---

[17] Passmore, *Ralph Cudworth*: 112.

BIBLIOGRAPHY

Primary Sources, Ralph Cudworth

Manuscript sources

Cambridge: Christ's College MS B.1.10, 11 (Christ's College Account Book), C.6.13.1 (Christ's College Order Book).

London: British Library MS Additional 4978-4987 (Works attributed to Dr Ralph Cudworth).

Oxford: Bodleian Library (Bod) MS D'Orvile 471 (letter to Issac Vossius).
MS Rawlinson, A28, A.38, A.43, A.58, A.63, C.982 (letters to John Thurloe).
MS Rawlinson, B.375 (subscription to the Act of Uniformity).
MS Selden Supra, 108, 109 (letters to John Selden).
MS Tanner, 39, 44, 46, 49, 58, 92, 290 (correspondence)
MS Western, 52546 (letter to John Selden).

Printed sources

'Additional Manuscript no.4981' (On the Nature of Liberum Arbitrium) introduced by J.L. Breteau, in *The Cambridge Platonists in Philosophical Context*, edited by G.A.J. Rogers et al. Dordrect: Kluwer, 1997.
A Discourse concerning the true notion of the Lord's supper, London: 1670.
'A Sermon Preached before the House of Commons. March 31st 1647' in *The Cambridge Platonists*, edited by C.A. Patrides. London: Edward Arnold, 1969.
A Sermon Preached to the Honourable Society of Lincolnes-Inne. London: 1664.
A Treatise Concerning Eternal and Immutable Reality, edited by Edward Chandler. London: 1731.
A Treatise Concerning Eternal and Immutable Reality, edited by Sarah Hutton. Cambridge: CUP, 1996.
A Treatise on Freewill, edited by John Allen. London: 1838.
'A Treatise on Freewill' in *A Treatise Concerning Eternal and Immutable Reality*, edited by Sarah Hutton. Cambridge: CUP, 1996.
'Two undated letter to John Stoughton' in Thomas Solly, *The Will Human and Divine*. London: 1856.
'Preface' to 'A Sermon Preached before the Honourable The House of Commons, On March 31st, 1647,' in Charles Taliferro and Alison J. Teply eds, *Cambridge Platonists Spirituality*. Mahwah NJ: Paulist Press, 2004.
Systema intellectuale huius universi, translated by Johann Lorenz Mosheim. Jena: 1733.
The True Intellectual System of the Universe: The First Part; Wherein, All the Reason and Philosophy of Atheism is Confuted; and Its Impossibility Demonstrated, London:1678.

The True Intellectual System of the Universe, 3 vols, edited by John Harrison. London: Thomas Tegg, 1845.
The Union of Christ and the Church in a shadow. London:1642.

Other Primary Sources

Manuscripts

Cambridge: Cambridge University Library (CUL) MS Mm.1.38 (Notes on the Expulsion and Recantation of Daniel Scargil).
MS Mm.5.24, 45, 48 (Notes on the Masters of God's House and Christ's College).

Cambridge: Christ's College MS Box 77 (Notes on Ralph Cudworth).
Box 188 (Letters of Edward Abney, and other related correspondence).
John Mitchell, 'Personalities of Christ's.'

Cambridge: Emmanuel College MS 48 (Directions for a Student of the University)

London: British Library MS Additional 4297 (Miscellaneous papers of Thomas Birch).

Oxford: Bodleian Library (Bod.) MS Rawlinson, C.982 (letter of H. Justel).
MS Rawlinson, D.1104 (letter of Ralph Brownrigge).

Printed sources

Anon., *An historical Account of Comprehension and Toleration. From the Old PURITAN to the new LATITUDINARIAN; with their continued projects and Designs, in opposition to our more orthodox Establishment*. London: 1706.
Anon., *Great and Good news for the Church of England, If they please to accept thereof: or the Latitudinarian Christians Most Humble Address and Advice To all the Imposing Clergy Men of the said church by What names or Titles soever Dignified or Distinguished*. London: 1688.
Aquinas, Thomas, *Summa Theologica*, 5 vols, translated by the Fathers of the English Dominican Province. Westminster MD: Christian Classics, 1981.
Augustine, *The City of God*, translated by Henry Bettenson. Harmondsworth: Penguin, 1984.
Bacon, Francis, *The Advancement of Learning* in *The Oxford Francis Bacon*, vol. 4, edited by Michael Kiernan: Oxford: The Clarendon Press, 2000.
Burnet, Gilbert, *A supplement to Burnet's History of my own time*, edited by H.C. Foxcroft. Oxford: The Clarendon Press, 1902.
—, *History of My own time*, 2 vols, edited by Osmund Airy. Oxford: The Clarendon Press, 1897-1900.
Calvin, Jean, *Institutes of the Christian Religion*, 2 vols, translated by Henry Beveridge. London: James Clark & Co., 1962.
Cicero, *De Fato*, translated by H. Rackham. Cambridge, MA: Harvard University Press, 1960.

—, *The Nature of the Gods*, translated P.G. Walsh. Oxford: The Clarendon Press, 1997.

Conway, Anne, *The Conway Letters: The Correspondence of Anne, Viscountess Conway, Henry More, and their friends, 1642-1684*, edited by Marjorie Nicolson, revised by Sarah Hutton. Oxford: The Clarendon Press, 1992.

Cudworth the elder, Ralph, *A Commentarie or Exposition, upon the first Chapters of the Epistle to the Galatians: penned by... Mr. W. Perkins. Now published for the benefit of the Church, and continued with a supplement upon the sixth chapter, by Rafe Cudworth*. Cambridge: 1604.

Culverwell, Nathaniel, *An Elegant and Learned Discourse on the Light of Nature*, edited by Robert A. Green and Hugh MacCallum. Toronto: University of Toronto Press, 1971.

Descartes, René, *The Philosophical Works of Descartes*, 2 vols, translated by Elizabeth S. Haldane and G.R.T. Ross. Cambridge: CUP, 1967.

Fowler, Edward, *Certain Propositions By which the Doctrine of the Holy Trinity Is so Explained, According to the Ancient Fathers as to speak it not Contradictory to Natural Reason*. London: 1719.

—, *The Principles and Practices, Of certain Moderate Divines of the Church of England. (greatly mis-understood) Truly Represented and Defended; Wherein (by the way) Some Controversies, of no mean importance, and succinctly discussed in A Free Discourse between to Intimate Friends*. London: 1670.

Gibbon, Edward, *The Decline and Fall of the Roman Empire*, 7 vols. London: Methuen & Co., 1906.

Hobbes, Thomas, *Behemoth or The Long Parliament*, edited by Ferdinand Tonnie. Chicago: University of Chicago Press, 1990.

—, *The Correspondence*, 2.vols, edited by Noel Malcolm. Oxford: Clarendon Press, 1994-1997.

—, *Leviathan*, edited by C.B. MacPherson. Harmondsworth: Penguin, 1968.

—, *Man and Citizen (De Homine and De Cive)*, edited and translated by Bernard Gert, Charles T.Wood, and T.S.K. Scott-Craig. Indianapolis: Hackett, 1991.

—, 'Of Liberty and Necessity' in *Hobbes and Bramhall on Liberty and Necessity*, edited by Vere Chappell. Cambridge: CUP, 1999.

—, 'The Question concerning Liberty and Necessity' in *Hobbes and Bramhall on Liberty and Necessity*, edited by Vere Chappell. Cambridge: CUP 1999.

Holdsworth, Richard, *Praelectiones Theologicae*, edited by Richard Pearson, London: 1661.

Hume, David, *Enquiries Concerning Human Understanding and Concerning the Principles of Morals*, edited by L.A. Selby-Bigge and P.H. Niddich. Oxford: The Clarendon Press, 1975.

Jackson, Thomas, *The Works of Thomas Jackson, D.D.* 12 vols. Oxford: OUP, 1844.

[Leslie, Charles], *The Charge of Socinianism Against Dr Tillotson considered. In Examination of Some Sermons He has lately Published on purpose to clear Himself from that Imputation... By a True Son of the Church*. Edinburgh: 1695.

Locke, John, *The Correspondence of John Locke*, edited by E.S. de Beer. Oxford: The Clarendon Press, 1976-89.

—, *An Essay Concerning Human Understanding*, edited by Peter H. Nidditch. Oxford: OUP, 1975.

—, *Some Thoughts concerning Education*, edited by John W. and Jean Yolton. Oxford: Clarendon Press, 1989.

—, *The Reasonableness of Christianity as delivered in scriptures*, edited by John C. Higgins-Biddle. Oxford: The Clarendon Press, 1999.

—, *Two Treatises of Government*, edited by Peter Laslett. Cambridge: CUP, 1960.

—, *Writings on Religion,* edited by Victor Nuovo Oxford: OUP, 2002.

Masham, Damaris, 'Letters between Damaris, Lady Masham and Gottfried Leibniz' in *Leibniz's 'New System' and associated contemporary texts*, edited and translated by R.S. Woolhouse and Richard Franks, Oxford: OUP, 1997.

Millington, Edward, *Bibliotheca Cudworthiana*. London: 1691.

Milton, John, *Political Writings*, edited by Martin Dzelzanis. Cambridge: CUP, 1991.

More, Henry, *An Antidote to Atheism or, An Appeal to the Naturall Faculties of the Mind of Man, Whether there be not a God, in A Collection of Philosophical Writings*. London: 1662.

—, *A Collection of Several Writings of Dr Henry More*, 2. vols. London: 1662.

—, *An Explanation of the Grand Mystery of Godliness*. London: 1660.

—, *The Complete Poems of Dr Henry More (1614-1687)*, edited by Alexander B. Grosart. Hildesheim: Georg Olms, 1969.

Nye, Stephen, *A Brief History of the Unitarians, Called also Socinians. In Four Letters, Written to a Friend*. London: 1697.

—, *Consideration of the Explications of the Doctrine of the Trinity By Dr Wallis, Dr Sherlock, Dr South, Dr Cudworth, and Mr Hooker*. London: 1693.

—, *Considerations on the explications of the Doctrine of the Trinity occasioned by Four Sermons preached by his Grace, the Lord Bishop of Canterbury*. London: 1697.

—, *Discourse concerning the Nominal and Real Trinities*. London: 1695.

Owen, John, *A Brief Declaration and Vindication of the Doctrine of the Trinity: As also of the Person and Sanctification of Christ*. London: 1676.

P[atrick], S[imon], *A brief account of the new sect of Latitude-men together with some reflections Upon the New Philosophy*. London: 1662.

Perkins, William, *The Works of that famous and worthie Minister of Christ... M.W. Perkins: gathered into one volume and newly corrected according to his owne copies*. London: 1605.

—, *The Works of William Perkins*, edited by Ian Breward. Appleford: The Sutton Courtney Press, 1970.

Pierce, Thomas, Αυτοκατακρισις *or Self-condemnation*. London: 1658.

Plato, *Crito*, translated by Hugh Tredinick, in *The Collected Dialogues of Plato, edited by Edith Hamilton and Huntington Cairns*. Princeton NJ: Princeton University Press, 1961.

—, *Euthyphro*, translated by Lane Cooper, in *The Collected Dialogues of Plato*, edited by Edith Hamilton and Huntington Cairns. Princeton, NJ: University Press, 1961.

—, *Laws*, translated by A.E. Taylor, in *The Collected Dialogues of Plato*, edited by Edith Hamilton and Huntington Cairns. Princeton, NJ: Princeton University Press, 1961.

—, *Meno*, translated by W.K.C. Guthrie, in *The Collected Dialogues of Plato*, edited by Edith Hamilton and Huntington Cairns. Princeton, NJ: Princeton University Press, 1961.

—, *Phaedrus,* translated by R. Hackworth, in *The Collected Dialogues of Plato*, edited by Edith Hamilton and Huntington Cairns. Princeton, N.J., Princeton University Press, 1961.

—, *Timaeus*, translated by Benjamin Jowett, in *The Collected Dialogues of Plato*, edited by Edith Hamilton and Huntington Cairns. Princeton, NJ: Princeton University Press, 1961.

—, *Theatetus*, translated by F.M. Cornford, in *The Collected Dialogues of Plato*, edited by Edith Hamilton and Huntington Cairns. Princeton, NJ: Princeton University Press, 1961.

Plotinus, *The Enneads*, translated by A.H. Armstrong. Cambridge, MA: Harvard University Press, 1967-1988.

Sherlock, William, *A Vindication of the Doctrine of the Holy and Ever Blessed TRINITY, and the Incarnation of the Son of God.* London: 1690.

Smith, John, *Selected Discourses.* London: 1821.

South, Robert, *Animadversions upon Dr Sherlock's Book entitled a vindication of the Holy and Ever-Blessed Trinity.* London: 1693.

The Racovian Catechism, translated by Thomas Rees. London: 1818.

Tillotson, John, *Sermons Concerning the Divinity and Incarnation of our Blessed Saviour.* London: 1693.

—, *The Works of the Most Reverend Dr John Tillotson, Late Archbishop of Canterbury: Containing Fifty Four Sermons and Discourses, on several Occasions. Together with the Rule of Faith.* London: 1696.

—, *The Works of the Most Reverend Dr. John Tillotson*, 3. vols, London: 1752.

Turner, John, *A Discourse Concerning the Messias ... To which is prefixed a large preface, asserting and explaining the Doctrine of the Blessed Trinity against the Late writer of the Intellectual System.* London: 1685.

Warner, John, *Anti-Haman, or an Answer to M.G. Burnet's "Mistery of Iniquiti unvailed" ... To which is annexed a letter to R. Cudworth, By W.E. Student of Divinity.* Amsterdam: 1679.

Whichcote, Benjamin, *Moral and Religious Aphorisms*, edited by W.R. Inge. London: Elkin Matthews & Marrot, 1930.

—, 'The Manifestation of Christ and the Deification of Man,' in *The Cambridge Platonists*, edited by C.A. Patrides. London: Edward Arnold, 1967.

—, 'The Unity of the Church maintained by sincere Christians,' in *The Cambridge Platonists*, edited by C.A. Patrides. London: Edward Arnold, 1967.

—, 'The Use of Reason in the Matter of Religion,' in *The Cambridge Platonists*, edited by C.A. Patrides. London: Edward Arnold, 1967.

Whichcote, Benjamin, and Anthony Tuckney, 'Eight Letters of Dr Anthony Tuckney and Benjamin Whichcote,' in Benjamin Whichcote, *Moral and Religious Aphorisms*, edited by Samuel Salter. London: 1753.

Wise, Thomas, *A Confutation of the Reason and Philosophy of Atheism being an abridgement of Dr Cudworth's True Intellectual System of the Universe:*

In which the arguments for and against atheism are clearly stated and examined. London: 1706.

Worthington, John, The *Diary and Correspondence of Dr John Worthington,* edited by James Crossely and Richard Copley Christie. Manchester: The Chetham Society, 1847-1886.

Secondary sources

Aaron, Richard, *John Locke.* Oxford: The Clarendon Press, 1971.

Anon., 'Ayscough's Catalogue of MSS. in the British Museum' in *The Critical Review* 55 (1783): 389-92.

Anon., 'Memoirs of Ralph Cudworth D.D.,' Author of The Intellectual System,' *The Present state of the Republic of Letters*, XVII, January (1736): 24-38.

Armour, Leslie, 'Trinity, Community, and Love,' in *Platonism and the Origins of Modernity*, edited by Sarah Hutton and Douglas Hedley. Dordrecht: Springer, 2008.

Armstrong, A.H. ed., *The Cambridge History of Later Greek and Early Medieval Philosophy.* Cambridge: CUP, 1967.

—, 'Plotinus,' in The *Cambridge History of Later Greek and Early Medieval Philosophy,* edited by A.H. Armstrong. Cambridge: CUP, 1967.

Armstrong, Brian, *Calvinism and the Amyrant Heresy: Protestant Scholasticism and Humanism in Seventeenth-Century France.* Madison, WI: University of Wisconsin Press, 1969.

Armstrong, Robert L., 'The Cambridge Platonists and Locke on Innate Ideas,' in *Journal of the History of Ideas*, 30 (1969): 187-202.

Ashcraft, Richard, 'Anti-clericism and authority in Lockean political thought,' in *The Margins of Orthodoxy: Heterodox Writing and Cultural Response, 1660-1750*, edited by Roger D. Lund. Cambridge: CUP, 1995.

Ashcraft, Richard, 'Latitudinarianism and toleration: historical myth versus political history,' in *Philosophy, Science and Religion in England, 1640-1700*, edited by Richard Kroll et al. Cambridge: CUP, 1992.

Ayres, Michael, *Locke: Epistemology and Ontology*, 2. vols. London: Routledge, 1991.

—, 'Mechanism, Superaddition, and the Proof of God's Existence in Locke's Essay,' in *The Philosophical Review*, 90 (1981): 210-251.

Baldi, M, 'Cudworth versus Descartes: Platonism et sens commun dans la critique de Meditations,' in *The Cambridge Platonists in Philosophical Context* edited by G.A.J. Rogers et al. Dordrecht: Kluwer 1997.

Barbour, Reid, *English Epicures and Stoics: Ancient Legacies in Early Stuart Culture.* Amherst, MA: University of Massachusetts Press, 1998.

Barnes, Jonathan, *The Ontological Argument.* London: Macmillan, 1972.

Beiser, Frederick C., *The Sovereignty of Reason: The defence of rationality in the early English Enlightenment.* Princeton, NJ: Princeton University Press, 1996.

Bendell, Sarah, Christopher Brooks, and Patrick Collinson, *A History of Emmanuel College.* Woodbridge, Suffolk: Boydell, 1999.

Benz, Ernst, *The Mystical Sources of German Romantic Philosophy*, translated by Blair Reynolds & Eunice M. Paul. Allinson Park, PA: Pickwick Publications, 1983.

Birch, Thomas, 'An Account of the Life and Writings of R. Cudworth D.D.,' in *Ralph Cudworth, The True Intellectual System of the Universe*. London: Richard Priestly, 1820.

Bouwsma, William, *John Calvin*. Oxford: OUP, 1988.

—, 'The Two Faces of Humanism: Stoicism and Augustinianism in Renaissance Thought' in *Itinerium Italicum: The Profile of the Italian Renaissance in the mirror of its European Transformations*, edited by Heiko A. Oberman and Thomas A. Brady Jr. Leiden: Brill, 1975.

Bray, John, *Theodore Beza's Doctrine of Predestination*. Nieuwkoop: B. De Graaf, 1975.

Breteau, J.-L., 'Chaos and Order in Cudworths Thought' in *Platonism and the Origins of Modernity*, edited by Sarah Hutton and Douglas Hedley. Dordrecht: Springer, 2007.

Breward, I., 'The Importance of Perkins,' in *The Journal of Religious History*, 4 (1966): 113-28.

Broad, Jacqueline, 'A Woman's Influence? John Locke and Damaris Masham on Moral Accountability,' in *The Journal of the History of Ideas*, 67 (2006): 489-510.

—, *Women Philosophers in the Seventeenth Century*. Cambridge: CUP, 2002.

Brown, David, *The Divine Trinity*. London: Duckworth, 1985.

Brooke, John Hedley, *Science and Religion: Some Historical Perspectives*. Cambridge: CUP, 1991.

Bush Jr, Sargent and Carl J. Rasmusse, *The Library of Emmanuel College Cambridge, 1584-1637*. Cambridge: CUP, 1986.

Butin, Philip Walker, *Revelation, Redemption, and Response: Calvin's Trinitarian Understanding of the Divine-Human Relationship*. Oxford: OUP, 1985.

Carter, Benjamin, 'Ralph Cudworth and the theological origins of Consciousness' in *The History of the Human Sciences*, (forthcoming).

Cassirer, Ernst, *The Platonic Renaissance in England*, translated by James P. Pettegrove. London: Thomas Nelson and Sons, 1953.

Chadwick, Henry, 'Philo and the beginnings of Christian thought,' in *The Cambridge History of Later Greek and Early Medieval Philosophy*, edited by A.H. Armstrong. Cambridge: CUP, 1967.

Champion, J.A.I., *The Pillars of Priestcraft Shaken: The Church of England and its Enemies, 1670-1730*. Cambridge: CUP, 1992.

Clark, J.C.D., *The English Society 1688-1832: Ideology, Social Structure and Political Practice during the Ancien Regime*. Cambridge: CUP, 1985.

Coffey, John, *Persecution and Toleration in Protestant England, 1558-1689*, Harlow, Middlesex: Longmans, 2000.

Coleridge, Samuel Taylor, *Coleridge on the Seventeenth-Century*, edited by Roberta Florence. Durham NC: Duke University Press, 1955.

Colie, Rosalie L., *Light and Enlightenment: A Study of the Cambridge Platonists and the Dutch Arminians*. Cambridge: CUP, 1957.

Colish, Marcia L., *The Stoic Tradition from Antiquity to the Early Middle Ages*, 2 vols. Leiden: Brill, 1985.

Collinson, Patrick, *English Puritanism*. London: The Historical Association, 1987.

Cope, Jackson I., '"The Cupri-Cosmits:" Glanvill on Latitudinarian Anti-Enthusiasm,' in *The Huntington Library Quarterly*, 17 (1954): 269-86.

176   'THE LITTLE COMMONWEALTH OF MAN'

Copleston, Frederick, *A History of Philosophy*, 9 vols. London: Burns and Oates, 1946-1975.
Costello, William T., *The Scholastic Curriculum at Early Seventeenth-century Cambridge*. Cambridge, MA: Harvard University Press, 1958.
Cottingham, John, *A Descartes Dictionary*. Oxford: Blackwell, 1993.
—, *Descartes*. Oxford, Blackwell, 1986.
—, 'Force, Motion, and Causality: More's critique of Descartes,' in *The Cambridge Platonists in Philosophical Context*, edited by G.A.J. Rogers, et al. Dordrecht: Kluwer, 1997.
Coudert, Allison, 'Henry More, the Kabbalah, and the Quakers,' in *Philosophy Science Religion*, edited by Richard Kroll et al. Cambridge: CUP, 1992.
Coudert, Allison, *The Impact of the Kabbalah in the Seventeenth-century: The Life and thought of Francis Mercury van Helmont (1614-1698)*. Leiden: Brill, 1999.
Coward, Barry, *The Stuart Age: England, 1603-1714*, third edition. London: Pearson, 2003.
Cragg, G.R., *From Puritanism to the Age of Reason: A Study of the Changes in Religious Thought within the Church of England, 1660-1700*. Cambridge: CUP, 1950.
—, *The Cambridge Platonists*. Oxford: OUP, 1968.
—, *The Church and the Age of Reason, 1648-1789*. Bristol: Hodder & Stoughton, 1962.
Cranston, Maurice, *John Locke: A Biography*. Oxford: OUP, 1985.
Crisp, Oliver, *Jonathan Edwards and the metaphysics of sin*. Aldershot: Ashgate, 2005
Curley, Edwin M., 'Calvin and Hobbes, or Hobbes as an orthodox Christian, in *The Journal of the History of Philosophy*, 34 (1996): 257-271, published with a reply by A.P. Martinich on 272-284, and Curley's reply to his reply on 285-287.
Darwall, Stephen, *The British Moralists and the Internal 'Ought': 1640-1740*, Cambridge: CUP, 1995.
Davenport, Paul Miles, *Moral Divinity with Tincture of Christ? An Interpretation of the Theology of Benjamin Whichcote, Founder of Cambridge Platonism*. Nimegen: Peeters, 1972.
Davis, Horton, *Worship and Theology in England: From Andrewes to Baxter and Fox, 1603-1690*. Princeton, NJ: Princeton University Press, 1975.
Dekker, Eef, 'Was Arminius a Molinist?' in *The Sixteenth Century Journal*, 27 (1996): 337-352.
Dixon, Philip, *Nice and Hot Disputes: The Doctrine of the Trinity in the Seventeenth Century*. London: T&T Clark, 2003.
Dockrill, D.W., 'The Authority of the Fathers in the Great Trinitarian Debates of the Sixteen Nineties,' in *Studia Patristica*, 18 (1990): 335-47.
—, 'The Fathers and the Theology of the Cambridge Platonists,' in *Studia Patristica*, 17 (1982): 427-39.
—, 'The Heritage of Patristic Platonism in Seventeenth-Century English Philosophical Theology,' in *The Cambridge Platonists in Philosophical Context*, edited by G.A.J. Rogers et al. Dordrecht: Kluwer, 1997.
Donelly S.J., John Patrick, *Calvinism and Scholasticism in Vermigi's doctrine of Man and Grace*. Leiden: Brill, 1976.

Emilson, Eyjolfur Krajalar, *Plotinus and Sense Perception: A Philosophical Study.* Cambridge: CUP, 1988.

Fletcher, H.F., *The Intellectual Development of John Milton,* 2 vols. Urbanna, IL: University of Illinois Press, 1961.

Frankel, Lois, 'Damaris Masham' in *A History of Women Philosophers, volume three: Modern Women Philosophers, 1660-1900,* edited by Mary Ellen Waithe. Dordrecht: Kluwer, 1991.

Friedman, Jerome, *Michael Servetus: A Case Study in Total Heresy.* Geneva: Librairie Droz S.A., 1978.

Gasccoigne, John, *Cambridge in the Age of the Enlightenment: Science, Religion, and Politics From the Restoration to the French Revolution.* Cambridge: CUP, 1989.

Gill, Michael B., *The British Moralists and the Birth of Secular Ethics.* Cambridge: CUP, 2006.

—, 'Rationalism, sentimentalism, and Ralph Cudworth,' in *Hume Studies,* 30 (2004): 149-182.

Goldie, Mark, 'The Reception of Hobbes,' in *The Cambridge History of Political Thought, 1450-1700,* edited by J.H.Burns, with the assistance of Mark Goldie. Cambridge: CUP, 1991.

—, *John Locke and the Mashams of Oates,* private publication by the Parish of High Laver, 2004.

Goldie, Mark, and John Spurr, 'Politics and the Restoration Parish: Edward Fowler and the Struggle for St Giles Cripplegate,' in *English Historical Review,* 109 (1994): 572-596.

Greene, Robert A., 'Whichcote, the Candle of the Lord, and Synderisis,' in *The Journal of the History of Ideas,* 52 (1991): 617-644.

Guibbory, Achsak, *Ceremony and Community from Herbert to Milton: Literature, religion, and cultural conflict in seventeenth-century England.* Cambridge: CUP, 1998.

Gysi, Lydia, *Platonism and Cartesianism in the Philosophy of Ralph Cudworth.* Bern: Herbert Lang, 1962.

Haakonssen, Knud, *Natural Law and Moral Philosophy: From Grotius to the Scottish Enlightenment.* Cambridge: CUP, 1996.

Hall, A. Rupert, *Henry More.* Cambridge: CUP, 1990.

—, 'Henry More and the Scientific Revolution,' in *Henry More (1614-1687) Tercentenary Studies,* edited by Sarah Hutton. Dordrecht: Kluwer, 1991.

Hall, Roland, 'New Words and Antedatings from Cudworth's "Treatise on Freewill,"' in *Notes and Queries,* 205 (1960): 427-32.

—, 'Cudworth: More New Words,' in *Notes and Queries,* 208 (1963): 313-14.

—, 'Cudworth and his Contemporaries: New words and antedatings,' in *Notes and Queries,* 220, (1975): 313-14.

Hasker, William, *God, Time, and Knowledge.* Ithaca, NY: Cornell University Press, 1989.

Harper, George, *The Neoplatonism of William Blake.* Chapel Hill, NC: University of North Carolina Press, 1961.

Harris, Ian, *The Mind of John Locke: A Study of Political Theory in its Intellectual Setting.* Cambridge: CUP, 1994.

Harrison, Peter, *'Religion' and Religions in the English Enlightenment.* Cambridge: CUP, 1990.

Hartshorne, Charles, *Anselm's Discovery: A Re-Examination of the Ontological Proof for God's Existence*, Lasalle, IL: Open Court, 1965.

Heawood, Edward, *Watermarks of the 17th and 18th Centuries*. Hilversum: The Paper Publications Society, 1950.

Hedley, Douglas, *Coleridge, Philosophy and Religion: Aids to Reflection and the Mirror of the Spirit*. Cambridge: CUP 2000.

—, 'The Platonick Trinity: Philology and Divinity in Cudworth's Philosophy of Religion,' in *Philogie und Erkenntnis, Beiträge zu Begriff und Problem frühneuzeitlicher >Philologie<*, edited by Ralph Häfner. Tübingen: Max Neimeyer Veralg, 2001.

Helm, Paul, *John Calvin's Ideas*. Oxford: OUP, 2004.

Henry, John, 'Henry More versus Robert Boyle: The Spirit of Nature and the Nature of Providence,' in *Henry More (1614-1687): Tercentenary Studies, edited Sarah Hutton*. Dordrecht: Kluwer, 1990.

—, *The Scientific Revolution and the Origins of Modern Science*. Basingstoke: Palgrave, 2002.

Higgins-Biddle, John C., 'Introduction' in John Locke, *The Reasonableness of Christianity as delivered in scriptures*, edited by John C. Higgins-Biddle. Oxford: The Clarendon Press, 1999.

Hill, Christopher, *Milton and the English Revolution*. New York: Viking Press, 1977.

—, *The World Turned Upside Down: Radical Ideas during the English Revolution*. Harmondsworth: Penguin, 1991.

Hutton, Sarah, *Anne Conway: A Women Philosopher*. Cambridge: CUP, 2004.

—, 'Aristotle and the Cambridge Platonists: the case of Cudworth,' in *Philosophy in the Sixteenth and Seventeenth Centuries: Conversations with Aristotle*, edited by C.T. Blackwell and S. Kusukawa: London: Ashgate, 2000.

—, 'Classicism and Baroque: A Note on Mosheim's footnotes to Cudworth's The True Intellectual System of the Universe,' in *Johann Lorenz Mosheim: Theologie im Sannhungsfeld von Philosophie, Philologie und Geschichte, 1693-1755*, edited by Martin Mulsow. Wiesbaden: Harrasowitz, 1997.

—, 'Cudworth, Boethius and the Scale of Nature,' in *The Cambridge Platonists in Philosophical Context: Politics, Metaphysics & Religion*, ed. G.A.J. Rogers, et al. Dordrecht: Kluwer, 1997.

—, 'Damaris Cudworth, Lady Masham: Between Platonism and Enlightenment' in *The British Journal for the History of Philosophy*, 1 (1993): 29-54.

—, 'Liberty and Self-determination: Ethics Power and Action in Ralph Cudworth,' in *Del necessario al possible. Determinismo e Libertà nel penserio Anglo-Olandese de XVII seculo*, edited by L. Simonutti. Angeli: 2001.

—, 'Plato in the Tudor Academies,' in *Sir Thomas Gresham and Gresham College: Studies in the Intellectual History of London on the Sixteenth and Seventeenth Centuries*, edited by Francis Ames-Lewis. Aldershot: Ashgate, 1999.

—, 'Platonism, Stoicism and Scepticism and Classical Imitation,' in *A Companion to English Renaissance Literature and Culture*, edited by Michael Hattaway. Oxford: OUP, 2000.

—, 'Ralph Cudworth: God, Mind, and Nature,' in *Religion, Reason and Nature in Early Modern Europe*, edited by Robert Crocker. Dordrecht: Kluwer, 2001.

—, 'The Neoplatonic Roots of Arianism: Ralph Cudworth and Theophilus Gale,' in *Socinianism and its Role in the Culture of XVI-th to XVIII-th Centuries* edited by L. Szczucki and Z. Ogonowski. Warsaw: PWN – Polish Scientific Publisher, 1983.

—, 'Thomas Jackson, Oxford Platonist, and William Twisse,' in *The Journal of the History of Ideas*, 39 (1978): 635-52.

Illiffe, Rob, 'Prosecuting Athanasius: Protestant Forensics and the Mirrors of Persecution,' in *Newton and Newtonianism: New Studies*, edited by James E. Force and Sarah Hutton. Dordrecht: Kluwer, 2004.

Inge, W.R., 'Introduction,' to Benjamin Whichcote, *Moral and Religious Aphorisms*. London: Elkin Matthews, 1930.

—, *The Platonic Tradition in English Religious Thought*. London: Longmans, Green & Co., 1926.

—, *The Philosophy of Plotinus*, 2 vols. London: Longmans, Green & Co., 1918.

Jacob, Margaret C., *The Newtonians and the English Revolution: 1689-1720*. Hassocks, Sussex: Harvester Press, 1976.

Jayne, Sears, *Plato in Renaissance England*. Dordrecht: Kluwer, 1995.

Jones, David Martin, *Conscience and Allegiance in Seventeenth-Century England: The Political Significance of Oaths and Engagements*. Rochester, N.Y, University of Rochester Press, 1999.

Jones, Rufus M., *Spiritual Reformers of the 16th and 17th Centuries*. London: Macmillan, 1928.

Jue, Jefferey K., *Heaven upon Earth: Joseph Mede (1586-1638) and the Legacy of Millenarianism*, Dordrecht: Springer, 2006.

Katz, David S., 'Henry More and Jews,' in *Henry More (1614-1687): Tercentenary Studies*, edited by Sarah Hutton, Dordrecht, Kluwer, 1991.

—, *The Jews in the History of England, 1485-1850*. Oxford: The Clarendon Press, 1994.

—, *Philo-Semitism and the Readmission of the Jews to England: 1603-1655*. Oxford: The Clarendon Press, 1982.

Kendall, R.T., *Calvin and English Calvinism*. Oxford: OUP, 1979.

Kenny, Courtney, 'Cudworth's Manuscripts on Future Punishment,' in *The Theological Review*, 61 (1878): 267-280.

Kenyon, J.P., ed., *The Stuart Constitution: 1603-1688*. Cambridge: CUP, 1986.

Krook, D, 'The Recantation of Daniel Scargill,' in *Notes and Queries*, 198 (1953): 267-280.

Lacugna, Catherine Mowry, *God for Us: The Trinity and the Christian Life*. San Francisco: Harper Collins, 1993.

Lake, Peter, 'The Laudian Style: Order, Uniformity and the Pursuit of the Beauty of Holiness in the 1630s,' in *The Early Stuart Church, 1603-1642*, edited by Kenneth Fincham. Oxford: Macmillan, 1993.

Leedham-Greene, E.S., *Books in Cambridge Inventories*, 2 vols. Cambridge: CUP, 1986.

Brian Leftow, 'Anti Social Trinitarianism,' in *The Trinity*, edited by Steven Davis and Daniel Kendall. New York: Oxford University Press, 1999.

Levine, Joseph M., 'Latitudinarians, Neoplatonists and the Ancient Wisdom,' in *Philosophy, Science and Religion in England, 1640-1700*, edited Richard Kroll, et al. Cambridge: CUP, 1992.

Locke, Louis G., *Tillotson: A Study on Seventeenth-Century Literature*. Copenhagen: Rosenkilde and Bagger, 1954.

Lovejoy, Arthur O., 'Kant and the English Platonists,' in *Essays Philosophical and Psychological: In honor of William James by his colleagues at Columbia University*. New York: Longmans, Green and Co., 1908.

Maclear, James Fulton, 'Popular anticlericism in the Puritan Revolution,' in *The Journal of the History of Ideas*, 17 (1956): 443-70.

MacPherson, C.B., *The Political Theory of Possessive Individualism: Hobbes to Locke*. Oxford: OUP, 1962.

Malcolm, Noel, 'Thomas Hobbes and Voluntarist Theology', PhD Thesis, University of Cambridge: 1982.

Manning, Brian, 'The Levellers and Religion,' in *Radical Religion in the English Revolution*, edited by J.F. MacGregor and B Reay. Oxford: OUP, 1984.

Marshall, John, *John Locke: Resistance, Religion and Responsibility*. Cambridge: CUP, 1994.

—, 'Locke, Socinianism, "Socinianism", and Unitarianism' in M.A. Stewart, ed., *English Philosophy in the Age of Locke*. Oxford: The Clarendon Press, 2000.

Martin, Raymond, and John Barresi, *Naturalization of the Soul: Self and Personal Identity In the Eighteenth-Century*. London: Routledge, 2000.

Martineau, James, *Types of Ethical Theory*, 2 vols. Oxford: The Clarendon Press, 1885.

Martinich, A.P., *Hobbes: A Biography*. Cambridge: CUP, 1999.

—, *The Two Gods of Leviathan: Thomas Hobbes on Religion and Politics*. Cambridge: CUP, 1992.

McAdoo, H.R., *The Spirit of Anglicanism: A Survey of Anglican Theological method in the Seventeenth century*. London: Adam and Charles Black, 1965.

McGrath, Alister E., *A Life of John Calvin: A Study in the Shaping of Western Culture*. Oxford: Blackwell, 1990.

—, *Christian Theology: An Introduction*. Oxford: Blackwell, 1997.

—, *Reformation Thought: An Introduction*. Oxford: Blackwell, 1993.

—, *The Intellectual Origins of the European Reformation*. Oxford: Blackwell, 1987.

McLachlan, H. John, *Socinianism in the Seventeenth-Century England*. Oxford: OUP, 1951.

McNeill, John T., *The History and Character of Calvinism*. Oxford: OUP, 1954.

Merlan, P., 'Greek Philosophy from Plato to Plotinus,' in *The Cambridge History of Later Greek and Early Medieval Philosophy*, edited by A.H. Armstrong. Cambridge: CUP, 1970.

Mill, J.S., *Dissertations and Discussions: Political, Philosophical, and Historical* 4. vols. London: Longmans, Green, Reader, Dyer, 1854-1875.

Miller, John, 'James II and Toleration' in *By Force or By Default? The Revolution of 1688-1689*, edited by Eveline Cruickshank. Edinburgh: John Donald, 1989.

Mintz, Samuel I., *The Hunting of Leviathan: Seventeenth-century Reactions to the Materialism and Moral Philosophy of Thomas Hobbes*. Cambridge: CUP, 1962.

Moore, Jonathan D., *English Hypothetical Universalism: John Preston and the Softening of Reformed Theology*. Grand Rapids, MI: William Eerdmans Publishing, 2007.

Muirhead, John H., *The Platonic Tradition in Anglo-Saxon Philosophy: Studies in the History of Idealism in England and America*. London: George Allen and Unwin, 1931.

Richard A. Muller, *After Calvin: Studies in the Development of a Theological Tradition*: Oxford, OUP, 2003.

—, *Post-Reformation Reformed Dogmatics: The Rise and Development of Reformed Orthodoxy, ca. 1520 to ca. 1725*, 4. vols. Grand Rapids, MI: Baker Academic, 1987 & 2003.

Mullet, Michael, *Calvin*. London: Routledge, 1989.

Mulsow, Martin and Jan Rohls, eds, *Socinianism and Arminianism: Anti-Trinitarianism, Calvinists, and Cultural Exchange in Seventeenth-Century Europe*. Leiden: Brill, 2005.

Newsome, David, *Two Classes of Men: Platonism and English and Romantic Thought*. London: John Murray, 1974.

Nicolson, Marjorie, 'Christ's College and the Latitude-Men,' in *Modern Philology*, 27 (1929-1930): 35-53.

Norbrook, David, *Writing in the English Republic: Poetry, Rhetoric, and Politics, 1627-1660*. Cambridge: CUP, 1999.

Nuovo, Victor, *John Locke and Christianity*. Bristol: Thoemmes Press, 1997.

—, 'Locke's Theology, 1694-1704) in *English Philosophy in the Age of Locke*, edited by M.A. Stewart. Oxford: The Clarendon Press, 2000.

O'Meara, Dominic J., *Plotinus: An Introduction to the Enneads*. Oxford: The Clarendon Press, 1993.

Oppy, Graham, *Ontological Arguments and Belief in God*, Cambridge: CUP, 1996.

Pacchi, Arigo, 'Hobbes and the Problem of God,' in *Perspectives of Thomas Hobbes*, edited by G.A.J. Rogers and Alan Ryan. Oxford: The Clarendon Press, 1988.

Parker, T.M., '"Arminianism and Laudianism" in Seventeenth-century England' in *Studies in Church History*, vol. 1, edited by C.W. Dugmore and Charles Duggan. London: Nelson, 1964.

Parkin, Jon, 'Hobbism in the Later 1660s: Daniel Scargill and Samuel Parker,' in *The Historical Journal*, 42 (1999): 85-108.

—, *Taming the Leviathan: The Reception of the Political and Religious Ideas of Thomas Hobbes in England 1640-1700*. Cambridge: CUP, 2007.

—, *Science, Religion, and Politics in Restoration England: Richard Cumberland's De Legibus Naturae*. Woodbridge: Boydell, 1999.

Passmore, John, *Ralph Cudworth: An Interpretation*. Cambridge: CUP, 1951.

Patrides, C.A. ed., *The Cambridge Platonists*. London: Edward Arnold, 1967.

Paul, Robert S., *The Assembly of the Lord: Politics and Religion in the Westminster Assembly and the 'Grand Debate'*. Edinburgh: T&T Clark, 1985.

Peile, John, *Biographical Register of Christ's College 1505-1905 and of the earlier foundation, God's house, 1448-1505*. Cambridge: CUP, 1913.

Plantinga, Jr., Cornelius, 'Social Trinity and Tritheism', in *Trinity, Incarnation, and Atonement: Philosophical and Theological Essays*, edited by Ronald

J. Feenstra and Cornelius Plantinga Jr. Notre Dame IN: University of Notre Dame Press, 1989

Pocock, J.G.A., *Barbarism and Religion: Volume One, The Enlightenment of Edward Gibbon, 1737-1764*. Cambridge: CUP, 1999.

—, 'Post-Puritan England and the Problem of the Enlightenment,' in *Culture and Politics: From Puritanism to the Enlightenment*, edited by Perex Zagorin. Berkeley: University of California Press, 1980.

—, *The Ancient Constitution and Feudal Law: A study of English Historical Thought in the Seventeenth Century*. Cambridge: CUP, 1957.

—, *The Political Works of James Harrington*. Cambridge: CUP, 1977.

—, 'Time, History, and Eschatology,' in *Politics, Language, and Time: Essays on Political Thought and History*. Chicago: University of Chicago Press, 1960.

—, 'Within the margins: The definitions of orthodoxy,' in *The Margins of Orthodoxy, Heterodox Writing and Cultural Response, 1660-1750*, edited by Roger D. Lund. Cambridge: CUP, 1995.

Porter, H.C., *Reformation and Reaction in Tudor Cambridge*. Cambridge: CUP, 1958.

Powicke, Frederick J., *The Cambridge Platonists: A Study*. London: J.M. Dent and Sons, 1929.

Rauser, Randal, 'Rahner's Rule: An Emperor without Clothes?' *International Journal of Systematic Theology*, 7 (2005): 81-94.

Redwood, John, *Reason, Ridicule and Religion: The Age of Enlightenment in England, 1660-1750*. London: Thames and Hudson, 1976.

Rist, John, *Plotinus: The Road to Reality*. Cambridge: CUP, 1967.

—, *Stoic Philosophy*. Cambridge: CUP, 1969.

Rist, John, ed. *The Stoics*. Berkeley: University of California Press, 1978.

Rivers, Isabel, *Reason, Grace and Sentiment: A Study of the Language of Religion and Ethics in England*, 2. vols. Cambridge: CUP, 1991 & 2000.

Rogers, G.A.J., 'Descartes and the English,' in *The Light of Nature: Essays in the History and Philosophy of Science presented to A.C. Crombie*, edited by J.D. North and J.J. Roche. Dordrecht: Kluwer, 1985.

—, 'John Locke: conservative radical' in *The Margins of Orthodoxy: Heterodox Writing and Cultural Response, 1660-1750*, edited by Roger D. Lund. Cambridge: CUP, 1995.

—, 'Locke and the Latitude-men: Ignorance as a Ground of Toleration,' in *Philosophy, Science, and Religion in England, 1640-1700*, edited by Richard Kroll, et al. Cambridge: CUP, 1992.

—, 'More, Locke, and the Issue of Liberty,' in *Henry More (1614-1687) Tercentenary Studies*, edited by Sarah Hutton. Dordrecht: Kluwer, 1991.

—, 'The Other-worldly philosophers and the real world: The Cambridge Platonists, Theology and Politics,' in *The Cambridge Platonists in Philosophical Context: Politics, Metaphysics & Religion*, edited by G.A.J. Rogers, et al. Dordrecht: Kluwer, 1997.

Rosenblatt, Jason P., *Renaissance England's Chief Rabbi: John Selden*. Oxford: OUP, 2006.

Sailor, Danton B., 'Cudworth and Descartes,' in *The Journal of the History of Ideas*, 23 (1962): 133-140.

Sandbach, F.H., *The Stoics*. London: Chatto and Windus, 1975.

Saveson, J.E., 'Differing Reactions to Descartes among the Cambridge Platonists,' in *The Journal of the History of Ideas*, 21 (1960): 560-567.

Schmitt, Charles B., *Aristotle and the Renaissance*. Cambridge MA: Harvard University Press, 1983.

Scott, Dominic, 'Reason, Recollection and the Cambridge Platonists,' in *Platonism and the English Imagination*, edited by Anna Baldwin and Sarah Hutton. Cambridge: CUP, 1994.

Scott, Dominic, *Recollection and Experience: Plato's Theory of Learning and its Successors*. Cambridge: CUP, 1995.

Selby-Bigge, L.A., ed., *British Moralists*, 2. vols. Oxford: The Clarendon Press, 1897.

Shapiro, Barbara J., *Probability and Certainty in Seventeenth-Century England: A Study of the Relationship between Natural Science, Religion, History, Law and Literature*. Princeton, NJ: Princeton University Press, 1983.

Skinner, Quentin, *Visions of Politics*, 3. vols. Cambridge: CUP, 2002.

Simmonutti, Luisa 'Bayle and Le Clerc as readers of Cudworth: aspects of the debate on Plastic Nature in the Dutch learned journals' in *Geschiedenis van de Wijsbegeerte in Nederland*, 4 (1993): 147-165.

Sobol, Peter G., 'The Cabala,' in *The History of Science and Religion in the Western Tradition: An Encyclopaedia*, edited by Gary B. Ferngren. New York: Garland, 2000.

Spellman, W.M., *The Latitudinarians and the Church of England, 1660-1770*. Athens GA: University of Georgia Press, 1993.

Spurr, John, 'The Church of England, Comprehension and The Toleration Act of 1689,' in *English Historical Review* 104, (1989): 927-946.

—, *English Puritanism: 1605-1693*. Basingstoke: Macmillan, 1998.

—, '"Latituinarianism" and the Restoration Church,' in *The Historical Journal*, 31 (1988): 61-82.

—, '"Rational Religion" in Restoration England,' in *The Journal of the History of Ideas*, 49 (1988): 563-585.

Stough, Charlotte, 'Stoic Determinism and Moral Responsibility,' in *The Stoics*, edited by John Rist. Berkeley: University of California Press, 1978.

Taliaferro, Charles, *Evidence and Faith: Philosophy and Religion since the Seventeenth-Century*. Cambridge: CUP, 2005.

—, 'The Trinity and Natural Reason: Lessons from Cambridge Platonism,' in *The Holy Trinity*, edited by Melville Y. Stewart. Dordrecht: Kluwer, 2003.

Thiel, Udo, 'Cudworth and Seventeenth-Century Theories of Consciousness' in *The Uses of Antiquity: The Scientific Revolution and the Classical Tradition*, edited by Stephen Gaukroger. Dordrecht: Kluwer, 1991.

—, 'Self-Consciousness and Personal Identity' in *The Cambridge History of Eighteenth-Century Philosophy*, edited by Knud Haakonssen. Cambridge: CUP, 2007.

—, 'The Trinity and Human Personal Identity' in *English Philosophy in the Age of Locke*, edited by M.A. Stewart. Oxford: OUP, 2000.

Thomas, Roger, 'Comprehension and Indulgence,' in *From Uniformity to Unity* edited by Geoffrey F. Nuttall and Owen Chadwick. London: SPCK, 1962.

Tigerstedt, E.N., *The Decline and Fall of the Neoplatonic interpretation of Plato*. Helsinki: Societas Scientiarum Fennica, 1974.

Todd, Richard, 'Stoicism,' in *The History of Science and Religion in the Western Tradition: An Encyclopaedia*, edited by Gary B. Ferngren. New York: Garland, 2000.

Torrance, Thomas F., 'Calvin's Doctrine of the Trinity' in *Calvin Theological Review*, 25 (1990): 165-193.

Toulmin, Joshua, *An Historical View of the State of the Protestant Church in England and the Progress of Free Enquiry and Religious Liberty from the Restoration to the Accession of Queen Anne*. London: 1814.

Trentmann, John A., 'The Authorship of "Directions for a Student in the University,"' in *Transactions of the Cambridge Bibliographical Society*, 7 (1978): 170-83.

Trevor-Roper, H.R., *Archbishop Laud, 1573-1645*. London: Macmillan, 1962.

—, *Catholics, Anglicans, and Puritans*. London: Seeker & Warburg, 1987.

—, 'The Religious Origins of the Enlightenment,' in *Religion, the Reformation and Social Change*. London: Macmillan, 1967.

Trowell, Stephen, 'Unitarian and/ or Anglican: The Relationship of Unitarians to the Church from 1687-1698' in *The Bulletin of the John Rylands Library* 78 (1996): 77-102.

Tuck, Richard '"The Ancient Law of Freedom": John Selden and the Civil War' in *Reactions to the English Civil War: 1642-1649*, edited by John Morrill: Basingstoke: Macmillan, 1982.

Tucker, Robert C., *Philosophy and Myth in Karl Marx*. Cambridge: CUP, 1972.

Tulloch, John, *Rational Theology and Christian Philosophy on England in the Seventeenth Century*, 2 vols. Edinburgh: William Blackwood and Sons, 1874.

Turner, Frank M., *The Greek Heritage in Victorian Britain*. New Haven, Yale University Press, 1981.

Twigg, John, *The University of Cambridge and the English Revolution, 1625-1688*. Woodbridge: Boydell, 1990.

Tyacke, Nicholas, *Anti-Calvinists: The Rise of Arminianism, c. 1590-1640*. Oxford: The Clarendon Press, 1987.

—, 'Arminianism and English Culture,' in *Britain and the Netherlands, volume 7, Church and State since the Reformation*, edited by A.C. Duke and C.A. Tamse. The Hague: Martinus Nijhoff, 1981.

—, 'Archbishop Laud,' in *The Early Stuart Church, 1603-1642*, edited by Kenneth Fincham. London: Macmillan, 1993.

Vickers, Brian, 'Introduction,' to *Occult and Scientific Mentalities in the Renaissance*, edited by Brian Vickers. Cambridge: CUP, 1984.

Von Leyden, Wolfgang, 'Locke and Nicole: their proofs of the existence of God and their attitude towards Descartes' in *Sophia* 16 (1948): 41-55.

Walker, D.P., *The Ancient Theology: Studies in Christian Platonism from the Fifteenth to the Eighteenth Century*. London: Duckworth, 1972.

Wallace Jr, Dewey D., *Puritans and Predestination: Grace in English Protestant Theology, 1525-1695*. Chapel Hill, NC: University of North Carolina Press, 1982.

Wallace, John M., *Destiny his Choice: the loyalism of Andrew Marvell*. Cambridge: CUP, 1968.

Ward, Richard, *The Life of the Pious and Learned Henry More*. London: 1710.

Wendel, François, *Calvin: The Origins and Development of his Religious Thought*, translated by Philip Mairet. London: Collins: 1963.

White, Peter, *Predestination, Policy, and Polemic: Conflict and Consensus in the English Church from the Reformation to the Civil War*. Cambridge: CUP, 1992.

Wiles, Maurice, *The Archetypal Heresy: Arianism through the Centuries*. Oxford: The Clarendon Press, 1996.

—, *Working Papers in Doctrine*. London: SCM Press, 1976.

Wright, George, *Religion, Politics, and Thomas Hobbes*. Dordrecht: Springer, 2006.

Wolterstorff, Nicholas, 'John Locke's Epistemological Piety: Reason is the Candle of the Lord,' in *Faith and Philosophy*, 1 (1984): 572-591.

Woolhouse, R.S., *Locke: A Biography*. Cambridge: CUP, 2007.

Yates, Francis A., *Giordano Bruno and the Hermetic Tradition*. London: Routledge and Kegan Paul, 1964.

Zaehner, R.C., *Mysticism: Sacred and Profane. An Inquiry into some Varieties of Praeternatural Experience*. Oxford: The Clarendon Press, 1957.

INDEX

Benjamin Carter: The Little Commonwealth of Man

STUDIES IN PHILOSOPHICAL THEOLOGY

1   H. de Vries, *Theologie im Pianissimo & zwischen Rationalität und Dekonstruktion*, Kampen, 1989
2   S. Breton, *La pensée du rien*, Kampen, 1992
3   Ch. Schwöbel, *God: Action and Revelation*, Kampen, 1992
4   V. Brümmer (ed.), *Interpreting the Universe as Creation*, Kampen, 1991
5   L.J. van den Brom, *Divine Presence in the World*, Kampen, 1993
6   M. Sarot, *God, Passibility and Corporeality*, Kampen, 1992
7   G. van den Brink, *Almighty God*, Kampen 1993
8   P.-C. Lai, *Towards a Trinitarian Theology of Religions: A Study of Paul Tillich's Thought*, Kampen, 1994
9   L. Velecky, *Aquinas' Five Arguments in the* Summa Theologiae *Ia 2, 3*, Kampen, 1994
10 W. Dupré, *Patterns in Meaning. Reflections on Meaning and Truth in Cultural Reality, Religious Traditions, and Dialogical Encounters*, Kampen, 1994
11 P.T. Erne, *Lebenskunst. Aneignung ästhetischer Erfahrung*, Kampen, 1994
12 U. Perone, *Trotz/dem Subjekt*, Leuven, 1998
13 H.J. Adriaanse, *Vom Christentum aus: Aufsätze und Vorträge zur Religionsphilosophie*, Kampen, 1995
14 D.A. Pailin, *Probing the Foundations: A Study in Theistic Reconstruction*, Kampen, 1994
15 M. Potepa, *Schleiermachers hermeneutische Dialektik*, Kampen, 1996
16 E. Herrmann, *Scientific Theory and Religious Belief. An Essay on the Rationality of Views of Life*, Kampen, 1995
17 V. Brümmer & M. Sarot (eds.), *Happiness, Well-Being and the Meaning of Life. A Dialogue of Social Science and Religion*, Kampen, 1996
18 T.L. Hettema, *Reading for Good. Narrative Theology and Ethics in the Joseph Story from the Perspective of Ricoeur's Hermeneutics*, Kampen, 1996
19 H. Düringer, *Universale Vernunft und partikularer Glaube. Eine theologische Auswertung des Werkes von Jürgen Habermas*, Leuven, 1999
20 E. Dekker, *Middle Knowledge*, Leuven, 2000
21 T. Ekstrand, *Max Weber in a Theological Perspective*, Leuven, 2000
22 C. Helmer & K. De Troyer (eds.), *Truth: Interdisciplinary Dialogues in a Pluralist Age*, Leuven, 2003
23 L. Boeve & L.P. Hemming (eds.), *Divinising Experience. Essays in the History of Religious Experience from Origen to Ricœur*, Leuven, 2004
24 P.D. Murray, *Reason, Truth and Theology in Pragmatist Perspective*, Leuven, 2004
25 S. van Erp, *The Art of Theology. Hans Urs von Balthasar's Theological Aesthetics and the Foundations of Faith*, Leuven, 2004
26 T.A. Smedes, *Chaos, Complexity, and God. Divine Action and Scientism*, Leuven, 2004
27 R. Re Manning, *Theology at the End of Culture. Paul Tillich's Theology of Culture and Art*, Leuven, 2004
28 P. Jonkers & R. Welten (eds.), *God in France. Eight Contemporary French Thinkers on God*, Leuven, 2005
29 D. Grumett, *Teilhard de Chardin: Theology, Humanity and Cosmos*, Leuven, 2005
30 I.U. Dalferth, *Becoming Present. An Inquiry into the Christian Sense of the Presence of God*, Leuven, 2006

PRINTED ON PERMANENT PAPER • IMPRIME SUR PAPIER PERMANENT • GEDRUKT OP DUURZAAM PAPIER - ISO 9706

N.V. PEETERS S.A., WAROTSTRAAT 50, B-3020 HERENT